The Unity of Music and Dance in World Cultures

The Unity of Music and Dance in World Cultures

David Akombo

McFarland & Company, Inc., Publishers
Jefferson, North Carolina

LIBRARY OF CONGRESS CATALOGUING-IN-PUBLICATION DATA

Names: Akombo, David Otieno.
Title: The unity of music and dance in world cultures / David
   Akombo.
Description: Jefferson, North Carolina : McFarland & Company,
   2016 | Includes bibliographical references and index.
Identifiers: LCCN 2015042360 | ISBN 9780786497157 (softcover :
   acid free paper) ∞
Subjects: LCSH: Music and dance. | Dance music—History and
   criticism.
Classification: LCC ML3400 .A4 2016 | DDC 781.5/5409—dc23
LC record available at http://lccn.loc.gov/2015042360

BRITISH LIBRARY CATALOGUING DATA ARE AVAILABLE

ISBN (print) 978-0-7864-9715-7
ISBN (ebook)978-1-4766-2269-9

© 2016 David Akombo. All rights reserved

*No part of this book may be reproduced or transmitted in any form
or by any means, electronic or mechanical, including photocopying
or recording, or by any information storage and retrieval system,
without permission in writing from the publisher.*

Front cover image © CastaldoStudio/iStock/Thinkstock

Printed in the United States of America

McFarland & Company, Inc., Publishers
   Box 611, Jefferson, North Carolina 28640
      www.mcfarlandpub.com

This work is dedicated to all world music enthusiasts including, but not limited to, the interdisciplinary scholars, friends, students, staff and faculty with whom I have interacted as professor in my teaching career. Others include two special people, Barbara Achando and Andrea Alali (a.k.a. Madam Lou).

Acknowledgments

Many people assisted and encouraged me in various ways during the writing of this book. The fact that you are reading this proves that you are one of the dedicated scholars interested in understanding global cultures. This book took hundreds of hours of preparation and a major commitment. An enormous debt of gratitude can hardly be repaid to Risa Polansky, who not only proofread multiple versions of all the chapters but also provided many stylistic suggestions to make it a suitable textbook for understanding world music. I also owe great appreciation to Joel Cárdenas of the University of Utah School Law and the librarians at various universities, including Harvard University and the University of Florida, who were always ready to help me in my research to find inspiring literature in both print and e-media on the subject. However, despite all the assistance provided by the above professionals and friends, I alone remain responsible for the content, including any errors or omissions that may unwittingly remain.

Table of Contents

Acknowledgments   vi
Preface   1

Part I: Africa

1. The Bikutsi Dance of Cameroon   3
2. The Egungun Dance of the Yoruba Culture of Nigeria   8
3. The Music and Dance of Côte d'Ivoire   14
4. The Gumboot Dance of South Africa   20
5. The Music and Culture of Botswana   29
6. Dances of the Mbuti People of the Democratic Republic of Congo   36

Part II: The Americas

7. The Bachata Dance of the Dominican Republic   45
8. The Merengue Dance of Latin America   51
9. The Merengue of the Dominican Republic   59
10. Folk and Mento Dance Traditions of Jamaica   68
11. The Reggae Dance of Jamaica   74
12. The Rumba Dance of Cuba   80
13. The Sun Dance of the Plains Indians   88
14. The Hula Dance of the Hula People of Hawaii   94
15. Swing Dancing of New York   101
16. American Jazz   106
17. Popular Dances of Mexico   111
18. The Slave Dances of North America   118

19. The Tango of Argentina	125
20. The Chacarera Dance of Argentina	131
21. The Capoeira Dance of Brazil	136
22. Brazilian Music and Dances	143

Part III: Asia

23. The Odissi, a Classical Indian Dance	151
24. The Bharata Natyam and Kathak Dances of India	158
25. The Kundiman, Sinulog and Tinikling Dances of the Philippines	165
26. The Santacruzan Dance of the Philippines	174
27. The Dances of the Khalkas People of Mongolia	180
28. The Dances of China	186
29. The Shomyo Dance of Japan	191

Part IV: South Pacific

30. The Kapa Haka Dance Tradition of New Zealand	197
31. Australian Aboriginal Music and Dances	203

Part V: Europe

32. The Ballet of Europe	211
33. Igor Stravinsky and the Ballets Russes	217
34. Traditional Music and Dance of Ireland	228
35. The Flamenco Dance Tradition of Spain	240

Part VI: Middle East

36. The Music and Dances of Afghanistan	247
37. The Saray Court Dance of the Turkish People	251
38. Traditional Music of Iraq	257

Index	263

Preface

In my professional teaching career, I have continued to be inspired by the amount of knowledge we can gather on humans simply based upon his or her musical culture. The world of music is rich with artifacts that make me want to know the correlations of these artifacts and the human sociocultural milieu. In my career as a music educator and ethnomusicologist, I have interacted with several scholars and researchers as well as honor students whose quest for knowledge about the human artistic phenomenon has remained unfulfilled. The questions of human culture, especially as they pertain to musical expressions, were the beginnings of my quest for insights into the old debate of whether music and dance are inseparable. They are an esthetic confluence of sonic energy with a response from receptive body parts moving in time, hence the creation of the whole: music and dance. There could not have been a better opportunity to add to the plethora of ideas regarding human artistic experiences.

It is believed that the true origins of music and dance are based on the divine power. Various nations of the world support this theory through their myths. Many different world traditions hold that music and dance have coexisted for millennia. Music and dance have indeed shared a compatible role in human cultural spheres without the need to separate them. Consequently, many scholars seem to agree that music and dance are inseparable.

Research into the dichotomies of music and dance began early in the nineteenth century. These studies have continued in the context of the search for the truth about music and dance. The idea of music existing in many non-Western cultures, without dance, continues to intrigue scholars. Similarly, dances without music have been viewed as incomplete. Dances without music do exist, however, hence a good reason for a scientific study to determine historical and modern contexts of music and dance and whether they are separable.

This debate has led some scholars to believe that music can exist on its own without the accompaniment of dance while others argue that dance can also be performed without music. In each case however, the interpretations of the terms "music" and "dance" are culture-bound. While in some cultures music means sound and body movement, in others, dance means body movement and sound. This book surveys music and dance around the world and tries to put dance and music back to the context in which they were first created by humans: as a composite whole to coexist and complement each other in the attempt to complete the human sphere.

In this book, I have tried to examine by way of defining and re-examining both music and dance from a global perspective. I have endeavored to portray music and dance as a composite whole by considering them inherent in every culture. I present and show the connection of the two units as complementing each other. In the course of the investigation, I observed instances where music is performed without dance, even though throughout the text, we find that dance can hardly exist without music. Although the intention of this book is not to decontextualize world cultures that subscribe to the confluence of music and dance as human activities, the book nonetheless provides an insight into the study to find the pre-historical and anthropological misconceptions on their unitary existence. A foray into the arts however shows that the *de facto* relationship between music and dance is high among non-Western cultures. Thus, every dance goes with some form of music as music goes with some form of dance notwithstanding the culture-specific definitions of the two. Indeed many scholars agree that in one way or another, music connects with movement in the repertory of all cultures.

Part I: Africa

1. The Bikutsi Dance of Cameroon

History

The Republic of Cameroon is located on the Central West African Coast, bordering Nigeria, Chad, and the Central African Republic. This country has a rich and varied cultural past, with traces of human activity dating back to the Neolithic period. Cameroon was divided into numerous kingdoms and chiefdoms since its beginnings. One can see this division today from the estimated 250 distinct ethnic groups living in the country. Several external influences from the European and the Western world in general have affected these cultures without eliminating the traditional values in the music and dances of Cameroonian tribes.

For instance, Portuguese explorers were the first Europeans to reach the coast of Cameroon in 1472. Upon arrival, the sailors immediately established trade relations and regularized themselves with the natives of the country. Over the next few decades, the natives of Cameroon frequently sold and traded slaves along with selling them raw materials to the Portuguese, who were heavily involved in the Atlantic Slave Trade. Due to the Atlantic Slave Trade's immense popularity during this time, Cameroon became one of the more significant sources for the acquisition of potential slave labor. Native Cameroonians were taken from all over the country and sent to the coastal ports of Douala and Bimbia where they were eventually sold into slavery. Although the sale of indigenous people tore many communities and their respective cultures apart, tribal chiefs often overlooked these effects for the prospect of more money.

As the slave trade started to decline in the early 1880s, Portugal began separating itself from contact with Cameroon. The Portuguese presence was largely superseded by the Germans, who claimed the territory as the colony of "Kamerun" in 1884. Once in Cameroon, the Germans established logging plantations in the southern forests along the coast and broke trade relations among the native tribes. They also initiated a harsh system of forced labor since many of the indigenous people were unwilling to work for them on the plantations. Due to the brutality that accompanied this form of labor, many native Cameroonians died serving German interests.

German influence was prevalent in Cameroon until the end of World War I. After the Germans were driven out by French and British forces, they were forced to give up their control of the territory. Both France and Britain gained control of a portion of the country in 1918 and subsequently introduced Cameroon to its official languages, French and English. Although French and English are Cameroon's official languages, about 24 distinct African dialects are spoken by its indigenous peoples today. Aside from the introduction of new dialects, cultural influences from France and England are apparent in the Cameroonian celebration of traditional European holidays such as New Year's Day and Christmas. French and English cultures also emphasized a formal education for Cameroon's youth, which has guided Cameroon to one of the highest literacy rates in Africa today.

By 1961, Cameroon gained full independence from all other nations that previously laid claims to its control. The country's first president was Ahmadou Ahidjo, who pledged to build a capitalist economy and keep close economic ties with France. To the dismay of many traditionalist Cameroonians, Ahidjo emphasized the importance of nationalism over tribalism and used his fears of ethnic violence to convey his message. Over the next few decades, Cameroon witnessed a number of economic troubles due to corruption and mismanagement in the government. Cameroon also witnessed shifts in political power from an authoritarian regime to a more democratic rule under President Paul Biya, who is still in power today. Although Biya and his Cameroon People's Democratic Movement preach democracy, many natives feel that he has turned to the harsh leadership style of his predecessor, Ahidjo. Regardless of all the political and economic controversy within their country, Cameroonians have witnessed their music and culture flourish beyond ethnic lines and across the world.

Culture

Due to the multitude of tribes in Cameroon, each tribe can be placed into one of five distinct cultural regions: Western Highlanders; Coastal Tropical Forest Peoples; Southern Tropical Forest Peoples; predominantly

Islamic people of the Central Highlands; and *Kirdi* or non-Islamic people of the Northern Deserts.

The Beti people have historically inhabited villages spread throughout the Southern Tropical region. Today one can see an influx of Beti people moving to Cameroon's capital of Yaounde. However, to witness Beti traditions in their purest form, one must visit the surrounding villages in the countryside.

Music

The Beti are best known for their traditional *bikutsi* music, which literally means, "beating the ground continuously." Traditionally, *bikutsi* music had many functions and was performed during several events ranging from market bazaars to communication. The traditional Beti people used bikutsi at the majority of their social gatherings and events. Some of the social context for which the music was performed, such as preparation for interethnic war, have since been abandoned due to a more modernized society. This music has gained contemporary popularity throughout Africa as well as outside of Africa. Historically, these traditional Beti ceremonies were divided into two phases: *Ekang* and *Bikutsi*. The Ekang phase dealt with imaginary, spiritual, and mythological elements, while the Bikutsi phase covered real-life issues that affected the community.

Throughout both phases of Beti gatherings, a double-sided harp with calabash amplification known as the *mvet* is used. Only played by Beti storytellers or griots, the mvet is viewed as an instrument of God to educate the people. During the Ekang phase, which is intensely musical and usually lasts all night, poetic recitations are accompanied by hand clapping, foot stomping, and dancing. At various points in the sacred Ekang phase, balafon (xylophone) players move into a more animated and provocative performance, signaling a shift to the Bikutsi phase which is usually less structured than the Ekang. In this phase of Beti ceremonies, women erotically sing and dance along with the music coming from the balafon; focusing their lyrics and dance movements on the trials and tribulations of everyday life, as well as sexual taboos and fantasies. These improvised female choruses are an integral part of traditional bikutsi music and generally make the core of the authentic Beti traditions.

Traditional bikutsi music is characterized by an intense 6/8 pounding musical rhythm, which is played by various rattles, drum, and the balafon. Since it is based on ancient war rhythms, outsiders often regarded bikutsi as music of savages. Therefore, it did not gain mainstream success until the 1950s. The urbanization of Cameroon during the 1950s had a major influence on the country's music, and is likely the main reason for the popularization of bikutsi music. The most important innovator in modern bikutsi music is Messi Me Nkonda Martin and his band, Los Camarões. The title of Martin's band is derived from the initial name given to Cameroon by the Portuguese, which were Rio dos Camarões (River of Prawns). Martin, a Cameroonian guitarist, has been credited for adding new elements like the electric guitar and synthesizer to bikutsi music. These new elements resulted from outside influences from Spain, Cuba, and Zaïre. Although Martin added these new components to bikutsi music, he was able to keep a traditional timbre, or quality of sound, by linking the strings of his guitar together with pieces of paper, creating a timbre very similar to the traditional balafon.

Over the next few decades, with the influx of foreigners into Cameroon, several instruments found their way into the musical repertoire of Cameroon's musicians. Keyboards, brass instruments, and complex jazz harmonies were added by several musicians, and these modernized bikutsi music. Bikutsi artists started touring across the globe, recording compact discs, making appearances on television and in Claire Denis' film *Man No Run*. The film used footage from the group Les Têtes Brulées, which had toured Europe. Although bikutsi music has recently declined in production, its influences can still be heard in the popular music styles of modern-day Cameroon. It is evident that through the years, bikutsi has evolved into one of Cameroon's most popular forms of cultural expression and is now the country's most recognizable music. Despite its fusion with other types of music, bikutsi has been able to retain much of its rich cultural and traditional heritage by retaining the Beti style elements that identify it as a Cameroonian genre.

Another type of music prevalent in Cameroon is makossa. Most common in urban areas, makossa is a popular dance rhythm that originated during the 1950s during the struggle for independence by the Union des Populations Camerounaises (UPC). Fast-paced bouncy melodies accompanied by strong bass and drum rhythms, characterize this type of music. Due to its flexible rhythmic structures, makossa is generally adaptable to a wide variety of instrumentation and has seen significant influences from American and African jazz, highlife, Latino music and rhumba. Although makossa music is not as traditional as bikutsi music, it occasionally uses traditional thumb pianos and drums of Cameroon.

Makossa witnessed its first major international success in 1972 when singer and saxophonist Emmanuel Manu Dibango released his single "Soul Makossa." Although his success was short-lived, Dibango had laid the foundation and set the precedent for future makossa artists. A large influx of new artists came into Cameroon's musical spectrum popularizing this new style of music. They added new electronic elements such as the electric guitar and synthesizer, which had a great appeal to the urban public. During the 1980s, makossa gained mainstream success throughout Africa and, to a lesser extent, abroad as these newly incorporated musical elements heightened its appeal. As the 1980s progressed, makossa evolved into a highly popular form of pop music in Cameroon. To the dismay of many traditional Cameroonian bikutsi artists, makossa artists seemed to abandon culturally authentic elements in favor of the modernized genre. Despite criticism from certain factions at home, makossa flourished and has ultimately continued to influence the popular music of Cameroon today.

In Cameroon today, traditional and animist religious practices have given way to new Christian practices like baptisms and first communions. A traditional ceremony that has lost almost complete practice in Cameroon is the *mevengu*. During this ceremony, young women would dance all night in order to abstain from sexual behavior. This ritual practice would last for nine days. Another formal tradition that has been almost completely abandoned is the *so* ritual. During this highly feared and anticipated Beti ritual, adolescent boys would have to pass a series of grueling tests. If they passed, the boys were deemed ready for their passage into manhood and were able to escape from the fears of their youth. Although these ceremonies and many other similar traditions have lost their importance in the contemporary culture of Cameroon, Christian practices have not fully overpowered traditional ways.

Cameroon, despite being influenced by foreign nations such as France and Britain, has been able to maintain much of its traditional music and culture. Even though some traditional practices of Cameroon have lost their significance in modern times, it is clear that most Cameroonians hold ancient traditions in high regard and respect their meanings. Through the success of its music and culture, Cameroon has been able to define itself as a prominent and highly influential country within the African continent.

References

Bailey, Robert C., Serge Bahuchet, and Barry S. Hewlett (1992). Development in the Central African Rainforest: Concern for Forest Peoples. In *Conservation of*

West and Central African Rainforests, ed. K. Cleaver, et al. Washington, DC: World Bank.
DeLancey, Mark W. (1990). *Historical Dictionary of the Republic of Cameroon*. Lanham, MD: Scarecrow.
Geschiere, P. (1998). *The Modernity of Witchcraft: Politics and the Occult in Postcolonial Africa*. Charlottesville: University Press of Virginia.
Graham, Ronnie (1988). *The DaCapo Guide to Contemporary African Music*. New York: DaCapo.
Konings, P., and F. B. Nyamnjoh (1996). The Anglophone Problem in Cameroon. *Journal of Modern African Studies* 35 (2): 207–229.
Mbaku, John Mukum (2005). *Culture and Customs of Cameroon*. Westport, CT: Greenwood.
Neba, Aaron. S. (1987). *Modern Geography of the Republic of Cameroon*. Camden, NJ: Neba.
Ngwa, J.A. (1987). *A New Geography of Cameroon*. London: Longman.
Nkwi, P. N., and A. Socpa (1997). Ethnicity and Party Politics in Cameroon: The Politics of Divide and Rule. In *Regional Balance and National Integration in Cameroon*, ed. P. N. Nkwi and F. B. Nyamnjoh. Leiden, Netherlands: African Study Centre.
Regis, Helen A. (2002). *Fulbe Voices: Marriage, Islam, and Medicine in Northern Cameroon*. New York: Westview.
Riesman, Paul (1977). *Freedom in Fulani Social Life: An Introspective Ethnography*. Chicago: University of Chicago Press.
Salamone, Frank A. (1985). Colonialism and the Emergence of Fulani Ethnicity. *Journal of Asian and African Studies* 20: 170–201.
Schultz, Emily A. (1981). *Image and Reality in African Interethnic Relations: The Fulbe and Their Neighbors*. Williamsburg, VA: Studies in Third World Societies.

2. The Egungun Dance of the Yoruba Culture of Nigeria

The Yoruba culture and ethnic group is one of the most widely studied in the world. Its attraction comes from the vast and rich traditions, values, practices, philosophies, and institutions of its culture. Yoruba beliefs focus on values of respect, honesty, care, and its extensive religion. These aspects are shown in daily life from work and industry, to artistic expression in music and dance.

The geographical location of the Yoruba homeland lies in Southwestern Nigeria; covering approximately 180,000 square kilometers. However, the Yoruba culture spreads all throughout Nigeria into the neighboring countries of Benin and Togo. Significant aspects of the culture can be found in all parts of West Africa as well as in Brazil, Cuba, Haiti, Trinidad, Puerto Rico, and the United States. A standard Yoruba language is spoken among the twenty-two major sub-ethnic groups although they each have distinct dialects. While most individuals identify themselves first by his or her sub-ethnic group, and only secondarily as Yoruba, there remains a unifying foundation of mythology and history linking all kingdoms to the ancient holy city of Ile-Ife. Along with these spiritual commonalities, music and dance have importance throughout all Yoruba culture.

The Music of the Yoruba

The music of the Yoruba exists in contexts of prayer, entertainment, or simply as folk tradition. Several distinct features characterize Yoruba music. While melodies are important to many Yoruba songs and prayers, no harmony is ever added to the song. Singing is either done in complete unison, or separated by octaves. Compared to harsh or raspy singing in many other African cultures, Yoruba singing is known to have clearer, more open vocal quality. Singing and drumming patterns of call-and-response are common, usually with an elder leading the song. Structurally, Yoruba songs follow verse and chorus forms (Waterman, 1990). Although other instruments have found their way into Yoruba music, especially in the last century, the only instruments employed in traditional Yoruba music are drums and human voice.

Yoruba drums can be classified into four categories: *Dundun, igbin, Bata* and *gudugudu. Dundun* drums, also known as *gangan*, are the most important drums of Yoruba music. In Western contexts, dundun drums are commonly referred to as "talking drums" for their similarity to the bending of pitches in human speaking. *Dundun* drums hang from a strap worn over the shoulder, and are played with a curved stick held in the opposite hand. The drum-side hand serves to pull and release tension strings to change the tightness of the drumhead, thus affecting the pitch produced when it is struck (Bascom, 1953). The next category, *igbin* drums, also known as *agba* or *apesi*, consists of a set of three drums. These thick, squat instruments sit on the ground when played. While the *dundun* drums are tuned by strings, the general pitches of the *igbin* drums are determined by their size and then further tuned by wooden pegs in the sides of the drums. These are played with either two sticks, or one stick and one hand. The third classification of Yoruba drums is the *bata* drum. These hourglass shaped instruments have two playable heads, one large and low-pitched, and one small and high-pitched. The *bata* drum is held with an elaborate strap over the player's shoulders and behind his neck. Lastly, the smallest drum of Yoruba music, the gudugudu, is a bowl-shaped drum made from a gourd, a hollow, dried shell of a fruit. This ornamental drum is held from a strap around the neck, and beaten with leather straps. Drums in Yoruba culture, however, serve purposes beyond simple musical function.

Drumming is used widely for worshipping the hundreds of deities. Yoruba religion recognizes one high-god, Olorun, also known as Olodumare. Although almost all prayer is directed to the many other gods known collectively as *orisha*. *Orisha* are assigned specific drums and are given songs unique to their purpose, but they are not consistent over the vast number of tribes and variations of mythology. The most notable, developed, and elaborate ritual of worship of the Yoruba people is the masquerade of Egungun.

The Dance of the Yoruba

Egungun is the younger brother of Shango, revered as the god of thunder and lightning. Egungun is customarily celebrated in the festivals of Elewe Egungun, also known as Ebora-Spirit music and dance. These festivals include not only elements of music and dance, but of theater, drama, poetry, mime, and costume as well. The worship of Egungun incorporates the use of *bata* drums accompanying intricately decorated dancers who wear wooden masks on top of their heads and are completely covered with appliquéd fabrics and leather. The body is completely covered, and the identity of the dancer is kept secret (Bascom, 1953). As the dancers sing, their voices change in order to communicate with the Egungun. The key aspect of Egungun dancing is communication and language of the drums. All of the rhythms played by the drummer translate to the dance sequences that, in turn, present to the community, or audience, the tales of Egungun mythology. A skilled drummer must not only be dexterous in his playing ability, but also well versed and fluent in the language and poetry of the tales (Euba, 1994). Egungun drum language can be roughly translated into three commands. Large, deep-pitched drums relate to the shoulders and chest of the dancer; medium drums imitate or follow the large drums; and smaller, high-pitched drums relate to the dancer's waist, hips, and feet (Sakeyfio, 1980). In the Egungun dances, the primary dancer and lead drummer are of equal importance. While the festive displays of Egungun dance worship are prominent in Yoruba culture, spiritual dance may have a much more serious nature.

In Yoruba religion, gods can be directly communicated with through dance. Along with dance, as with prayer and worship, dance can be a direct language of the deities. In some ceremonies, dancers reach a state of trance, allowing their bodies to serve as a vessel for the god. When this trance leads to complete possession by the god, the dancer is believed to be moving only by the god's will ("Dances of Ecstasy"). Only a few people in each ceremony may become possessed, or none at all. Those whose bodies are chosen by the gods to dance in are considered lucky and blessed. These traditional religious rituals have maintained great value in Yoruba culture despite the Western influences since the British colonial period and the arrival of Christian missionaries. That is not to say, however, that secular music and dance have remained traditional as well.

The Evolution of the Yoruba Music

The evolution of Yoruba music has produced international stars and influenced genres around the world. With colonialism came new instruments and consequentially, new music. In the early 1920s, Juju music was born in Lagos, Nigeria. The term Juju has multiple stories of origin. One story recalls the antics of a Juju musician in Tunde King's band who would throw his tambourine into the air to the amusement of the audience. That music became known as Juju from a doubling of the Yoruba word *"ju,"* meaning "toss" or "throw." Melodies, influenced by western instruments such as the guitar, banjo, ukulele, and mandolin, could now have harmonic accompaniments. To match the harmonic variety given by the stringed instruments, musicians began incorporating percussion instruments from other Western and African cultures. The tambourine, samba drum, *shekere* (gourd-shaker surrounded by woven beads), cowbells, bongos, and claves were just some of the new instruments to arrive. After the 1930s, small ensembles and bands were forming (Thomas, 1992). Juju bands could be soon found on street corners, in cafes, and all social gatherings in Lagos.

The first great icon of Juju was Tunde King. Growing up in the Lagos music scene, Tunde was quick to catch on to the new sounds of the city.

Leading on vocals and guitar, Tunde King was accompanied by three percussionists who added strong harmonies to the elevating melodies for which the King would become known. His songs spoke to the citizens of Lagos and beyond, reminiscing about the "good old days" and simple life before the problems that came about with the colonial governments. The colonial government in place in Nigeria from 1900 to 1932 was that of Oba Esugbayi Eleko; his reign was one of great disorder and little social or economic development for the country (Thomas, 1992). Another significant figure in Juju was Akanbi Wright. While Juju musicians embraced all aspects of the Western music that was being exposed to them, many considered this new style to be completely absurd and rejected it. Akanbi Wright, however, played a large role in increasing Juju's appeal to the more stubborn or traditional people. Wright was the first musician to incorporate the use of the *dundun*, or talking drum, into Juju music. The sound of the *dundun* helped Juju music to keep its Yoruba identity while it continued to develop. Juju music maintained its own progress at the rate of the technological developments of music all around the world. Inevitably, this evolution led to the use of electronic instruments and amplifiers and therefore bigger concerts and larger followings. Wright also became famous for his skills as a composer. Most notable was a song of his that became a school anthem sung by children all across Nigeria.

King Sunny Ade also made great strides in the movement of Juju music. Sunny Ade presented the use of the organ and slide guitar. His tremendous band, which even included dancers and sideshows, introduced the concert-style shows and brought his act to big venues. King Sunny Ade became very successful and set out on multi-city tours around West Africa. Eventually, his popularity led him overseas. King Sunny Ade was the first Juju musician to tour the United States with great success, opening many doors for exchange of styles between American and African music.

One particular fusion was created completely by a single man: Fela Anikulapo Kuti. After studying music in London, Fela traveled to the United States, where he was exposed to jazz, funk, soul, and rock. However, the music of the United States was not the only aspect to influence him. Fela Kuti was very moved by the pride of the Black Power movement and struggles of the Civil Rights era. Icons like Malcolm X and Dr. Martin Luther King, Jr., inspired Fela to focus on human and civil rights issues. Fela Kuti returned to Nigeria and put together a band, blending Juju music with the sounds of Charlie Parker and James Brown, all to the rhythm of heavy African drumming (Thomas, 1992). He called this music Afrobeat, and with its lyrical messages of protest against government corruption and injustice, it quickly became the music of the people. With his sharp, controversial lyrics, Fela became a thorn in the side of the Nigerian government. Fela Kuti took all risks in speaking out against the officials, and they did not hesitate to attempts to silence him. This reached its peak when a few dozen soldiers came to his home in Lagos, setting fire to the building only after committing atrocities of rape and violence to the over fifty people that lived in his home. Most importantly, Fela's mother was thrown out of an upstairs window and soon died of her injuries. The successes of Juju music and its child, Afrobeat, have served as a medium through which contemporary Yoruba culture can spread.

Yoruba culture can be seen not only in Southwestern Nigeria but also in thousands of miles from the homeland as well. The slave trade brought millions of Africans to the Americas and, inevitably, it also about their cultures. The influence of Yoruba traditions exists in all areas. From the Rumba music of Cuba to the Candomble dance of Brazil. Yoruba music and dance exemplify the essence of the culture. Whether in the context of traditional religious rituals or simply for fun and entertainment, Yoruba music and dance is always performed with deepest love and sincerity.

References

Bascom, W. (1953). *Drums of the Yoruba of Nigeria*. Folkways Records.
Brandon, G. (1993). *Santeria from Africa to the New World*. Bloomington: Indiana University Press.
Dances of Ecstasy (2003). Prd. Ferenc van Damme. Opus Arte.
Drewal, M. T. (1998). Art in Yoruba Life and Thought and Descriptive Catalogue. In *Yoruba—Art in Life and Thought*, ed. David Dorward. Bundoora, Victoria, Australia: La Trobe University.
Euba, A. (1994). Drumming for the Egungun: The Poet-Musician in Yoruba Masquerade Theater. In *The Yoruba Artist*, ed. Rowland Abiodun, Henry J. Drewal, and John Pemberton III. Washington: Smithsonian Instution.
King, A. (1961). *Yoruba Sacred Music from Ekiti*. London: Ibadan University Press.
Sakeyfio, G. O. (1980). *Yoruba Music and Dance at Ila Rangun Odun Egungun Festival*. Folkways Records.
Thomas, T. A. (1992). *History of Juju Music*. Jamaica, NY: Thomas Organization.
Waterman, C. A. (1990). *Juju*. Chicago: University of Chicago Press.
White, H. (1994). *Art from Nigeria*. Rotterdam, Holland: Steens Schiedam.

3. The Music and Dance of Côte d'Ivoire

Côte d'Ivoire, also known as the Ivory Coast, is a tropical West African country. At the turn of the nineteenth century, Côte d'Ivoire was the most economically prosperous Tropical African country mainly due to the ivory trade. The Ivory Coast is located along the western coast of Africa. The country is surrounded by Liberia and Guinea on its west coast, Mali and Burkina Faso on its north coast, and Ghana to its east. To the south of Ivory Coast lies the Gulf of Guinea. The capital of Côte d'Ivoire is Yamoussoukro. France made initial contact as early as 1637 but it was not until 1893 when the French took control amidst strong rebellion from freedom fighters led by a Malinke chief named Almany Samory. The Neolithic culture, which was thought to have existed before then, was infiltrated by France formally from about 1899 until 1960 when Ivory Coast gained her political independence from France. Ivory Coast government leaders including the current president, Laurent Gbagbo, have maintained strong ties with the French since the country gained independence during the 1960.

Economy

The economy of is Côte d'Ivoire is market-based economy and relies heavily on agriculture. Almost 70 percent of all people in the Ivory Coast are involved in agriculture. The Ivory Coast is one of the largest cocoa and palm oil exporters in the world and the world's largest producers of Robusta coffee. Political instability has ravaged the country within the past decades. The civil war that broke out in 2002 rumbled the country's market and severely affected the country's economy.

Culture

The natives of the Ivory Coast are known as Ivorians and comprise 77 percent of the country's population. The country also consists of Spanish, French, British, and Arabian people. There are about 65 different languages spoken in Ivory Coast; the most common of them is Djoula, which acts as the national trade language. However, French is considered the country's first language.

The culture of Ivory Coast has its influences from the Spanish, French, British, and the Arabs. The people of these cultures reach into the realm of music and dance of Ivory Coast as well as in everyday life. However, the Ivory Coast's neighboring countries have played a larger role in the development of music in the region. The roots of traditional music of the Ivorians such as the *balonyè* (one-stringed harp) of the Fodonbele tribe have led to the contemporary style of Ivorian music thus; the mixture of influences of the past has led the Ivory Coast to produce a sound of its own.

Music

The music of the Ivory Coast can be classified and named according to the tribal groups found in Ivory Coast. Thus, every tribe has its characteristic style of music. For example, the Baule people play the Baule style while the Gur people play the Gur style. The Baule style of music however is generally considered to represent the Ivory Coast as a whole. In their style of music, common features include the traditional rhythmic patterns played on drums being accompanied by a harp. Yao Kuadio, a performer of traditional music is well known in this tradition and performs on two harps at the same time. Harps are still found throughout the continent and can range from the portable kora used by itinerant musicians in West Africa, to the lutes found in South Africa, to the human-shaped harps of the Azande and the Mangbetu peoples of the Democratic Republic of Congo (Lee, 1999). Another characteristic associated with the Ivorian style traditional music is polyrhythm or many separate rhythms occurring simultaneously during one song. In the performance excerpt on the Video Anthology of World Music and Dance, it shows that the performer who plays the harps actually plays two completely different rhythms at the same time and his accompanists contribute their own separate rhythms to make one fluid sound. Much of Baule music also involves the use of various types of idiophones such as the *sekeseke*, a woven rattle used to keep time in a performance.

One characteristic of Ivorian music that differentiates it from that of other African music is its rhythmic pattern. In many songs the rhythms are similar to each other. They do not share the common 4/4 count that is characteristic of Western European music. However, in the Ivory Coast, some of its music does have this common count time signature because of the European musical influence.

Music has many purposes for the people of the Ivory Coast and Africa in general. Often times drumming is used as a type of communication between and within communities, comparable to Morse code in the United States. Drumming as a form of communication however is different from Morse code in that it actually imitates the words they are attempting to say across town. Their drumbeats imitate their actual speech patterns or inflections of speech. They have songs that ask their gods for assistance during hunting or farming seasons. In turn, they have songs of praise to their gods thanking them for successful hunts or agricultural seasons.

Gender has little effect on the performance of most Ivorian music. Since a large portion of their music is performed in full costume, including masks, it is okay for women to participate in the singing and dancing. The masks of each dance help tell the dances. Masks are made of not only people but also animals and ghosts as well as other non-living organisms. The females are able to wear these masks and perform just as any male would in most dances. However, there are dances and songs that are only to be performed by one particular group. There are dances specifically for men and some for women only and still others only for children.

During the movement from traditional to contemporary music in the Ivory Coast, the style of the music and the motives behind creating it has changed a great deal. In the past the music has been made almost entirely for spiritual, communicative, or healing purposes. The traditional spiritual songs praising God for watching over a community or asking God for help are seen less and less in the music of modern times. The drum speaking in the villages is still very prevalent in some of the rural villages or towns but in the larger, industrialized places, it plays a lesser role from a functional standpoint. In many rural towns and villages, traditional music is still used for healing despite the diminishing practices due to modern technologies and medical practices. In Ivory Coast, contemporary music is floating down the main stream, similar to that of the United States. Many young performers are seeking successful careers in the music industry for better lives. Although the music itself still maintains many of the instrumental sounds of traditional music, it has shifted drastically toward the use of electrophones.

Abidjan, the country's administrative center, is one of the most influential contributors to all the music of Ivory Coast both locally and throughout Africa. The music industry plays a much larger role than ever before in the Ivory Coast. Artists are not only seeking to succeed financially within their own country, but also to be idolized by other countries as well. One popular contemporary artist is Ivorian pop star, Orentchy. He and his brother developed their own style of music with traditional roots but with a lot of modernization as well. Orentchy sings his songs in French, English, Yoruba, Nzema, and Swahili in order to reach a wide variety of people. His audience is huge and travels all over Africa to listen to and to talk about his music. In this way, Orentchy is much like that of a popular singer in America. In technologically advanced countries like the United States for example, after a record is released, the artists go around and promote their record all over the country and the world. Ivory Coast artists are similar in some ways to their American counterparts. Music is becoming mainstream activity for Ivorians. In the city of Abidjan for instance, there are more than five major recording studios. In the USA, artists visit from all across the continent to record their singles in order to be signed.

Contemporary Music

Another popular style of contemporary music in the Ivory Coast is reggae. The Ivorian reggae music is somewhat different from the traditional reggae music of the West Indies, but it contains the same time counts as well as many of the same instruments. You can hear the rhythmic membranophones and idiophones being accompanied by various types of chordophones from the Ivory Coast but with occasional use of an acoustic guitar. The reggae musicians make use of the keyboard in much of their music. In a lot of the reggae music, there is some voice synthesizing as well. The reggae style music has become a very prevalent style in the Ivory Coast in recent years and it is continuing in growth.

Another common style of Ivorian music that has more recently been popularized is the rap and hip-hop. This genre has become a large part of the music industry in the country since it landed in the mainstream in 1998. In the Ivory Coast, they hold an annual event called "Le Défi," during which rappers face off against each other with new rhymes as well as freestyles. It is very comparable to the American Freestyle Battles. Two big names in rap and especially the "Le Défi" shows are Stezo of the Flotte Imperiale Posse and Almighty from the group Ministère Authentik Fame. The rivalry of these two rappers is even greater than that experienced in the contests in the United States. They are so famous in "Le Défi" because of their heated battles against one another. With the wave of hip-hop music comes another wave of hip-hop style. Hip-hop has become very important in the city of Abidjan. One is bound to experience more of this than in London or the United States. This wave of hip-hop style has hit the Ivory Coast just as suddenly as the rap scene hit. While it is a new genre to the Ivory Coast, some originals initiated the transition early, although it did not catch on right away. Artists like Erik B, Big Daddy Kane, and K-Solo are just some of the early hip-hop artists comparable to early American artists like Tupac Shakur and Run DMC. Some of the hip-hop is fused with the country's native styles such as Zouglou. Rap as a genre is taking over the mainstream scene in the Ivory Coast in much the same way it has hit America.

There are exceptions to the money-seeking performers however. Ivory Coast's city of Man, which is mostly comprised of the Dan people, has been the center of a major religious revival through music throughout the 1990s. During the '80s, a man by the name of Gba Gama was at the center of this revival. With an increasing number of Muslims and Christians in the city, Gama thought it was a good idea to construct a place where people could congregate and enjoy all cultures in their area. He built a bar and acted as a booking agent for people in the city to play or enjoy music and festivals. His business quickly grew, and the festivals he began to organize became larger. In his article "Pop Goes the Sacred: Dan Mask Performance and Popular Culture in Postcolonial Côte d'Ivoire," Daniel Reed, an avid researcher of the African culture endeavors to demonstrate to the diverse crowd of thousands that despite the fact that many of their elders had embraced Islam and abandoned Ge, despite the growing influence of Christianity, despite the ubiquitous presence on the streets of Man of mediated popular music and expressive traditions of other ethnic groups, Ge was still central to their lives (Reed, 2001; 2003a). The article Reed wrote discusses a faltering religion and how the recent festivals have not only brought a revival to the old religion, but the festivals have also put amateur artists into the music circuit. Many of these artists have reached the mainstream without abandoning their traditional music roots. They have maintained the same patterns and style of music as their ancestors, and they continue to sing songs of praise and healing to their gods.

The transition of music from traditional to contemporary in the Ivory Coast has turned towards the contemporary style of the United States. Their music has shifted its emphasis from religious values and purposes more toward moneymaking and fame purposes. The country still has a few small but strong groups bringing about a revival of the religious music of the region. These groups alone have changed the modern music in the Ivory Coast a great deal by putting their reasons for singing before their benefits from singing. They choose to sing songs of healing and praise. If that brings them fame then so is it but the music is what really matters. Many of these people have stood by the values of traditional music. They are maintaining their roots even though their country is always continuously borrowing cultures from elsewhere including the United States.

References

Barber, Karin (1997). Introduction to *Readings*. In *African Popular Culture*, ed. Karin Barber. Bloomington: Indiana University Press.

Barber, Karin, and Christopher Waterman (1995). Traversing the Global and the Local: Fuji Music and Praise Poetry in the Production of Contemporary Yoruba Popular Culture. In *Worlds Apart: Modernity through the Prism of the Local*, ed. Daniel Miller. London: Routledge.

Barz, Gregory F. (1997). Confronting the Field (Note) In and Out of the Field: Music, Voices, Text, and Experiences in Dialogue. In *Shadows in the Field: New Perspectives for Fieldwork in Ethnomusicology*, ed. Gregory F. Barz and Timothy J. Cooley. New York, Oxford: Oxford University Press.

Bauman, Richard (1971). Differential Identity and the Social Base of Folklore. In *Toward New Perspectives in Folklore*, ed. Americo Paredes and Richard Bauman. Austin: University of Texas Press.

Bauman, Richard, and Charles Briggs (1992). Genre, Intertextuality, and Social Power. *Journal of Linguistic Anthropology* 2 (2):131-72.

Ben-Amos, Dan (1976). Analytical Categories and Ethnic Genres. In *Folklore Genres*, ed. Dan Ben-Amos. Austin: University of Texas Press.

Comaroff, Jean, and John Comaroff (1993). Introduction to *Modernity and Its Malcontents: Ritual and Power in Postcolonial Africa*. Chicago, London: University of Chicago Press.

Davidson, Basil (1966). *A History of West Africa*. Garden City, NY: Anchor.

Duranti, Alessandro (1994). *From Grammar to Politics: Linguistic Anthropology in a Western Samoan Village*. Berkeley: University of California Press.

Fischer, Eberhard. (1978). Dan Forest Spirits. *African Arts* 11 (2):16-23, 94.

Fischer, Eberhard, and Hans Himmelheber (1984). *The Arts of the Dan in West Africa*. Zurich: Museum Rietberg.

Gba, Daouda (1982). Les masques chez les Dan. Master's thesis, Université National de Côte d'Ivoire.

Goueu, Tia Jean-Claude (1997). Drum lesson with author (DR97C31). Man, Côte d'Ivoire, 26 May.

Gueu Gbe, Gonga Alphonse (1997). Interview by author (DR97C44). Man, Côte d'Ivoire, 18 August.

Gyekye, Kwame (1997). *Tradition and Modernity: Philosophical Reflections on the African Experience*. New York and Oxford: Oxford University Press.

Hannerz, Ulf. [1987] 1997. The World in Creolization. In *Readings in African Popular Culture*, ed. Karin Barber. Bloomington: Indiana University Press.

Hopkins, A. G. (1973). *Economic History of West Africa.* London: Longman.
Kamara, Mamadou Koble (1992). *Les Fonctions du Masque dans la Société Dan de Sipilou.* Zurich: Museum Rietberg.
Kisliuk, Michelle (1997). (Un)doing Fieldwork: Sharing Songs, Sharing Lives. In *Shadows in the Field: New Perspectives for Fieldwork in Ethnomusicology,* ed. Gregory F. Barz and Timothy J. Cooley. New York, Oxford: Oxford University Press.
Kisliuk, Michelle (1998). *Seize the Dance! BaAka Musical Life and the Ethnography of Performance.* New York and Oxford: Oxford University Press.
Koetting, James (1970). Analysis and Notation of West African Drum Ensemble Music. *Selected Reports, Institute of Ethnomusicology, UCLA* 1 (3):115–46.
Kristeva, Julia (1986). The Bounded Text. In *Contemporary Literary Criticism,* ed. R.C. Davis. New York: Longman.
Lee, C. Carole (1999). The Reach of African Music. *Humanities* 6, no. 20 (November/December).
Piot, Charles (1999). *Remotely Global: Village Modernity in West Africa.* Chicago: University of Chicago Press.
Reed, Daniel B. (2001). Pop Goes the Sacred: Dan Mask Performance and Popular Culture in Postcolonial Côte d'Ivoire. *Africa Today* 48(4): 67–85.
Reed, Daniel B. (2003a). *Dan Ge Performance: Masks and Music in Contemporary Côte d'Ivoire.* Bloomington: Indiana University Press.
Reed, Daniel B. (2003b). *Old Masks, Old Music, New Realities: Dan Ge Performance in Contemporary Côte d'Ivoire.* Bloomington: Indiana University Press.
Stone, Ruth M. (1985). "In Search of Time in African Music." *Music Theory Spectrum* 7 (1985):139–48.
Stone, Ruth M., and Verlon L. Stone (1981). "Event, Feedback, and Analysis: Research Media in the Study of Music Events." *Ethnomusicology* 25 (2):215–25.
Vandenhoute, P.J. (1948). *Classification Stylistique du Masque Dan et Guéré de la Côte d'Ivoire Occidentale (A.O.F.).* Leiden: E.J. Brill.
Waterman, Christopher A. (1990). "Our Tradition Is a Very Modern Tradition: Popular Music and the Construction of a Pan-Yoruba Identity." *Ethnomusicology* 34 (3): 67–79.
Zemp, Hugo. (1964). Musiciens Autochtones et Griots Malinké chez les Dan de Côte d'Ivoire. *Cahiers d'Etudes Africaines* 24 (6–4): 370–82.

4. The Gumboot Dance of South Africa

The gumboot dance was created by a combination of different cultures dances. Using film as depicted in multiple cultural dances that exist in South Africa, this short chapter gives the history of the gumboot dance. Some of the different South African ethnic dances that appear to have influenced the gumboot dance are also discussed.

The Birth of the Gumboot Dance

The birth of the gumboot dance occurred in the 1880s. Its fruition coincided with the introduction of gold mining in South Africa. Of course, with the opening of mines, many jobs were filled. The state of poverty and subsistence economies that existed all over South Africa encouraged Africans from all over the country to migrate to work in the mines. The train system was the primary channel used by the miners to be transported thousands of miles from their homes for work (*Gumboot* movie). The people who owned the mines made working conditions difficult for the native South Africans. It is not to say that the workers were slaves; however, conditions were poor and they employed various strategies to adapt to their situation. The workers would work in three-month shifts. After their three months were over, they would return home to their families for a short stay before returning to the mines. When the miners came to the mining camps, they were stripped of their ethnic decorations or clothing. The miners were all given the same uniforms. The owners of the mines did not want any problems between the multitudes of ethnic groups working in the mines together. Many different tribes represented their tribal cultures through their decor. The uniforms did not allow different tribes to be recognized by their clothing. In addition, by taking away the South African miners' clothes, they were stripping them of their heritage, which the mine owners also thought would keep the South Africans from starting an uprising against them.

Language was also restricted. The miners were not allowed to talk to each other inside of the mines because of the fear that the mine owners had of a workers rebellion. As a method to control workers, they were often chained to a workstation. The social and physical conditions that were created by the mine owners are what facilitated the necessity for the gumboot dance. The mentality of mine owners was that if they could remove symbolic aspects of culture, the workers would form a homogenized group. Therefore, these people formed the dance as a way of dealing with their unbearable situation.

The Elements of the Gumboot Dance

One of the main ingredients of the gumboot dance is stomping of the feet, which simulates the miners at work. The cost to pump the water out of the mines was higher than the mine owners cared to pay. They could not ignore the problem of water in the mines because the miners were having health problems that caused them to be unable to work. As a result, mine owners issued their gumboots to protect their feet from fungi and other skin infections.

There were two main functions for the gumboot dance in the beginning. First was to communicate and second was to entertain the miners during the very hard and dangerous work. Oral communication proved difficult for people at varied levels of the mining hierarchy. Many of the miners did not speak a common language because of their different ethnic backgrounds. The miners had to find a way to communicate. The way the miners learned to communicate was using rhythm and music. In the mines, the miners did not have traditional musical instruments that they might have used to communicate, such as drums. As a result, the miners used what they had to make rhythms. These rhythms came from the chains that were around their ankles and their gumboots. With the use of what miners had, they were able to communicate inside of the mines without the mine owners knowing that they were actually speaking a language with rhythm. Some scholars concur that this rhythmic language compares to Morse code (Mosley, 2001).

With gumboot dance as a universal language, it also evolved into a dance men performed in their spare time in the mining communities. The miners would use the dance to cope with the bad situation of the mining conditions. In general, the gumboot dance became a social event for these miners. At a point, the mine owners discovered the dance. The more tolerant ones allowed the best dancers to create dance troops to perform gumboot dance as a way of promoting the company and as a tourist attraction.

Singing during the dances became popular at this time, and the miners would often sing a song in an African language that would mock the working conditions and wages, but the employers would never know that they were singing negatively about the mining industry. It is obvious here that the oppressive conditions were transgressed by the miners. As they transcended their confines, something that is today considered art emerged.

Gumboot's Survival

The gumboot dance has continued to exist through time even though it is no longer needed to communicate in the mines to express the discontent of the miners. One way that it has survived as a dance is through the work of Mrs. M. Makhuda. During the Apartheid, Makhuda opened a youth center in 1974 in Soweto to keep children off the streets and in safe care (Forbes, Askeni & Lewis 1999). Makhuda thought it would be good to teach the children traditional dances to keep them in touch with their native culture. This sentiment of returning to tradition was especially important in the Apartheid era. The gumboot dance became so popular amongst some of the dances at the youth center that a special group was formed called the Rishile poets. The Rishile poets performed all over South Africa. As their popularity grew their dance company bonded with other partnerships such as SFX back row, and Columbia Artist theatricals. A new group was created to perform the dance in 1999 and was called Gumboots. This show is so popular that the dancers tour internationally right from the United Kingdom to The United States. The show has helped to keep the gumboot dance alive and, with international success, has spread the dance around the world.

The Dance Form of Gumboot

Men usually perform the gumboot dance. This is because mining work was exclusively performed by men. Even though men created the dance, there is no evidence that it is taboo for women to perform the gumboot dance. The dance is usually composed of five to ten people, but the ensemble could be even larger depending on how many people want to partake in the dance. The dance is performed in linear rows so you can see all the dancers dancing at the same time. It is imperative that participants are coordinated with each other. The linear style illuminates the synchronicity of body movements. Clapping hands, stomping, and slapping gumboots are central to the movements of the dance. There are usually no drums in the dance, thus the use of clapping and slapping of the gumboots allows there to be a strong pulsing rhythm that substitutes drums. To enhance the sound of the slapping of their gumboots, the dancers put bolt washers on fishing line to add a certain timbre. When the boots are struck, the washers on the fishing line would make a jingle-like sound. In the later forms of gumboot dance, around the 1970s, singing and playing the guitar during the performance became popular. Singing and playing guitar while performing existed before the 1970s, but it was not as prevalent as during this time. The primary aspect of the singing that occurs is a call and response format where a lead singer would sing a phrase and the rest of the dancers would respond.

Many contemporary dances in Africa have connections to other traditional dances. The borrowing of dance or musical techniques is not exclusive to one cultural tradition. The gumboot dance has emerged from various ethnic dances found in South Africa. To gain a better understanding of the gumboot dance, some traditional South African dance forms are analyzed to identify any similarities between the gumboot dance and traditional dance forms of South Africa. Specifically, one of the largest tribes in South Africa, The Zulu, and a much smaller tribe, the !Kung San are analyzed.

Zulu Dance

In order to trace the potential roots of the gumboot dance, it is helpful to examine other traditional African dances, such as the Zulu wedding dance. An initial observation about the dance was the attire of the dancers varied. Both male and female dancers were wearing similar colors but the styles of clothing were different. The respect of attire in this dance is different from the gumboot dance because it has already been stated that everyone who performs the gumboot dance wears the same clothing because of the mandatory uniforms that were issued in the mines.

During a visit to South Africa in the spring of 2001, not only was the attire of the Zulu dances but their dance moves were closely observed. Their first movement was similar to the gumboot dance, including the stomping of the dancers' feet. In the wedding dance, the only instruments used were singers' voices, stomping, and clapping of the hands and feet. These sounds and movements are very reminiscent of the gumboot dance. The premier gumboot dancers were unable to use instruments in their performances. To keep time, they stomped their feet and clapped their hands. The use of the body and instruments seems to be an aspect that exists in both the gumboot dance and the Zulu dance. This elaboration of similarities displays South African elements that derive from their ethnic groups. These ethnic groups comprised the majority of miners.

In the Zulu wedding dance, the singing followed a call and response form. It seemed that one person would sing a phrase, and the majority of the people performing the dance would respond. In the later forms of gumboot, we find the dancers singing while dancing such as the dance company that performs "gumboots." There tends to be a "front man" that sings first and the rest of the dancers respond. The singing structure of the Zulu wedding dance and the gumboot dance follow the same form. You could infer that the call and response singing of the gumboot dance could have been adopted from the Zulu wedding dance or another Zulu dance that uses call and response. Call and response is found in various African musical and dance traditions. Identities that share call and response traditions are reiterated in the mines as a way of creating a new identity; therefore, they are especially important to the cultural aspect of these dances.

The !Kung San Dance

The next dance that was analyzed was a dance by the *!Kung San*. The purpose of the dance was enter a trance-like state to heal sickness. In this book, tangible connections between that of the *!Kung San* and the gumboot dances are made. The first was the use of hand clapping in the performance. It has already been stated that hand clapping and feet stomping are a large part of the gumboot dance performance. Elements of clapping in the *!Kung San* dance suggest it is possible that *!Kung San* dance influenced the gumboot dance. The next element of the *!Kung San*'s dance performance that could have a relationship with gumboot dance is the use of ankle rattles. In the *!Kung San* performance, the dancers tied a strand of shells around their ankles when they danced. The shells created a sound that added to the texture of the music that went along with the performance. In the gumboot dance, rattles were not made of shells but of nut washers that they would tie to fishing line and tie around their ankles. In the gumboot dance, the ankle rattles were used to add a rhythmic text to the dance. The utilization of the ankle rattles in both the gumboot dance and the *!Kung San* dance, suggest one could say that the use of the ankle rattle could be an element of the gumboot dance that was borrowed from the *!Kung San*.

The last element of the *!Kung San* dance that was similar to the gumboot dance is the use of call and response. In the *!Kung San* performance, the Shaman would sing a phrase, and the rest of the ensemble would respond. As it has already been shown, call and response is used in the gumboot dance. Because call and response is also used in *Zulu* song and dance traditions, it is hard to say whether call and response was adopted from *Zulu* or the *!Kung san* dance. These elements existed in both of these South African dances, therefore, one could infer that that call and response is an important aspect of many kinds of music and dance in South Africa.

Zulu dances and !Kung San dances have been likened to the gumboot dance. The parallels made between dances may appear broad. Arguably, the dances and their respective ethnic groups are not mutually exclusive. The combination of ethnic migration and dance similarities allows one to make conclusions. One may argue that some of the similarities found among these dances are found across the African continent. This may be true, however, the migratory connections, especially for the Zulu into mining communities, cannot be refused. Therefore these miners, despite the attempts of mine owners, could not be completely removed from their traditional pasts.

Step Dancing

The gumboot dance lends a familiar image to an American eye. Even though the gumboot dance is from a culture that is far away from the United States, it shares a vast number of similarities to some step show dances. Step dancing is a phenomenon that is very popular with many African American fraternity and sororities in high schools and universities across the United States. Even though the origins of step dancing do not directly link up with the origins of the gumboot dance, the two dances have many similarities that liken them together. The relationship is so linked together that step dancing has been a way of helping the gumboot dance survive by Step dancing in The United States.

Step dancing's true beginnings are unknown but some believe that it started in 1922 during an Inter Fraternity Conference in Washington, D.C. In between events at the conference, fraternities would sing, chant, and do marches to impress women (Forbes, Askeni & Lewis 1999). After World War II, different elements of military marching were added to dance steps for the step shows. These included the use of a cane in the step show performances and the use of line formation in the dances (Forbes, Askeni & Lewis 1999). During this time, stepping became an important part of pledging and initiation in African American fraternities and is still an important part of pledging today. Many step show performances have influences from Masonic marching and African influence from great

African marching armies such as The Warriors of Carthage by Hannibal Ruler of Carthage, Nubian warriors of King Piankhy of Nubia, and the Zulu Legion by general Chaka of the Zulu nation (Forbes, Askeni & Lewis 1999).

Even though the fraternities acknowledge that there are African influences in step show dances, some people who are involved with step shows believe that stepping is a separate entity with a different historic background than the gumboot dance of South Africa. This quote expresses that sentiment, "Please note that some people want to give the credit to the South African boot dance, but it would be unfair to ignore everything that stepping was in the beginning and it is now" (Forbes, Askeni & Lewis 1999). The history of step dancing in America has its own history that should be acknowledged separately from gumboot dance. The social and stylistic ingredients of that step dancing and the gumboot dance have in common are helping the gumboot dance live on vicariously through the use of step dancing in the United States. There is a line from Shakespeare's *Romeo and Juliet* that states "...a rose by any other name would smell as sweet." This quote expresses the relationship between the gumboot dance and step dancing, because if you showed a South African an American Step show dance, they would probably call it gumboot dance. Moreover, if you showed gumboot dance to an American, they would probably call it step dance. The assumption has not been tested; however, it provides cause for further research. Even though these two dances have different historic backgrounds, the dances themselves are so similar that if you were not completely familiar with both dance forms, you could mistake one form for the other.

Just because the gumboot dance and step dancing have varied elements, it does not discredit their commonalities. For it is not only the dance movements that link these two dances together, but also a social context. Both dances have been used to create a social solidarity. In the early years of gumboot dancing in the mining communities, it was danced by the workers and by the workers only. The dance was used to help relieve the stressful times of working in the mines. Therefore, it was almost like a sub-culture exclusive to its members. The mineworkers took pride in having the dance belong to them and not to anyone else. There appears to be a similar sense of ownership with step dancing. Only members of the fraternities perform step dances, making it a restricted club of people. In both cases, only the people who belong in the solidarities perform the gumboot and step dances. It is also important to note that the populations that perform these dances are both marginalized and therefore need the sense of solidarity and pride to persevere. A sense of ownership also accompanies these sentiments. The relationship that exists between the gumboot dance and step dances, therefore, helps to bind the two dances together without homogenizing the cultural groups and discrediting their respective histories.

The Gumboot Dance Today

The gumboot dance is not a ritualistic or social dance in modern South Africa. Gumboot is primarily performed by few people included in a dance company called gumboots, which makes it available in South Africa and throughout Europe. Global exposure coupled with the newfound meanings of gumboot dancing has allowed it to evolve into a novelty dance. The dance is no longer danced to communicate in mines or for groups of miners nor is it used to dance in relief of working in a harsh environment. The dance is now performed to show African identity. It expresses the hardships that South Africans have endured, such as the mining conditions and Apartheid. The step show dances can also be paralleled in a similar fashion, because step dances are part of the identity of African American fraternities. In both cases, these dances are used to express African identity and African American identity. Even though the gumboot dance is no longer used as a functional dance in South Africa, it still expresses African identity, which is why the dance is still valued and performed.

Visual similarities between the gumboot dance and the step dance allow the viewer to see them as related despite their different histories and cultural contexts. The eyes of an onlooker who is familiar with one of these dances will recognize the sounds and movements of the other dance. The analogy then can be drawn to genres of music or language families, one may not know all Bantu languages or Rock 'n' Roll artists, but to know Swahili or the music of Led Zeppelin is to know a representation of a common foundation. In a way, the shared foundational elements of the gumboot dance and the Step dance could allow them to be grouped together into a genre. Even if these dances are categorized together in an academic sense or simply if the viewer makes the connection, it ties them to a shared identity that cannot be separated.

Music and dance are always borrowing and evolving to make new forms. If you look at a dance close enough, you can look into the past and find music and dance forms from past generations. These dances, whether it is in their historical or contemporary analysis, are connected through identity and cultural context.

References

Dixon, Norm (2005). Rishile Gumboot Dancers of Soweto. http://www.greenleft.org.au/back/1998/343/343p22.htm, November.
Forbes, Rapheal, Ahab Askeni & Terrence Lewis (1999). The Genesis. Retrieved November 2005. http://www.stompshow.com/information.php?info_id=3.
Gumboots (2001). Choreography by Rishile Gumboot Dancers of Soweto and Zenzi Mbuli. Warner Vision International, Columbia Artists Theatricals. Chatsworth, CA: Image Entertainment.
Gumboots History: Rhythm Is a Language (2004). www.gumbootsworldtour.com/english/history/html.
The JVC Video Anthology of World Music and Dance. Vol. 19 (1988). Tokyo: JVC Victor Company of Japan [production company].
Let the People Speak (1994). Shosholoza Mandela. Produced and directed by Zeph R. Makgetla. Marshalltown, Johannesburg.
Mosley, Albert (2001). On the Aesthetics of Black Music. *Journal of Aesthetic Education* 35(3), 94–98.
South African Dance: Gumboot in Dance Style Locator (2005). http://www.worldartswest.org/plm/guide/locator/southafrican.shtml.

5. The Music and Culture of Botswana

Botswana, known officially as the Republic of Botswana, is a landlocked country in southern Africa. Botswana is made up of numerous ethnic groups and draws much of its music, as well as its culture, from those ethnic groups and its surrounding countries. The countries of South Africa, Namibia, Zambia and Zimbabwe border Botswana. The population of Botswana is 1,765,000, and is unusually diverse. The official language of Botswana is English, even though it is only spoken by only about 3 percent of the people, whereas the national language of Botswana is Tswana—the language of the largest ethnic group. Botswana is also one of the most AIDS-ridden countries in the world (World Health Organization, 2007). Adult prevalence rates of over 38 percent give Botswana the second highest rate of infection in the world behind Swaziland. One out of every three Botswana residents has AIDS, meaning 350,000 people are living with AIDS each year, and over 30,000 die each year from the disease. Due to this extremely high rate, the government of Botswana has instituted a free antiretroviral drug program, as well as nationwide AIDS prevention education. The major food/waterborne illnesses in Botswana are: bacterial diarrhea, hepatitis A, and typhoid fever. The main vector borne disease is malaria. All of these diseases are so prevalent because of the lack of proper medical advances as well as the inability and knowledge of how to stop the diseases from spreading. The other aspect of the demographics is what truly shows the diversity within Botswana. It involves aspects of ethnic groups, languages, and religions. Botswana is made up of six different ethnic groups, with the Tswana people being the largest at 79 percent of the population. The Kalanga people make up the next largest ethnic group totaling to about 11 percent of the population. The next ethnic groups all make up 3 percent of the population and they are the Basarwa, Kgalagadi and Caucasians. The last ethnic group makes up only 1 percent of the population, and is labeled simply as "other"—meaning it is most likely people who simply have not registered or live in a remote place. The languages are a reflection of the ethnic group's representation in the population. Tswana is the most widely spoken, followed by Ikalaganga and English. Another diverse aspect of Botswana's demographics is religion. The country is predominantly Christian, practiced by 74 percent of Botswana, followed by the religion of Badimo, which is practiced by 6 percent of the population. The other 20 per cent is made up of the religious specification of other/unspecified/none.

History

The history of Botswana is very rich and shows just how far the country has come from a small British colony to an independent country. Botswana's most well-known music is its traditional folk music, but it also has a lot of popular music that it uses from other countries. Another music style that is emerging is the hip-hop style of music. One aspect of the music industry in Botswana is music education within the school systems. Aside from the music, other important things to look at about Botswana are all of the aspects that make up the country: demographics, history, geography, politics, economics, and education.

Demographics

To understand the diversity of Botswana, one needs only to look at the demographics. The demographics themselves are extremely diverse; they tell a tale of good, bad and a happy medium. Some of the more harrowing details within the demographics are the statistics of life and death. The overall population growth rate is actually a negative growth rate, –0.04 to be exact. This negative growth rate is directly reflected when looking at the birth and death rates: for every 1,000 people, there are 23 births. Consequently, for every 1,000 people there are also 29 deaths. This negative growth rate is a reflection of the AIDS epidemic and other diseases that are prevalent in Botswana. Even though there is this negative growth rate, a positive fact is that for every woman, 2.79 children are born. The hope is for this to increase, as well as for the death rate to diminish greatly. Another negative aspect of Botswana's demographics is that the life expectancy is very low at only 33 years for the entire population. Unlike in the U.S., where there is a gap between men and women's life expectancies, there is no gap between men and women's life expectancies in Botswana. This low life expectancy can also be related to the prevalence of AIDS and other fatal diseases. Aside from AIDS, the other major diseases found in Botswana were discovered when Botswana was known as Bechuanaland. Bechuanaland was formed by the British government after tribal leaders in this part of Africa asked the British for help in order to stop problems such as war and to regulate migration. Bechuanaland was split into two sections: the Northern Province, which later became Botswana, and the southern, which is now part of South Africa. In 1910, the Union of South Africa was created, but it left Bechaunaland out of its borders. The idea was to add Bechuanaland to South Africa, but the election of the National Party government in 1948, which instituted the idea of Apartheid, officially ended the process of including Bechuanaland to South Africa. In 1964, the people of Bechuanaland petitioned the British government for democratic self-rule. The British government accepted this proposal, and the seat of Bechuanaland's government was moved from the city of Mafikeng to Gabome, which is now the present-day capital of Botswana. In 1965, leaders of Botswana drafted a constitution that allowed the citizens of Botswana to vote for their own leader. On September 30, 1966, Seretse Khania was elected as the first president of the Republic of Botswana. He was reelected twice and then died in office in 1980. His vice president stepped in as president and was later elected in his own right by the people. He was reelected two more times. He then retired and passed the presidency on to Festus Mogae in 1998 and he is still the president to this day.

Geography

Although the culture of Botswana is diverse, the physical geography of the country itself is not. It is made up primarily of the Kalahari Desert, the Okavango Delta, a large saltpan in the north called the Makgadikgadi Pan, and flat rolling grasslands. At 231,788 square miles, Botswana is comparable in size to both Madagascar and Texas. Botswana is also the world's 45th largest country, after Ukraine.

Although the physical aspects are not that diverse, the wildlife within these areas is extremely diverse. Wildebeest, antelope, mammals and birds gather in many savannas.

Government and Economy

With both a government and economy much like what we have in the U.S., Botswana is a very fast growing and stable country. The government of Botswana is that of a parliamentary republic. This type of government is a blending of both the British and the United States' forms of government. It reflects the government of England in that part of the government is made up of the parliament of Botswana. However, the type of government is similar to that of the U.S.A. because the president of Botswana is both head of state and head of the government. There are also three branches of government: legislative, executive and judicial branches. Each branch of the government functions almost exactly as the governmental branches of the U.S.

Another important aspect of the government of Botswana is the Botswana Defense Force (BDF). Although Botswana has no enemies, the BDF is a well-trained and capable army. As of late, the BDF's missions have been focused on anti-poaching activities, disaster-preparedness, and foreign peacekeeping.

Since becoming independent, Botswana has become one of the fastest growing economies in the world. It produced a growth rate of 9 percent from 1966 to 1999. Although the government has had to deal with budget deficits and small amounts of foreign aid, it has maintained a strong fiscal policy. Botswana has the highest credit rating of all African countries and has stockpiled foreign exchange reserves of over 5 billion USD. The reserves of Botswana have largely been built by using revenue from diamond mining and cautious foreign policy. The only mining company in Botswana is called Debswana, and it is owned by both a private company and the government—each owning a 50 percent share. Although countries such as the United States and most of Europe have been slow to invest and expand to Botswana, the country has been able to remain fully self-sufficient. Because it is landlocked, Botswana imports many things, mostly from the countries surrounding it. The country it deals most with is South Africa. The currency of Botswana is the Pula and is convertible with the South African Rand. Another large factor in the success of Botswana's economy is tourism. With multiple national parks and game reserves, Botswana is highly sought after by regular tourists as well as hunting expeditions.

Education

Since gaining its independence in 1966, Botswana has come extremely far in the area of education. Although there are still some deficiencies within the educational system, the government has plans to increase funding in order to get rid of these deficiencies. Because of diamond mining and the resulting increase in government revenue, there was a large increase in the need for education. Since there were sufficient funds, the government was able to provide the necessary funding for education. Each student was guaranteed 10 years of schooling; after which he or she would earn a junior certificate.

From there, half of the eligible students had the opportunity to go to secondary school for another two years. After the completion of secondary school, the student received the award of the Botswana General Certificate of Education. After leaving school, students could attend one of six technical colleges in Botswana, or take vocational training in either nursing or teaching. The brightest students in Botswana eventually go on to take classes at the University of Botswana—a large, modem, well-resourced university in Gaborne. After more than two decades of free education, the government of Botswana reinstated the schooling fee in January of 2006. The reinstatement of the fee will be used in order to pay for advanced school equipment, better schools, teacher's pay, and other programs.

Music

The music of Botswana is made up of three different types of music: traditional/folk, popular music and hip-hop. The most well-known of music within Botswana that is actually from Botswana is that of the traditional/folk style of music. In turn, the most popular traditional music is that of the largest ethnic group: the Tswana people. Tswana music differs greatly from most traditional African music because of lack of drums, when they are utilized as well as the use of drums overall. Instead of focusing on drumming, Tswana music relies heavily on singing and the use of string instruments. Some of the instruments used are: the *segaba*, which is a one-string version of the violin; and the *setinake*, which is made of several different kinds of forks and played like a keyboard. Originally, Tswana music was looked down upon as it was considered a hindrance to the proper development of the country. However, since gaining its independence, Botswana has seen a return to the popularity of Tswana music, with many Tswana groups performing worldwide in competitions and bringing home many awards.

The most well liked music in the country of Botswana is what is known as popular music. As in most African countries, this popular music is labeled as "jazz," but it sounds nothing like what we would describe jazz as in America. Although this music is definitely popular in Botswana, it is actually foreign to the country itself. There has recently been a push to focus on putting new life into the music industry in Botswana instead of importing foreign music. Most of the foreign music in Botswana comes from South Africa, Europe, and the United States.

The other popular form of music, which is relatively new to Botswana, is hip-hop. Hip-hop is something that has carried its influence over to Botswana from the United States, and has inspired musicians and singers in Botswana to write their own hip-hop songs. One of the most popular hip-hop groups in Botswana is called the Wizards. They are a long-standing group that mixes reggae, R&B, and hip-hop. The record label Phat Boy has been extremely helpful in popularizing hip-hop in Botswana due to its ability to sign artists and provide them with the necessary means to write and record music. Another important group that has pushed hip-hop into Botswana's culture is the duo of Draztik and Slim; two friends who star in the television/radio show *Strictly Hip-Hop*. These two have helped to popularize hip-hop by letting it be seen and heard by the large population within the country.

In conclusion, the music of Botswana is like a melting pot. The music is influenced heavily by the ethnic groups within Botswana, and by the countries around it. Botswana has kept its traditional music alive and is extremely proud of its musical traditions. However, Botswana is behind in that it does not really have its own artists to play the popular style of music described as "Jazz." Once Botswana is able to revive its own music industry, resulting in not having to purchase foreign records, the people of Botswana will be proud of yet another type of their own music. In looking at both the culture and the music of Botswana, one can see many parallels. The country, like the music, is continually evolving and making it more advanced in so many aspects of life. Although it still has a long way to go, all Botswana has to do is continue its forward progress, which will lead to better days for both the country itself and the help of music of Botswana reach amazing highs.

References

Addo, A. O., E. Miya, and H. Potgieter (2003). Integrating the Arts. In *Musical Arts in Africa: Theory, Practice and Education,* ed. A. Herbst, M. Nzewi, and K. Agawu, 236–260. Pretoria: University of South Africa.

Agawu, K. (2003). *Representing African Music: Postcolonial Notes, Queries, Positions.* New York: Routledge.

Bachmann, M. (1991). *Dalcroze Today: An Education Through and Into Music.* Oxford: Clarendon Press.

Balfour, Henry (1902). The Goura, a Stringed-Wind Musical Instrument of the Bushmen and Hottentots. *Journal of the Anthropological Institute of Great Britain and Ireland* 32:156–176.

Brearley, John (1989). Music and Musicians of the Kalahari. *Botswana Notes* 20:77–90.

Chernoff, J. M. (1979). *African Rhythm and African Sensibility: Aesthetics and Social Action in African Musical Idioms.* Chicago: University of Chicago Press.

England, Nicholas M. (1995). *Music among the Zu'/wã-si and Related Peoples of Namibia, Botswana, and Angola.* New York: Garland.

Farber, A. (1991). Speaking the Musical Language. *Music Educators Journal,* 78(4). Retrieved 23 April 2005 from 0-web29.epnet.com.innopac.up.ac.za.

Kreutzer, N. (1996). Toward a Primary School Music Curriculum that Builds on the Strengths of Informal Music Learning in the Community. *The Talking Drum* 6:14–17.

Kubik, G. (1983). Musikgestaltung in Afrika. In *Musik in Afrika,* ed. A. Simon, 27–40. Berlin: Museum fUr Vi.ilkerkunde.

Merriam, A. P. (1964). *Anthropology of Music.* Evanston, IL: Northwestern University Press.

Midweek Sun (Botswana). (2004). Arts review, 25 August, D.

Morton, Fred, and Jeff Ramsay (1987). *The Birth of Botswana: A History of the Bechuanaland Protectorate from 1910 to 1966.* Gaborone: Longman Botswana.

Tlou, Thomas, and Alec Campbell (1977). *History of Botswana*, 2d ed. Gaborone: Macmillan.

Valiente Noailles, Carlos (1993). *The Kua: Life and Soul of the Central Kalahari Bushmen*. Rotterdam: Balkema.

Waterman, C. A. (1991). The Uneven Development of Africanist Ethnomusicology: Three Issues and a Critique. In *Comparative Musicology and Anthropology of Music*, ed. B. Nettl and P. V. Bohlman, 169–186. Chicago: Chicago University Press.

Wood, Elizabeth N. (1983). The Use of Metaphor and Certain Scale Patterns in Traditional Music of Botswana. *African Music* 6:107–14.

World Health Organization (2007). Botswana. Retrieved September 22, 2007, from http://www.who.int/hiv/HIVCP_BWA.pdf.

Wylie, Diana (1990). *A Little God: the Twilight of Patriarchy in a Southern African Chiefdom*. Hanover, NH: Wesleyan University Press/University Press of New England.

6. Dances of the Mbuti People of the Democratic Republic of Congo

Mbuti pygmies are located in the Ituri forest of the Democratic Republic of the Congo, formerly known as Zaïre. Their culture is unique at its core but it does share some ties with the music and history of Zaïre. First, an overview of various aspects of the country is presented to provide a better understanding of its people, followed by an analysis of the musical culture of the Mbuti pygmies. Their music and its purpose are both complex and original in many ways, as communicated here. A brief history of the country is presented, dating back to the Bantu migration and the settling of Bantu speakers near the Zaïre River.

History

Prior to the Bantu migration from West Africa, hunting and gathering were the primary ways of obtaining food. According to Toylin Falola's book *Africa*, farmers and stock raisers, the Bantu had a more reliable food supply, and eventually the hunter-gatherers lost out in the competition

(Falola, 2003). As previously mentioned, this led to the settling of people in Zaïre around 500 BC. This settling of people is responsible for "bringing an economy based on yam and palm farming" (Zaïre XV). Around the mid–4th century AD, iron and copper technology, as well as salt, began a system of trade. At this time, there were long periods of drought that prompted a development of chieftaincies with the Luba kingdom at the forefront. This kingdom stayed small until the eighteenth century in which the Luba Kingdom underwent a period of great expansion (Falola, 2003). The death of King Ilunga Kabale in 1874 resulted in a competition for succession that resulted in the fall of the Luba Kingdom.

The next period of Zaïre's history begins with European exploration backed by King Leopold II of Belgium from the 1870s to 1920. During this time, he acquired the territory and established it as The Congo Free State. It is here that the present day Zaïre underwent a series of changes consisting of wars and political crisis. During this time, many people were exploited for Leopold's desire to make money in the rubber market. Between five million and fifteen million Congolese have died because of exploitation and several diseases. Due to the exploitation of this corruptness, outside pressure forced the Belgian Parliament to take control of the territory in 1908.

In 1960, the Congolese achieved their independence and renamed their country of Zaïre which six years later was changed to the Democratic Republic of Congo. Under the backing of European Nations, as well as the U.S., Mobutu Sese Seko came to power in 1971. Mobutu's corruptive ruling led to his fleeing the country in the late 1990s. The country was renamed the Democratic Republic of Congo soon afterward. In the past 10 years, the Congo has experienced both domestic and external conflicts that have been perhaps the bloodiest in history since World War II. An estimated 4 million people have lost their lives in the conflicts.

Demographics

The demographics of the democratic Republic of Congo exemplify the diversity of culture in which the pygmies live. The country's population is close to 57 million people. There are 250 different ethnic groups living in the country as well as 242 different languages spoken. Of those 242 languages, Kongo, Lingala, Tshiluba, and Swahili are recognized as the national languages. The geography of Zaïre is separated into mountains, plateaus, savannas, and tropical rain forest. There are also many religions existing within the country. Catholicism and Protestantism constitute the majority, but there are many who practice Islam and Kimbaquist, as well as many other indigenous religions. The combination of different ethnic groups, languages, geography, and religions complicates defining the culture in a simple way. As one could probably guess, the same is the case in their music.

Music

It is difficult to define the many different musical styles of these different ethnic groups within Africa and/or Zaïre. Musicologist John Roberts (1977) reaffirms this in his argument about writing coherently about the music of a continent covering 52 independent nations, between 800 and 1600 languages and at least five major cultural groupings. For this reason, the musical culture of the Mbuti Pygmies of the Ituri rain forest located in northeastern Zaïre is analyzed. Mbuti are a people with unique philosophies and lifestyles that are reflected in their music. They were chosen because their music and way of life is almost unintelligible compared to that of westerners. It is believed that this culture reflects the diversity of cultures existing within Zaïre, as these pygmies live only within that region in the world.

Mbuti music is a reflection of their culture and religion. They sometimes use it for the most important rituals of their people and other times it is used recreationally. They are a people independent from that of other Africans in some ways and connected in others, but religiously, they have remained consistent with their beliefs. There is still much to learn about the Mbuti and their culture, especially from a musical standpoint.

Pygmies History

Originally, pygmies were believed to have lived in the Ituri forest prior to the Bantu Migration. There is believed to be around 40,000 living in the world today. They were thought to be identifiable by their physical appearance, as Mbuti stand at an average height of four and a half feet. Recent research has proved this stereotype untrue, because the Bantu peoples' physiology has been altered by their diet and lifestyle as hunter-gathers in the rain forest (Falola 2003). The Mbuti live in primary rain forest, which means that the forest is dense with tall trees preventing much sunlight from passing through the canopy of treetops. The conditions and foods of the rainforest caused their physical change, and for many it is striking. Reference to the existence of pygmies dates back to the records kept by an Egyptian expedition from the Fourth Dynasty, which shows how long they have preserved this way of life in the forest.

The political structure of the Mbuti has no head figure. There is no president or chief of tribe. For the Mbuti, the basis of decisions affecting the entire camp among old respected men is their informal consensus hence the egalitarian spirit. It appears as though the authority of the elder men is understood and not questioned. They have adopted some political structure from outside influences like clan systems and funeral customs. As noted by Turnbull (1961) that the Pygmies voluntarily followed the Negro custom but at the same time, they were able to independently govern their own destiny. This is significant because it reflects the nature of the relationship the Mbuti have with outsiders. One thing they do not adopt was religious practices, for the Mbuti ware of the forest and others are not.

To most, the forest is an uninhabitable place. Villagers living outside of the forest fear it because it is a place of evil. They enter it from an etic (outsider's) perspective. To the Mbuti it is something entirely different. The Mbuti love the forest, for this is their world, and in return for their affection and trust, the forest supplies them with all of their subsistence and other primary needs for survival. Even though from this, we can see that the Mbuti way of life is different from that of their neighboring plantation owners in many ways owners, the Mbuti have adopted from their neighbors many customs including musical instruments.

Instruments

Trade occurs between the African plantation owners and the Mbuti and it is through this trade that some musical instruments are believed to have found their way into Mbuti culture. Examples of these instruments are water drums, bow harps, harp zithers, and limbindis. These instruments are generally used more for recreational purposes of music. They have also learned to use tools and weapons as instruments, such as blowing on the strings of hunting bows to produce their own sound. Whistles and flutes were also mentioned by Turnbull (1965) to be used during the Mbuti during his years of living with them, but, they were generally for recreation. The most important of all Mbuti instruments is the molimo, a type of sacred trumpet made out of a piece of hollowed woods.

Pygmy Music

The style of music of pygmies is based on repetition of musical periods of equal length, which means that it could be based on a scale system. The Mbuti do not chart their music theory but instead learn it growing up. Although they do use instruments, their music is mainly vocal. They have developed a polyphonic complexity, or the combination of two or more simultaneous but relatively independent melodic lines. This ability was not developed by Europeans until the fourteenth century, but a comparison as to who developed it first cannot be made because the Mbuti have no written history. This does however indicate that the Mbuti have evolved the complexity of their musical ability over time. Their music comes from spiritual stories, singing, and instruments, much like our own, but the sounds and rhythms are much different from the standard four/four measures and scales that we use.

Dance

As previously mentioned, much of their music is used recreationally, such as when hunting or singing a child a lullaby, which Turnbull (1965) witnessed during his time of living with the pygmies. There were rituals, which often included dance. One of the most prominent of these ceremonies was circumcision, a custom very common to some African societies. The Mbuti conducted this ceremony with the African villagers, which again exemplifies outside influence on their culture. Circumcision served to initiate boys into manhood, and immediately after they are circumcised, they are made to sit down and join the other initiates in singing and dancing many songs. They continuously sing and dance for many months during the initiation period. Here we see both music and dance being integrated into the ceremonies of the Mbuti. Another example of dance is the Molimo "Dance of the Honeybee," which they conducted during the honey season. In this dance

> The men and women were divided, and while the men pretended to be honeybee gatherers, dancing through a long curling line through the camp, the women danced in another long line through the trees at the edge of the camp, pretending they were the bees [Turnbull, 1961, p. 231].

From this example we can see imagery of the style of dances they did. Dances and singing also occurred before and after hunts, which were conducted only by men. However, these examples fail to compare to the true musical culture of the Mbuti, for even the circumcision ceremony was performed with the African plantation owners. What is truly important to the Mbuti is the Molimo.

Religion

At first sight, the Molimo would appear to be nothing more than a wooden trumpet. Turnbull reveals that when he first heard the Molimo, it was a deep, gentle, lowing sound, sometimes breaking off into a quiet falsetto, sometimes growling like a leopard (Turnbull, 1965). However, the physical presence of the Molimo is of no importance. It is designed to imitate the more respected animals of the forest, but its true importance is its essence. To understand this essence, the philosophy and religion of the Mbuti must first be understood.

To the Mbuti, all things are good because the forest is a good place. They believe that people should not grieve the way that people outside of their culture do. This is best exemplified in their views of death. For the Mbuti it is better to forget the dead quickly instead of making yourself remember them all the time, as the villagers do (Turnbull, 1961). This is not to say that they are not saddened by the death of a loved one, but they view that death as the forest's way of saying something is wrong. In his book review of *The Forest People*, Turnbull (1961) emphasizes that Mbuti imagination constructs the forest as benevolent and powerful, capable of giving strength and affection to all its children. This helps in understanding the way the pygmies viewed the forest, for they see it as a parent figure, and when something went wrong it was because the forest was asleep. As one cannot prevent a wrong from occurring when they are asleep, so too is the case for the forest. By waking the forest up, they are returning things to normal state of natural goodness.

In an attempt to better relate this religion to readers, Falola uses the Pantheism to define the Mbuti religion. Pantheism fails to do this though because pantheism is defined as a doctrine that equates god with forces of law and the universe; and unlike other indigenous African religious systems, it did not recognize a pantheon of human-like gods (Falola & Jennings, 2003). The forest was thought to be living and the forest was good. Turnbull (1961) expresses his original recognition of belief by the

Mbuti. They were a people who had found in the forest something that made their life more that just worth living, something that made it, with all its hardships and problems and tragedies, a wonderful thing full of joy and happiness and free of care.

This positive perception of the world by the Mbuti is unique in the sense that they do not perceive evil. This is the religion of the Mbuti based on their philosophy that their supreme caretaker (the forest) is good and bad results from its unawareness of things gone wrong. With this understanding we can now proceed to understanding the essence of the Molimo, which is achieved through music.

The Molimo

Turnbull made many observations of the ceremony of the Molimo; he originally perceived the Molimo as the sound and look of the trumpet. The ceremony begins with the initiated men of the tribe running to find the Molimo in the forest. During this process, they go and get the trumpets that they made to bring back to the camp. Women and children are not allowed to see the Molimo, so they retreat to their houses leaving the men to stand by the fire alone. The men sing songs in response to the call of the *Molimo*, or trumpets. Turnbull recognizes that at no time do their songs ask for this or that to be done, for the hunt to be made better or for someone's illness to be cured; it is not necessary (Turnbull, 1965). They do not desire from their god in their singing and they do not ask favors of it. It was as though the nightly chorus were an intimate communion between a people and their god, the forest (Turnbull, 1965). He finally understood the essence of Mbuti music.

Singing is the form of music by which the Mbuti communicate to the forest that they are experiencing darkness, or sadness. However, to the Mbuti, if darkness is of the forest, then darkness must be good (Turnbull, 1965). In other words, even bad is good because it is part of this world. They desire normality and embrace pain as a part of it, which provides them with a life where evil does not exist. Music allows them to achieve inner peace in all that happens and it is the means by which they show their appreciation for that which they have been provided. The use of music in the *Molimo* ceremony is its purpose, but the restoration of peace in the world is the essence of Mbuti music.

The uniqueness of the Mbuti shows a difference in culture that can exist in one society alone. On the surface, the Mbuti are a naturally short people; but in coming to understand their music, they can be understood more intimately.

References

Aron, Simha (1991). *African Polyphony and Polyrhythm*. Cambridge: Cambridge University Press.
Falola, T., and C. Jennings, C., ed. (2003). *Sources and Methods in African History: Spoken, Written, Unearthed*. Rochester Studies in African History and the Diaspora. Rochester: University of Rochester Press.
Hochschild, Adam (1999). *King Leopold's Ghost*. Boston: Houghton Mifflin.
Meditz, Sandra W., and Tim Merrill (1994). *Zaire: A Country Study*, 4th ed. Washington, D.C: Library of Congress.
Polgreen, Lydia (2006). Wars Chaos Steals Congo's Young by the Millions. *The New York Times*, July 30.
Robert, John (1977). *Black Music of Two Worlds*. New York: Folkways Records.
Turnbull, Colin M. (1961) *The Forest People*. New York: Clarion.
Turnbull, Colin M. (1965). *Wayward Servants: The Two Worlds of the African Pygmies*. Garden City, NY: Natural History.
World Views. The Music of Africa. Africa: An African World Press Guide 1997 11 27 200. http://worldviews.igc.org/awpguide/music.html.

PART II: THE AMERICAS

7. The Bachata Dance of the Dominican Republic

The term *bachata* is both a music genre and dance movement that is an important part of the culture of the Dominican Republic. This is evidence that in this tradition, music and dance have subsisted. The *bachata* style of music and dance is one of the Dominican Republic's most revered traditions and has been a part of its culture for almost half a century. It is often said that much can be told of a country's existence by the arts that flourish within her and *bachata* works very well in this capacity to symbolize the ever-changing social and political climates of this island nation. The history of the Dominican Republic, the musical influences of the Latin-American world, and the introduction of the *bachata* footwork have all shaped *bachata* and helped to make it what it is today. Each element has both unique and borrowed qualities from other parts of the world. In today's global village, an attempt to isolate one culture from another is futile. The music and dance of any culture are constantly expanding and being reshaped over time, and *bachata* is no exception.

History of the Dominican Republic and the Bachata

The voyage of Christopher Columbus in 1492 began at a time when Europeans first got a glimpse of the New World and one of his first stops was Hispaniola (modern day Haiti and the Dominican Republic). Always looking to spread European culture, the Spaniards first encountered the Taino, the native people of the Dominican Republic. Like many other native peoples of North America, the Taino were primarily a nature-worshipping people who had music and dances that were devotional to their gods and spirits. In a typical European fashion of the time, these nature dances were strictly banned and considered obscene, so little information still exists about the original Taino culture.

With the establishment of La Navidad, a European fort on the island, the Old World influences were sure to stay on the island for many years to come. In 1795, the Spanish ceded the colony of the Dominican Republic to the French. Not long after, Haitian blacks led by Toussaint L'Ouverture conquered it in 1801. A revolt in 1808 led to the first republic and in 1814, the Spanish regained the colony. 1822 brought another conquest by the Haitians but, in 1844 Pedro Santana established a republic. Finally, in 1861, the Dominican Republic once again became a Spanish province.

In less than 100 years, the control of the Dominican Republic changed more than five times. In such a politically unstable environment, the arts and culture cannot flourish. From 1916 to 1934, a new element was a part of the culture—the United States. In these years, the United States stationed marines to maintain peace in this troublesome area. The 1960s plagued the nation with more instability. Even within the past two decades, political control has always been looked at with insecurity and anxiety.

Despite these harsh political and economic times, the people of the Dominican Republic still managed to create some forms of fine arts. One of the first music styles to take root in the area was *musica de guitarra*, or guitar music. This musical genre was a long-standing tradition in the Latin American world and had been passed back and forth between the Spanish-speaking parts of the world for many years. In some regions, the styles of guitar music even took their own names and identities. In the Dominican Republic, one such style was the *bachata*, a sub-category of *music de guitarra* that was primarily characterized by romantic guitar ballads. This pure form of romantic guitar music was originally not intended for dancing at all and was viewed simply as an acoustic art form. Not long after, more instruments were added to create *bachata* ensembles. The guitar was complemented by the *requinto*, a smaller guitar that produced sounds of a higher pitch. Percussion instruments also added a new element to the genre. Such instruments included the bongos, the *maracas* (rattles), the claves (wooden sticks clapped together), and a *guiro* (ridged piece of wood or metal that was scraped to create sounds).

The Changing Face of Bachata

The *bachata* style of guitar music has roots in many parts of the Hispanic world. Rural guitar music was influenced by many of the Latin American "cowboys," often known as *rancheros* or *corridos*. These farmer types would entertain themselves by playing guitar music often to relax after a hard day of working in fields or ranches. In the 1960s, the influences of these groups reached the Dominican Republic as guitarists formed trios and began to play this rural guitar music at recreational events. On Saturdays, informal parties known as *pasadias*, were held to alleviate the stress of work and poverty for many Dominicans. Those of the lower socio-economic status usually played this music because of its ability to take minds off their harsh living conditions. Thus, *bachata* was scorned by the upper classes as "vulgar" and "full of debauchery." In the 1970s, technological advances made it possible to record and commercialize this romantic guitar music. Coined *bachata*, which meant "fun, merriment," the music was supposed to have become widely accessible. The only problem was that the only people who could afford such recordings were those of the upper class who looked upon it with disgust. The efforts to bring *bachata* to people on a national level had failed, and *bachata* was still something played house to house to pass the time.

The 1970s also brought a new element to *bachata*: a face. Edilio Paredes, a native of the small country town of La Galana, near San Francisco de Macoris, and a noted guitarist and pioneer of the genre, is often referred to as "the father of *bachata*." With his unique, creative guitar skills and warm sound, Edilio became one of the first distinguishable *bachata* artists on a national level. Unfortunately, however, the economic and political stability of the Dominican Republic was simultaneously worsening. Harsh living conditions made it even more difficult for *bachata* music to take root in the national culture and the arts were often put aside to make more time for things more pertinent to survival (Wayne, 2006). These arts, far from being lost, were altered just as the living conditions had been. The once romantic guitar music of *bachata* suddenly became much faster in tempo. The subject matter of the songs became more centered on raw sexuality and the maltreatment of women. Alcohol often joined the mix, adding to the chaotic nature of this once docile music form (Hernandez, 2005).

In the 1980s, a break from this new, violent *bachata* formed. This new movement was called *musica de amargue*, which translates to the "music of bitterness." This was in essence a return to the more traditional, romantic *bachata* of the 1960s. This new revival came under much scrutiny; however, it was radically different from the violent *bachata* of the 1970s, which in itself was not traditional at all. Through this entire complicated mess emerged this music of bitterness, a new take on old *bachata*. Old speeds and themes were resurrected and as the economic conditions began to stabilize, so did the *bachata*. The *bachata* that is popular today is mostly of the *musica de amargue* style adapted to today's ever-changing world.

Bachata *as Dance*

The music of *bachata* also gave way to forms of dance. In the beginning, *bachata* dance was simply improvisational: an audience heard the music and that audience reacted physically in whatever way they felt. Even the simple motion of beating one's hand to the beat of the bongos is a form of dance. The *bachata* that is danced today has a very simple basic structure. The *bachata* dance is usually danced in pairs, with some physical contact between the two dancers. This physical contact can be hand-to-hand, hand to waist, or any other combination, but there must be some connection between the participants. Most *bachata* music can be broken into measures of 4 beats, and if one were to speak out these beats; it would sound like 1–2–3–pop. The first three beats are steps in one direction, one partner's left and the other partner's right. The 4th beat, or pop, is a popping of the hip in the direction from which the dancers began. For most tyros or beginners of *bachata*, the 4 beats are danced along an imaginary straight line, back and forth. If all of these conditions are met, the dancers are dancing *bachata*: it's quite simple (Germani, 2005). More advanced dancers like to add some spice to their *bachata* as well. Such additions are circular motions, variations in contact, and most importantly, upper body movement. The hips and feet of all *bachata* dancers move in very similar fashions. The upper body movements individualize a *bachata* dancer and gives one a distinct identity.

Bachata *Takes Flight*

With today's technology and the ability to access the music and dance of any part of the world, *bachata* is becoming renowned internationally. Several festivals are held annually in the Dominican Republic in honor of this and other long-standing Latin American musical traditions. The *Bachata* and Merengue Festivals in Santo Domingo and Puerta Plata attract tourists every year to visit and view and participate in this Dominican dance.

Now that *bachata* has begun to spread to other parts of the world, it can truly be understood as an art form that reflects the social and economic status of the Dominican Republic. In order to convey these ideas effectively, *bachata* needed a poster child, a fresh new face with whom new generations of music lovers can relate and empathize. In 1998, *bachata* received such a face. Monchy y Alexandra is a vocal duo comprised of Ramon E. Rijo (Monchy) and Alexandra Cabrera. Producers Martires de Leon and Victor Reyes, both of whom envisioned a young and vibrant group that could spread *bachata* to the young masses, brought the two together (Mejia, 2006).

According to Mejia (2006), following unprecedented success in the genre, more than 500,000 copies of their records have been sold including, *Hoja en Blanco, Unplugged,* and *Confesiones.* The two have done what not even Edilio Paredes could do: "unified the Dominican Republic under one form of *bachata*" (Mejia, 2006).

The style has become a point of pride for the country along with other styles such as merengue. In a country that was constantly being handed back and forth between powers of the time, it has taken up until the present day to establish musical traditions that could be appreciated not only within the country, but also exported as symbols of the rich culture of the Dominican Republic.

Contributions to World and Cultures

The transmission of *bachata* on a worldwide scale has truly added yet another piece to word culture and music. Now that *bachata* can be heard in places other than the Dominican Republic, it will almost certainly be adapted to each region's styles. In Eastern Europe, folk traditions and dances may be mixed with traditional *bachata* music, or the dance steps from the Dominican Republic may be changed to incorporate such traditions. Within the Latin American world, *bachata* has skyrocketed in popularity and is danced alongside such important dances as the merengue, salsa, and rumba. The younger generations in the Far East, stepping away from traditional Asian music, have embraced *bachata* and many other parts of the Hispanic culture. With so much intermingling of cultures and adaptations from different parts of the world, the global perspective of music has changed drastically. Decades ago, one looked at their own styles of music with pride and nationalism, viewing other cultures as foreign and "not for them." In today's society, this ethnocentrism is no longer an option. On a daily basis, people are interacting with others who may be from parts of the world they have never even heard of. To truly cooperate and understand one another on a global level, certain cultural ideas must be examined and appreciated (Willoughby, 2003).

The *bachata* music and dance of the Dominican Republic, while new on the time scale, is quickly becoming embedded in cultures around the world. Through its rocky political history, the people of the Dominican Republic have done something amazing: they have created a genre of music and dance, held onto it through adversity, and are now able to use this as a window into their culture. The *bachata* is not about glamour and adornment, ideas that many of the people of this region have never attained. The romance of the music is a symbol that despite the poverty and the labor, these are still a sensitive, artistic people. The people of the Dominican Republic are survivors, and in order to keep spirits up and keep striving, it takes something as powerful as music and dance. Willoughby (2003) observes that throughout history, music and dance have always been studied with wonder and amazement. In some cultures, they were thought to have healing powers. Some believed them to be windows to the upper world, to a realm where gods and demons ruled. *Bachata*, in some respects, upholds these traditions. While it has never had religious connotations, one cannot help but notice the spirits of the dancers and audience be uplifted just by participating.

Music and dance are two incredibly powerful parts of a culture because it is not something that can be forced upon a people. Music and dance flow from the souls of the very people of the country, and these two fundamental ideas can help shape an entire region and help spread its culture to the entire planet.

References

Associated Press. (2005). This Is Travel. Retrieved January 20, 2006, from http://www.thisistravel.co.uk/index.html.

Germani, A. (2005) Bachata. Retrieved January 20, 2006, from http://www.thedancestoreonline.com/ballroom-dance-instruction/bachata-free-lessons.htm.

Hernandez, D. (2005). History of Bachata. Retrieved January 20, 2006, from http://home-3.tiscali.nl/~pjetax/historias/history_bachata.html.

Manuel, L., and B. Urena (1997). *El meringue y la relidad existencial de los Dominican: bachata y nueva cancion*. Santo Domingo, Dominican Republic: Unigraf.

Manuel, P., K. Bilby & M. Laregy (1995). *Caribbean Currents: Caribbean Music from Rumba to Reggae*. Philadelphia: Temple University Press.

Mejia, M. (2006). No Es Una Novela. Retrieved January 20, 2006, from http://www.monchyyalexandra.com/.

Tejeda, D. (2002). *La Pasion danzaria: musica y baile en el Caribe a trayes del marengue la bachata*. Dominican Republic: Academia de Ciencias de República Dominicana.

Valesquez, C., and A. Urena (2004). *De Santo Domingo al Mundo: el merengue y la bachata*. New York: Galos.

Wayne, D. (2006). Edilio Paredes and the Birth of Bachata. IASO Records. Retrieved January 20, 2006, from http://www.iasorecords.com/index.cfm?secid=4&subsecid=77.

Willoughby, D. (2003). *The World of Music*. New York: McGraw-Hill.

8. The Merengue Dance of Latin America

The Evolution of Merengue

Many dances are fusions of dances from different cultures and origins. *Merengue*, one of the most popular and widespread dances from Latin America, is no exception. However, there are often confusions about its origins. Some scholars believe that the Haitian *mereng*, a derivative of the European *contredanse*, traveled across the border in the nineteenth century shortly after the 1844 war of independence.

Most believe that *merengue* formed from the Cuban dance *upa*. Cuban marching bands brought *upa* to Puerto Rico in 1842. *Upa* was a mix of the Spanish ballroom (*contradanza*) *danza* and African elements. The elites thought it to be overtly sexual and rejected it. The Puerto Ricans organized new steps from the Spanish *danza* and put those to *upa*. This new dance was sometimes known as *merengue*. The Puerto Rican government passed laws against *merengue* and anyone who danced or played it was arrested. After 40 years since its conception, *merengue* died in Puerto Rico. However, from Puerto Rico the dance found its way to Santo Domingo (now the Dominican Republic).

Despite confusion about its origins, each theory hints at the *merengue*'s mixture of European and African elements. *Merengue* combines pronounced hip movements common in African dances with the hold of a

European ballroom *contredanse*. In addition, there is a collaboration of heavily syncopated rhythms with ensemble music.

The European and African influences are best noted in the type of instruments used in *merengue*. Back then, *Merengue* was played on instruments like the *tres* and *cuarto*, however, Germans in the late nineteenth century traded weapons for instruments and brought the one row button accordion. Other *merengue* instruments include bass guitar, guitar, *güira*, *tambora*, and, in recent years saxophone. The *tambora* is a double-sided drum of African origin played on one side with a stick and on the other the palm of your hand, marking a downbeat. The *güira*, a sheet of metal shaped into a cylinder, is brushed steadily on the downbeat. It adds a regular hissing, scratchy pulse.

When *merengue* was introduced to the Dominican Republic salons in the 1850s, it received opposition from the elite class. The intellectual elite rejected it because of the swinging hip movement and the fact that couples danced individually and very closely. *Merengue* music of the time contained African syncopated rhythms similar to the Cuban *danza*. The ruling classes consider *merengue* (*danza*) as a symbol of Cuban/Afro-Caribbean cultures whose African aesthetics they abhorred. The elites were urbanites, so *merengue* became a rural song and dance style, danced at informal festivals, *galleras* (cock-fighting rings), and brothels. In the Dominican Republic in 1880, however, 97 percent of the population was rural (Yeo).

Variations of the Merengue

Merengues were regional and varied, so there are many subgenres. They include *merengue cibaeño* (*perico ripiao*), *merengue estilo yanquí* (*pambiche*), and *merengue palo echao* (*prí-prí*).

Merengue cibaeño, also known as *merengue típico* or *perico ripiao* (a term coined for a brothel where it was allegedly played), is the most common form of *merengue* and what is known internationally. The Cibao region is in the center of the Dominican Republic, economically most important, had the highest population, and contained the largest city—Santiago de los Caballeros. *Marengue* was generally the dance of the elite in the regional hierarchy because the population was predominantly white. Therefore, *merengue cibaeño* dominated all other forms of *merengue*.

Merengue cibaeño is sung with a tight, nasal technique and has a monotonous 1–2–3–4 drumbeat. The tempo of the *merengue* dance as a whole can be frantic, but the turns are slow. There are usually four beats per turn. The steps are side to side: left, right, left right to match the beat, but can have a limping appearance. There are three main parts: the *paseo de la empalizada*, the *merengue*, and the *jaleo*. The music of the *paseo* is an eight measure march-like introduction, signaling the couples to take the floor. They hold each other in closed position like in the European ballroom dances and walk sideways or circle each other in small steps. This movement is called *merengue de salón* or ballroom *merengue*. The couples can switch to a double-handed position and do separate turns without letting go of each other's hands, something called *merengue de figura*. The *merengue* section is an eight measure European influenced melody, sung and played instrumentally several times to the accompaniment of major-mode harmonies.

The last part, the *jaleo*, features a two measure repeating pattern with interlocking rhythms performed on the *tambora*, *güira*, accordion and saxophone (if present). The rhythmic qualities of the *jaleo* are African derived and the vocals are often call and response, a practice unique to Africa.

The African influence in *merengue* may seem obvious. Nevertheless, to distance themselves from Haiti, the first black independent Caribbean nation, the Spanish elite in the Dominican Republic downplayed *merengue*'s African influences. Until as recently as the 1970s, some Dominican musicologists refused to recognize African contributions to *merengue*. Ethnomusicologist Martha Davis says Dominican scholars:

> have, at least, ignored African influence in Santo Domingo. At the worst, they have bent over backwards to convince themselves and their readers of the one hundred per cent Hispanic content of their culture. This is not an uncommon Latin American reaction to the inferiority complex produced by centuries of Spanish colonial domination [Austerlitz, 1997, p. 2].

At first, the *merengue* was used as a means of social entertainment and expression. That changed around 1916. Due to the Dominican Republic's contact with Germany during and after World War II, the United States military occupied the republic from 1916 to 1924. The Dominicans resisted this occupation in four ways.

In the east, *gavilleros* (bandits) led by local *cuadillos* (warlords) engaged the U.S. Marines in guerrilla warfare. In addition, the citizens created a hostile environment for the troops. The upper classes in El Cibao even participated by starting a campaign to sway international opinion against the occupation. Finally, *merengue cibaeño* became a symbol of cultural resistance and defiance. Songs were made denouncing the occupation and the U.S. government.

During that time there were two forms of *merengue* played that are still played today. One is the sectional *merengue cibaeño* discussed earlier. The other is a simpler style of *merengue* called *merengue estilo yanquí* or *pambiche*. This style of *merengue* got its name from a song about a fabric called Palm Beach. *Pambiche* uses *tambora* rhythms related to the *cinquillo* (a five note pattern used in Haitian and Cuban music), major dominant harmonies, and a melody repeated with improvised variations. As Ramón Jiménez, a Dominican alive during the occupation, says, this new style is nothing other than a slow, elongated *jaleo* with a syncopated rhythm that was easier for a foreigner, who does not have the sensibility of the native, to dance (Austerlitz, 1997, p. 41).

Besides *pambiche*, another result of the U.S. occupation was that it was easy to move up in the ranks of the military because not many Dominicans joined. One man who took advantage of this opportunity was Rafael Trujillo. A man of working class background, he understood the rural people and resented the upper class.

Merengue in Government

In 1930, Trujillo ran for president, basing his campaign on the *merengue*, which he used as a tool to unify the country. During his campaign, he toured with top *merengueros* (*merengue* players). Propaganda songs were written for him, and *merengue* bands bore his name, for instance Luis Albertí's Orquesta Presidente Trujillo.

Trujillo began to dominate *merengue*. He made the upper classes play *merengue* at every social event and he even put his brother Petán in charge of the major radio station "La Voz Dominicana." The station broadcasted only live music, so *merengue* bands seldom recorded. If they did, they could only do so with Petán's permission. As a result of these restrictions, many artists went to New York and Puerto Rico in search of recording opportunities.

The *merengue* under Trujillo's thirty-one year rule was stripped of its African influences, even though his grandmother was Haitian. According to journalist and dancer Hernando Ospina (1995), Trujillo's government was intent on "whitewashing" the countryside and its culture, in order to get rid of any African influences or any similarity with the poor, black culture of neighboring Haiti.

As soon as Trujillo was assassinated in 1960, artists began experimenting with *merengue*. They increased its speed, brought back the suggestive lyrics it was known for, and added aggressive arrangements with the *tambora* drum and saxophone. *Merengue* also absorbed other influences to keep with the times. Traditional Latin American ballads were turned to *merengues*. Furthermore, *merengueros* began incorporating *el maco*, a percussion pattern mixing the Haitian *konpa* with the Puerto Rican African-based *plena*. The four-beat Cibao style *merengue* was superseded by the two beat *maco* rhythm, which made *merengue* easier to dance to and more interesting. *El maco merengue* has a rhythmic pulse similar to disco, and by the 1980s it was more common than the original *merengue cibaeño*.

The Growth and Movement of Merengue

Since *merengue* was in competition with other forms of music such as rock 'n' roll and later, salsa, musicians began basing *merengue* arrangements on foreign hits, a practice called *fusilamiento*. Musician Johnny Ventura practiced *fusilamiento* and experimented with *merengue* during his "Combo Show." He used two to five wind instruments, a format known as *conjunto*, made popular by salsa, and for the first time, *merengueros* played standing up. He also boosted the *tambora*'s rhythm and added a Congo drum.

Another musician, Juan Luis Guerra and his quartet the 4:40, invented something called "*merengue dual*." He made party music with lyrical commentary that made people dance and think. He also fused *merengue* with jazz and African music, creating new and unique sounds.

One more creative musician, Wilfrido Vargas, transformed *merengue*'s sound. He and his sextet Los Beduinos practiced *fusilamiento*-using ideas from all of the Caribbean and Latin America. They used Trinidadian *soca* horns, electric guitar solos, Bach piano riffs, New Orleans brass, African American *doo wop*, splashing cymbals used by Haitian bands, and Martiniquan *zouk*. He did anything to keep *merengue* current and heavily played on radio stations in the Dominican Republic and abroad.

While Dominicans in the 1970s and 1980s were enjoying *merengue*, the people of New York City were enjoying another Latin dance: salsa. Soon, however, they got tired of salsa and were looking for a new dance craze. *Merengue* filled their void. For economic and political reasons, many Dominicans migrated to New York, bringing *merengue* with them. People started learning this new dance because it was easier to learn that salsa.

Soon *merengue* was playing in salsa clubs all over the United States.

Moreover, it is taught in dance studios alongside salsa and rumba. The club version is more erotic than ballroom *merengue*, containing a suggestive way of dancing. In addition, the *paseo* is superseded by an exaggerated Cuban motion taught in chain dance studios for Latin American dances.

Once it hit the clubs, *merengue* rapidly gained popularity. Elvis Crespo, who sings hard-hitting *merengue* in Spanish, made the U.S. Top 50 in 1999 with his hit "Píntame." New fusion genres of *merengue* were also developed including *mereng-house* and *mereng-rap*. *Mereng-house* mixes *merengue*, hip-hop, and electronic music. *Mereng-rap* is basically Dominican *merengue* with rapping. Santi y Sus Duendes and Lisa M. are credited with birthing the genre in 1990 with their song "Soy Chiquitos (No Inventes Papito, No Inventes)."

No matter where it is played, *merengue* reflects Dominican life and identity. It represents the national and racial identity of the Dominican Republic. Trujillo's whitewashing of the music echoed the Eurocentric feelings of many members of society. However, to deny *merengue*'s African influence is to deny a part of the Dominican heritage. Some variants of *merengue* kept its African roots though, such as *merengue palo echao*. Although it has had to compete with other forms of music across Latin America and the United States, *merengue* has managed to stay alive. Its popularity has even spread to places like the United States and United Kingdom, taking Dominican culture with it.

References

Alcantara, A. (1990). *Los escritores dominicanos y la cultura*. Santo Domingo: Instituto Tecnológico de Santo Domingo.

Alcantara, J. (1987). Black Images in Dominican Literature. *New West Indian Guide* 61(3–4): 161–173.

Aparicio, Frances R. (1998). *Listening to Salsa: Gender, Latin Popular Music, and Puerto Rican Cultures*. Hanover, NH: Wesleyan University Press.

Austerlitz, Paul (1997). *Merengue: Dominican Music and Dominican Identity*. Philadelphia: Temple University Press.

Baez Evertsz, F. (1986). *Braceros haitianos en la República Dominicana*, 2d ed. Santo Domingo: Instituto Dominicano de Investigaciones Sociales.

Behague, G. (1985). Popular Music. In *Handbook of Latin American Popular Culture*, ed. Harold E. Hinds, Jr., and Charles M. Tatum, 3–38. Westport, CT: Greenwood.

Bilby, K. (1985). The Caribbean as a Musical Region. In *Caribbean Contours*, ed. Sidney W. Mintz and Sally Price, 181–218. Baltimore: Johns Hopkins University Press.

Brito Ureña, Luis Manuel (1997). *El Merengue y la Realidad Existencial de los Dominicanos: Bachata y Nueva Canción*. Santo Domingo, Dominican Republic: Unigraf.

8. The Merengue Dance of Latin America

Bryan, P. (1985). The Question of Labor in the Sugar Industry of the Dominican Republic in the Late Nineteenth and Early Twentieth Centuries. In *Between Slavery and Free Labor: The Spanish-Speaking Caribbean in the Nineteenth Century*, ed. Manuel Moreno Fraginals, Frank Moya Pons, and Stanley L. Engerman, 235–251. Baltimore: Johns Hopkins University Press.

Coopersmith, J. (1949). *Music and Musicians of the Dominican Republic/Música y músicos de la República Dominicana*. Washington, D.C.: Pan American Union.

Davis, M. (1980). Aspectos de la influencia africana en la musica tradicional dominicana. *Boletín del Museo del Hombre Dominicano* 13: 255–292.

Davis, M. (1980). That Old-Time Religion: Tradición y cambio en el enclave "Americano" de Samana. *Boletín del Museo del Hombre Dominicano* 14:165–196.

Davis, M. (1982). Folklore como antropologia. *Erne Erne: Estudios dominicanos* 11(61): 61–78.

Davis, M. (1987). *La otra ciencia: El vodu dominicano como religión y medicina populares*. Santo Domingo: Editora Universitaria de la Universidad Autónoma de Santo Domingo.

Deive, C. (1981). La herencia africana en la cultura dominicana actual. In Bernardo Vega, et al., *Ensayos sobre cultura dominicana*, 105–141. Santo Domingo: Ediciones del Museo del Hornbre Dominicano.

del Castillo, J. (1978). *La inmigración de braceros azucareros en la República Dominicana, 1900–1930*. Santo Domingo: Universidad Autonoma de Santo Domingo.

del Castillo, J. (1979). Las emigraciónes y su aporte a la cultura dominicana (finales del siglo XIX y principios del XX). *Erne Eme: Estudios dominicanos* 8(45):3–43.

del Castillo, Jose (1984). *Ensayos de sociología dominicana*. Santo Domingo: Taller.

del Castillo, J. (1985). The Formation of the Dominican Sugar Industry: From Competition to Monopoly, from National Semiproletariat to Foreign Proletariat. In *Between Slavery and Free Labor: The Spanish-Speaking Caribbean in the Nineteenth Century*, ed. Manuel Moreno Fraginals, Frank Moya Pons, and Stanley L. Engerman, 214–234. Baltimore: Johns Hopkins University Press.

del Castillo, J. (1988). *Antología del merengue/Anthology of Merengue*. Santo Domingo: Banco Antillano.

del Castillo, J., and G. Manuel (1987). *Carnaval en Santo Domingo/Carnival in Santo Domingo*. Santo Domingo: Radisson Puerto Plata/Banco Antillano.

del Castillo, J., and F. Martin (1987). Migration, National Identity, and Cultural Policy in the Dominican Republic. *The Journal of Ethnic Studies* 15(3): 49–68.

Duany, J. (1984). Popular Music in Puerto Rico: Toward an Anthropology of Salsa. *Latin American Music Review* 5(2): 186–216.

Duany, J. (1985). Ethnicity in the Spanish Caribbean: Notes on the Consolidation of Creole Identity in Cuba and Puerto Rico, 1762–1868. In *Caribbean Ethnicity Revisited*, ed. Stephen Glazier, 15–39. New York: Gordon and Breach.

Duany, J., ed. (1990). *Los dominicanos en Puerto Rico: Migración en la semi-periferia*. Rio Piedras: Huracán.

Enciclopedia dominicana. (1978). Merengue. *Enciclopedia dominicana*. Volume IV, 2d ed. Santo Domingo: Enciclopedica Dominicana.

Estrellas del Merengue (1986). Dir. Augusto Guerrero. VHS. Miami Lakes, FL: Kubaney.

García, J. (1947). *Panorama de la música dominicana*. Ciudad Trujillo: Publicaciones de la Secretaria de Educación y Bellas Artes.

González, N. (1970). Social Functions of Carnival in a Dominican City. *Southwestern Journal of Anthropology* 26(4): 328–342.
González, N. (1975). Patterns of Dominican Ethnicity. In *The New Ethnicity: Perspectives from Ethnology*, ed. John W. Bennett, 110–123. St. Paul, MN: West.
Haidar, J. (1991) La música como cultura y como poesía: Juan Luis Guerra y el Grupo 4.40. *Claridad* (San Juan), Part I, 19–26 December; Part II, 3–9 January.
Hoetink, H. (1971). The Dominican Republic in the Nineteenth Century: Some Notes on Stratification, Immigration, and Race. In *Race and Class in Latin America*, ed. Magnus Morner, 96–121. New York: Columbia University Press.
Hoetink, H. (1985). *El pueblo dominicano: 1850–1900. Apuntes para su sociología historica*. Santiago: Departamento de Publicaciones, Universidad Católica Madre y Maestra.
Hutchinson, Sydney. Merengue: Popular Music of the Dominican Republic. *IASO Records—Caribbean Soul*. 2003. IASO Records, New York. 15 October 2005. http://www.iasorecords.com/index.cfm?secid=1&subsecid=82.
Jorge, B. (1982). Bases ideológicas de la práctica musical durante la era de Trujillo. *Erne Erne: Estudios dominicanos* 10(59): 65–99.
Lewis, G. (1983). *Main Currents in Caribbean Thought: The Historical Evolution of Caribbean Society in Its Ideological Aspects, 1492–1900*. Baltimore: Johns Hopkins University Press.
Lizardo, F. (1974). *Danzas y bailes folklóricos dominicanos*. Santo Domingo: Fundación García Arévalo.
McLane, D. (1991). Uptown and Downhome: The Indestructible Beat of Santo Domingo. *Rock and Roll Quarterly* (Winter): 13–15, 19.
Mercado, D. (1983). Memorias de un músico rural. Parte II. *Eme Eme: Estudios dominicanos* 12(67): 83–111.
Moya Pons, F. (1986). *El pasado dominicano*. Santo Domingo: Fundación J.A. Caro Alvarez.
Ospina, Hernando Calvo (1995). *Salsa: Havana Heat, Bronx Beat*. London: Latin American Bureau.
Pacini, D. (1989). Social Identity and Class in Bachata, an Emerging Popular Music in the Dominican Republic. *Latin American Music Review* 10(1): 69–91.
Pacini H. (1991). La lucha sonora: Dominican Popular Music in the Post-Trujillo Era. *Latin American Music Review* 12 (2): 105–123.
Roberts, John Storm (1998). *Black Music of Two Worlds: African, Caribbean, Latin, and African-American Traditions*. New York: Schirmer.
Rodriguez, D. (1971). *Música y baile en Santo Domingo*. Santo Domingo: Librería Hispaniola.
Rodriguez, D. (1975). *Lengua y folklore de Santo Domingo*. Santiago: Universidad Católica Madre y Maestra.
Rodriguez, D. (1979). *Poesía popular dominicana*. Santo Domingo: Universidad Católica Madre y Maestra.
Silie, R. (1988). Aspectos culturales en la formación nacional dominicana. Paper presented at the Symposium on Culture and Society in Latin America, University of Puerto Rico, Bayamon, 26 October.
Steward, Sue. *Música! The Rhythm of Latin America: Salsa, Rumba, Merengue and More*. San Francisco: Chronicle, 1999.

Torres-Saillant, S. (1991). *Cuestion haitiana y supervivencia moral dominicana.* Unpublished manuscript.

---

9. The Merengue of the Dominican Republic

Music and dance occupy a very important place in the culture of the Dominican Republic. Among the most popular and universal dances is the merengue. Its appeal spreads across the diversity of the country, and encompasses the Dominican spirit. Dominican artist Juan Luis Guerra has been quoted as saying, "because it's the music I have in my heart." Guerra speaks for Dominicans throughout every region of this vibrant island.

The Roots of Merengue

Although the Spanish influence is the dominant element in the Dominican folk music tradition today, the African slaves left their distinctive features (Haywood, 1966). There are two popular versions of how the merengue originated. One claim is that the dance began with slaves who were chained together and forced to drag one leg as they cut sugar to the beat of drums. The second story tells of a great hero who was wounded in the leg during a revolution. He was welcomed home with a victory celebration, and everyone dancing felt obliged to limp and drag one foot out of sympathy (Moya Pons, 1995). Regarding its roots and influences, the merengue has many. It is similar to the Haitian méringue (*mereng*), except in its accordion-based sound, instead of the Haitian guitar version. Another influence comes from the UPA, a Cuban form that arrived in Santo Domingo in the mid–1800s imported from Puerto Rico. Contact with major trading partner, Germany, brought the accordion (Moya Pons, 1995). The African and the French Minuet, from the late 1700s—early 1800s, are said to have had an impact. The slaves observed the ballroom dances in the big houses and when they had their own festivities they started imitating the "masters' dances." The slaves added a special upbeat (the drums), as a slight skip or a hop. The original merengue was a circle dance not danced by individual couples. They didn't hold each other intimately and the original movements included only the shaking of the shoulders and rapid movement of the feet. There was no obvious movement of the hips like today (Moya Pons, 1995).

The core of the merengue dance is a very simple two-step, but the opposing hip movement to the right makes it fairly difficult to learn. The music has a lot of variety and the tempos may differ a great deal. Dominicans prefer a sharp speeding up toward the climactic end of the dance. It usually has either two beats or four beats to the bar. What sets the merengue apart, though, from this fairly typical structure, are certain traditional key instruments and their role. Swift beats from guiro or maracas percussion section are accompanied by a wild accordion or saxophone. Often a sax, box bass, tambora drum or guyano are included. The rhythm dominates the music, and is the most characteristic feature. It is unsyncopated and includes an aggressive beat on the one and three (Moya Pons, 1995).

Forms of Merengue

The physical geography of the Dominican Republic is one with very distinct areas; the remoteness and readiness of their people to adapt instrumentation to whatever was available created many variants distinct to each region. Several different types of merengue have developed. In ballroom merengue, where couples are never separated, men and woman hold each other in a vals-like position and step to their side in a "*paso de la empalizada*" or "stick-fence step." They can turn clockwise or counterclockwise. It is slow and has a much more conservative hip action. Figure merengue (*merengue de figura*) also exists where dancers also make turns individually but still never let go the hand of their partner. Two dance versions of merengue *cibaeño* exist. Sectional merengue *cibaeño* starts with a short *paseo* (walk) as a signal for couples to take the floor followed by a longer European melody-driven section and ending with a *jaleo* featuring African rhythmic qualities and simpler chordal harmonies. The second type, *merengue estilo yanqui* (yankee merengue), received its name from the U.S. servicemen who preferred a simple and syncopated rhythm. This later became known as the *pambiche*, from the Palm-Beach fabric spoken of in the lyrics of a popular song of this style. Accordion-based merengue *cibaeño* called *Perico Ripiao* (ripped parrot) became prominent in the 1930s. It is unsure how it received its name, but two theories exist: a parrot is of little gastronomic substance and was used as a metaphor for the musical simplicity of early accordion-based merengue. *Perico Ripiao*, referring to the male genitals, was also the name of a popular brothel in Santiago where this music was often performed (Allen, 1998).

Dominican History

The first people of the island of Hispaniola, the Taino Indians, literally meaning "gentle," were serene and self-sufficient. The Spanish ran down their numbers with disease. Spanish explorations on the island of Hispaniola, what became known as Santo Domingo, led to the importation of Africans causing even more diversity on the island. In 1795, the French took control of Santo Domingo and in 1822; Santo Domingo was again invaded, this time by Haiti. The Dominican Republic became sovereign in 1844 despite economically and politically insecure conditions.

Financial mismanagement left the Dominican Republic in an unstable state at the beginning of the twentieth century. Sensing a threat to the Panama Canal, America reached a deal with the Dominican Republic in 1905 to take control of customs houses and regulate payments to creditors. Tensions between the two countries grew with the Republic's contact with Germany in World War I. In 1916, U.S. Marines began a military occupation. Dominicans resisted with guerrilla warfare in the East, waged by local *caudillos* (warlords), a campaign led by the upper classes of El Cibao in efforts to sway international pinion against the occupation and, in general, establishing the nation as a culturally hostile environment for U.S. forces (Moya Pons, 1995).

Merengue and the Nation

Merengue was part of a movement that heightened nationalism. Merengue *cibaeño* was created as a symbol of cultural resistance, while celebrating patriotism in the face of U.S. troops (who attempted to dance the merengue, creating the mid-tempo version known as *pambiche*). The upper classes also took on the merengue in nationalism yet only after making changes in instrumentation and arrangement to allow it to agree with their waltzes, polkas and *danzas*. For, at first, merengue was insulted by the upper class, which preferred an older form of dance music called *tumba*, calling the merengue vulgar and obscene, largely due to scandalous lyrics. In contrast to their *tumba*, the merengue was a couple's dance with scandalous swinging hip movement. Its music had African syncopated rhythms also found in the Cuban *danza*. To the ruling classes, the merengue stood for Cuban/Afro-Caribbean cultures whose African (Haitian) ideals they hated (Moya Pons, 1995).

Major public acceptance began with Rafael Trujillo in the early 1930s. After joining the military during the U.S. occupation and rising rapidly through the ranks, Trujillo was granted the opportunity to take advantage of his position after the departure of U.S. troops left a power vacuum. Dominican politics had previously been strictly regional. When Trujillo ran for president in 1930, he campaigned on a national platform, eliminating regional leaders. The key to his success, however, was his understanding of the power of rural aesthetic forms as symbols of national identity. He based his campaign around the merengue, acknowledging that the masses were rural and would react well to it. Trujillo toured the regions with top merengueros. Once in power, Trujillo continued to promote the merengue as a national and political symbol. Popular merengue bands were renamed after him, and his brother Petán ran a major radio station, *La Voz Dominicana*, that broadcasted live merengue (Allen, 1998). Yet, this also meant that merengue bands hardly ever recorded. Because of this, many artists, artistically suffocated, left for Puerto Rico and New York, spreading the merengue.

The Spread of the Merengue

Trujillo's assassination in 1961, after a 30-year reign, brought changes to the development of merengue. Songs surfaced in which he was the subject of disdain. The calm and prescribed merengues he favored so much gave way to new interpretations with increases in speed, sexually suggestive lyrics, and more aggressive arrangements of the tambora drum and saxophones (Moya Pons, 1995). This new edge reflected the political optimism in the country and the introduction of fresh ideas through the lifting of travel restrictions.

One of the most significant catalysts was the arrival of Rock & Roll from the United States. An important influence, Johnny Ventura, led the merengue's transition into the popular culture of Latin America. His lack of contact with the Trujillo era gave his songs a fresh agile quality. His

9. The Merengue of the Dominican Republic

group, the Combo-Show, was also revolutionary. The "combo" part referred to a smaller line-up, with just two to five brass instruments. The "show" was the visual spectacle, where all the musicians played standing up and even danced while singing (Allen, 1998). In addition, in the '70s and '80s, trumpeter/bandleader Wilfrido led great increases in tempo, encountering stiff competition from the disco and hustle. Yet, through this competition, the merengue absorbed new influences. The first was *fusilamiento*, literally meaning, "firing," as in a gun. This describes the practice of converting popular Latin American *baladas* (ballads) into merengues. *Fusilamiento* could be negatively taken to mean the "assassination" of a perfectly decent song or, positively, that a song was "fired up." The second result of these outside influences was the increased incorporation of *"El Maco"* (the toad), a percussion pattern with elements of Haitian *konpa* and Puerto Rican *plena*. The rhythmic pulse is similar to disco, which allowed both genres to compete (Allen, 1998).

Joaquín Balaguer took power in 1966 with the help of a U.S. intervention. The huge emigration numbers grew even more with the collapse of land reform policies and the presence of pro-government death squads. There was also a great ease in U.S. immigration policy, so migrants escaped to New York City and Puerto Rico (Moya Pons, 1995). Puerto Rico has a history of adopting other Caribbean music in preference to its own *bomba* and *plena*. This pattern continues with the merengue *cibaeño*. Merengue became part of Puerto Rican culture making the island a hub for the genre and creating a market for immigrating Dominicans to supply (Reyes-Schramm, 1989). By the 1990s, nearly a million Dominican immigrants made New York the city with the second largest Dominican population in the world. The combination of Hispanic and black communities spawned a trading of ideas, which started new movements in merengue-house and merengue-rap. New York had the necessary musicians, recording facilities, mass media and distribution networks. The lack of those necessary tools was hindering growth in the Dominican Republic (Allen, 1998). For these immigrants, the merengue is more than just a music and dance; it's a reminder of who they are and where they come from.

Juan Luis Guerra, known as the Dominican Republic's greatest son, though not born to the lower class, bridged the gap between classes through his music. In his music, Guerra utilizes a diverse mix of Caribbean sounds and jazz. His merengues and *bachatas* are party music for the masses and at the same time tied with keen lyrics for the intelligentsia. He calls his music *"el merengue dual"* (dual merengue): music to make you dance and think at the same time. Guerra's lyrics have been most important to his success. While merengue lyrics typically have little depth, Guerra has been called a musical poet many times. Guerra sang in English on only one occasion, in a song called "Guavaberry," rooted in his native island that tells the story of a descendant of ex-slaves who migrated to the Dominican Republic from America, forming a small, English-speaking community that still exists. Guerra learned from the failure of crossover attempts that, by singing in English, only offended their Latin fans and made no impact in the mainstream market. Yet, staying true to his ideals, his album *Bachata Rosa* sold five million copies and won the 1991 Grammy for Best Tropical Album, making him an unofficial spokesman for the Dominican Republic (Moya Pons, 1995).

The appearance of merengue came as a breath of fresh air when salsa was vulnerable. Salsa in the late seventies was suffering from creative depression, brought on by the formulaic output of the major record labels. Lyrics were almost identical between songs and sung by artists with weak voices. Merengue held what salsa used to: a new sound with lyrics describing real events and performed by singers of substance. Its rhythmic structure is similar to pop, making keeping up with musical trends and the remaking of non–Latin songs much easier (Allen, 1998). It has overtaken salsa as the music of choice in Latino dance clubs. It is often played at twice the speed of salsa.

More modern merengue incorporates electronic instruments and influences from salsa, rock and roll, and hip-hop. Though rooted in folk rhythms, current versions mix in synthesizers, sampled sounds, electronic drums, and funk-influenced electric bass. Choruses are usually in groups of three and often in a call and response pattern. Live, wild dancing has always been a defining characteristic. Lyrically, references to issues of sexuality and politics are usual in the past as well. Appropriate to the small, crowded dance floors, it is a dance that is easy to learn and, in essence, "fun." Today, genuine merengue only carries on in rural areas. The traditional form has changed since the disappearance of the paseo. The body has been extended from 8 or 12 beats, to 32 or 48. The jaleo now also includes more exotic rhythms (Allen, 1998).

The estimated population composition of the Dominican Republic is 16 percent white, and 11 percent black, while 73 percent claims to be some mix of the various ethnicities (Moya Pons, 1995). The exchanges between these different cultures as the Dominican Republic struggled to discover its own national identity gave way to the union of the many faces of the island which can be seen its music; the merengue. The merengue has become a source of national pride and identity, allowing the Dominican

Republic to inject it in all parts of daily life. When visiting this fascinating island, one has the opportunity to discover firsthand how close the merengue is tied to the core of the nation and each person in it. The music and dance is a way of life, from birth and lives within them. As former New York mayor Ed Koch puts it, the merengue is "the one dance you can do from the moment you're born" (Allen, 1998). No special occasion is required, as mini-performances can break out at any moment, and everyone takes part. As the Dominican Republic grows and spreads further into the world, the merengue will follow suit. The national identity of a nation is always changing due to outside factors. Yet the merengue will always be the traditional music of the Dominican Republic.

References

Alcantara, A. (1990). *Los escritores dominicanos y la cultura*. Santo Domingo: Institute Tecnológico de Santo Domingo.
Alcantara, J. (1987). Black Images in Dominican Literature. *New West Indian Guide* 61(3–4): 161–173.
Allen, R. (1998). *Island Sounds in the Global City: Caribbean Popular Music and Identity in New York*. New York: New York Folklore Society and the Institute for Studies in American Music, Brooklyn College.
Aparicio, Francis R. (1998). *Listening to Salsa: Gender, Latin Popular Music, and Puerto Rican Cultures*. Hanover, NH: Wesleyan University Press.
Austerlitz, Paul. (1997). *Merengue: Dominican Music and Dominican Identity*. Philadelphia: Temple University Press.
Baez Evertsz, F. (1986). *Braceros haitianos en la República Dominicana*, 2d ed. Santo Domingo: Instituto Dominicano de Investigaciones Sociales.
Behague, G. (1985). Popular Music. In *Handbook of Latin American Popular Culture*, ed. Harold E. Hinds, Jr., and Charles M. Tatum, 3–38. Westport, CT: Greenwood.
Bilby, K. (1985). The Caribbean as a Musical Region. In *Caribbean Contours*, ed. Sidney W. Mintz and Sally Price, 181–218. Baltimore: Johns Hopkins University Press.
Brito Ureña, Luis Manuel. (1997). *El Merengue y la Realidad Existencial de los Dominicanos: Bachata y Nueva Canción*. Santo Domingo, Dominican Republic: Unigraf.
Bryan, P. (1985). The Question of Labor in the Sugar Industry of the Dominican Republic in the Late Nineteenth and Early Twentieth Centuries. In *Between Slavery and Free Labor: The Spanish-Speaking Caribbean in the Nineteenth Century*, ed. Manuel Moreno Fraginals, Frank Moya Pons, and Stanley L. Engerman, 235–251. Baltimore: Johns Hopkins University Press.
Coopersmith, J. (1949). *Music and Musicians of the Dominican Republic/Música y músicos de la República Dominicana*. Washington, D.C.: Pan American Union.
Davis, M. (1980) Aspectos de la influencia africana en la música tradicional dominicana. *Boletin del Museo del Hombre Dominicano* 13: 255–292.

Davis, M. (1980). That Old-Time Religion: Tradición y cambio en el enclave "americano" de Samana. *Boletin del Museo del Hombre Dominicano* 14: 165–196.
Davis, M. (1982). Folklore como antropologia. *Erne Erne: Estudios dominicanos* 11(61): 61–78.
Davis, M. (1987). *La otra ciencia: El vodu dominicano como religión y medicina populares.* Santo Domingo: Editora Universitaria de la Universidad Autónoma de Santo Domingo.
Deive, C. (1981). La herencia africana en la cultura dominicana actual. In Bernardo Vega, et al., *Ensayos sobre cultura dominicana*, 105–141. Santo Domingo: Ediciones del Museo del Hornbre Dominicano.
del Castillo, J. (1978). *La inmigración de braceros azucareros en la República Dominicana, 1900–1930.* Santo Domingo: Universidad Autonoma de Santo Domingo.
del Castillo, J. (1979). Las emigraciones y su aporte a la cultura dominicana (finales del siglo XIX y principios del XX). *Erne Eme: Estudios dominicanos* 8(45):3–43.
del Castillo, Jose. (1984). *Ensayos de sociología dominicana.* Santo Domingo: Taller.
del Castillo, J. (1985). The Formation of the Dominican Sugar Industry: From Competition to Monopoly, from National Semiproletariat to Foreign Proletariat. In *Between Slavery and Free Labor: The Spanish-Speaking Caribbean in the Nineteenth Century*, ed. Manuel Moreno Fraginals, Frank Moya Pons, and Stanley L. Engerman, 214–234. Baltimore: Johns Hopkins University Press.
del Castillo, J. (1988). *Antología del merengue/Anthology of Merengue.* Santo Domingo: Banco Antillano.
del Castillo, J., and F. Martin. (1987). Migration, National Identity, and Cultural Policy in the Dominican Republic. *The Journal of Ethnic Studies* 15(3): 49–68.
del Castillo, J., and G. Manuel. (1987). *Carnaval en Santo Domingo/Carnival in Santo Domingo.* Santo Domingo: Radisson Puerto Plata/Banco Antillano.
Duany, J. (1984). Popular Music in Puerto Rico: Toward an Anthropology of Salsa. *Latin American Music Review* 5(2): 186–216.
Duany, J. (1985). Ethnicity in the Spanish Caribbean: Notes on the Consolidation of Creole Identity in Cuba and Puerto Rico, 1762–1868. In *Caribbean Ethnicity Revisited*, ed. Stephen Glazier, 15–39. New York: Gordon and Breach.
Duany, J., (ed.) (1990). *Los dominicanos en Puerto Rico: Migración en la semiperiferia.* Rio Piedras: Huracán.
Enciclopedia dominicana. 1978. Merengue. *Enciclopedia dominicana.* Volume IV, 2d ed. Santo Domingo: Enciclopedica Dominicana.
Estrellas Del Merengue. Dir. Augusto Guerrero. VHS. Miami Lakes, FL: Kubaney, 1986.
Garcia, J. (1947). *Panorama de la música dominicana.* Ciudad Trujillo: Publicaciones de la Secretaria de Educación y Bellas Artes.
Glass, Barbara (2005). Introduction, The Africanization of American Movement. In *When the Spirit Moves*, 1999, National Afro-American Museum and Cultural Center. Retrieved November 28, 2005, from http://www.savoystyle.com/african.html.
Gonzalez, N. (1970). Social Functions of Carnival in a Dominican City. *Southwestern Journal of Anthropology* 26(4): 328–342.
Gonzalez, N. (1975). Patterns of Dominican Ethnicity. In *The New Ethnicity: Perspectives from Ethnology*, ed. John W. Bennett, 110–123. St. Paul, MN: West.

9. The Merengue of the Dominican Republic

Haidar, J. (1991) La música como cultura y como poesía: Juan Luis Guerra y el Grupo 4.40. *Claridad* (San Juan), Part I, 19–26 December; Part II, 3–9 January.

Haywood, Charles (1966). *Folk Songs of the World*. New York: John Day.

Hoetink, H. (1971). The Dominican Republic in the Nineteenth Century: Some Notes on Stratification, Immigration, and Race. In *Race and Class in Latin America*, ed. Magnus Morner, 96–121. New York: Columbia University Press.

Hoetink, H. (1985). *El pueblo dominicano: 1850–1900. Apuntes para su sociología historica*. Santiago: Departamento de Publicaciones, Universidad Católica Madre y Maestra.

Hutchinson, Sydney. (2003). Merengue: Popular Music of the Dominican Republic. *IASO Records—Caribbean Soul*. IASO Records. October 15, 2005, http://www.iasorecords.com/index.cfm?secid=1&subsecid=82.

Jorge, B. (1982). Bases ideológicas de la práctica musical durante la era de Trujillo. *Erne Erne: Estudios dominicanos* 10(59): 65–99.

Lewis, G. (1983). *Main Currents in Caribbean Thought: The Historical Evolution of Caribbean Society in Its Ideological Aspects, 1492–1900*. Baltimore: Johns Hopkins University Press.

Lizardo, F. (1974). *Danzas y bailes folkloricos dominicanos*. Santo Domingo: Fundación García Arévalo.

McLane, D. (1991). Uptown and Downhome: The Indestructible Beat of Santo Domingo. *Rock and Roll Quarterly* (Winter): 13–15, 19.

Mercado, D. (1983). Memorias de un músico rural. Parte II. *Eme Eme: Estudios dominicanos* 12(67): 83–111.

Moya Pons, F. (1986). *El pasado dominicano*. Santo Domingo: Fundación J.A. Caro Alvarez.

Moya Pons, F. (1995). *The Dominican Republic: A National History*. New Rochelle, NY: Hispaniola.

Ospina, Hernando Calvo. *Salsa: Havana Heat, Bronx Beat*. London: Latin American Bureau, 1995.

Pacini, D. (1989). Social Identity and Class in Bachata, an Emerging Popular Music in the Dominican Republic. *Latin American Music Review* 10(1): 69–91.

Pacini, H. (1991). La lucha sonora: Dominican Popular Music in the Post-Trujillo Era. *Latin American Music Review* 12 (2): 105–123.

Reyes-Schramm, Adelaida. (1998). Music and Tradition from Native to Adopted Land Through the Refugee Experience. *Yearbook for Traditional Music* 22(1989): 22–35.

Roberts, John Storm. *Black Music of Two Worlds: African, Caribbean, Latin, and African-American Traditions*. New York: Schirmer, 1998.

Rodriguez, D. (1971). *Música y baile en Santo Domingo*. Santo Domingo: Librería Hispaniola.

Rodriguez, D. (1975). *Lengua y folklore de Santo Domingo*. Santiago: Universidad Católica Madre y Maestra.

Rodriguez, D. (1979). *Poesía popular dominicana*. Santo Domingo: Universidad Católica Madre y Maestra.

Silie, R. (1988). Aspectos culturales en la formación nacional dominicana. Paper presented at the Symposium on Culture and Society in Latin America, University of Puerto Rico, Bayamon, 26 October.

Steward, Sue. *Musica! The Rhythm of Latin America: Salsa, Rumba, Merengue and More*. San Francisco: Chronicle, 1999.

Torres-Saillant, S. (1991). *Cuestion haitiana y supervivencia moral dominicana*. Unpublished manuscript.

---

10. Folk and Mento Dance Traditions of Jamaica

Jamaica, a small but prominent island of the West Indies, is a country that has belied its small size by influencing culture throughout the world. The medium through which this island and many of her peoples have made themselves outstanding international figures is music.

Jamaica is mainly known for her Reggae music. In fact, if a person were to ask another about the type of music produced by the island, the expected answer would refer to reggae. A fact unknown to many, however, is that Jamaica has birthed many genres of music. Amongst these are Ska, Rock Steady, Dub, Ragga, and Dancehall. The least recognized of these genres is the type responsible for the birth of all other forms of Jamaican music—the island's folk song and dance.

Jamaica's Musical Beginnings

Jamaicans are a singing, dancing people (Lewin, 1976). The most prominent derivative of Jamaican folk music is *Mento*—the original music of the island (Jamaican Cultural Development Commission. To understand what *Mento* is, a look at the history of the island, in terms of European domination and the influence of African slavery, is necessary. Folk dances of the island evolved from the religious and cultural celebrations of African slaves as well as from dances created in European courts.

Both African and English musical styles helped Jamaican folk music evolve. The island's folk music features drum rhythms, "singing voice," and scale types akin to those found in West African culture. Thus, African influence through slavery is the most prominent component of present-day Jamaican music. Due to slavery and the European imposition of cultural standards from about 1655, the British melodies of hymn tunes and folk songs also form the basis of many Jamaican folk songs. Work songs, which too helped create Jamaican folk culture, were developed during slavery. The slaves were prohibited from either drumming or talking to one another while they worked. The slave overseers, however, did not mind if they sang. Therefore, these indefatigable workers developed music addressing their toils and day-to-day plantation labor.

The first African slaves to inhabit the island were brought by the Spanish in 1517. When the British captured the island from the Spanish, these first slaves were freed and soon became identified as the Maroons. For decades to come after their liberation, the Maroons disputed with the English settlers over land rights. The conflict was finally resolved in 1739 when the English signed a treaty that upheld the Maroons' rightful claim to the land. Jamaica's second wave of African slaves was brought to the island by the English to work the crop plantations.

The rich culture of the Africans now inhabiting the small island was maintained through their music and dance festivities. During the Christmas season, the slaves celebrated by dressing in various costumes and masks representing certain characters. The slaves sang and danced to different instruments, which included the fife—a bamboo flute about 30cm long—and the drum—the central instrument of African celebrations—while joyously parading the "streets" of their particular area. This celebration called *Jonkunnu* was derived from the *Jonkanoo*—a dance performed by the Ashanti people of West Africa during harvest time, and is still performed at Christmastime in various parts of the island.

A second type of Afro-centric, Jamaican folk dance is *Kumina*. After the slaves were emancipated in 1838, Africans continued to arrive on the island as indentured servants. These new plantation indefatigable workers settled in the eastern parish of St. Thomas. This sect of Africans evolved the dance of *Kumina* where they used drumming. It is hard, almost impossible, to kill deep-seated almost instinctive behavior, and as a result, drumming has persisted as an integral part of the music traditions in Jamaica (Lewin, 1976). The *Kumina* emerged from a fusion of Christianity, animism from the southern region of Africa, and Pocomania—a Jamaican revivalist, religious denomination of Christianity. *Kumina* is a distinctly African word from the Congo. *Kumina* features strong, distinct drumming rhythms that are meant to entice the presence of the gods and spirits who then provide the help to the participants through their dance drumming ritual. *Kumina* dancing follows the liveliness of the dance's drum rhythms. Common features of the dance are bodies that are tilted forward, bent elbows, and swinging hips. Various body parts such as the shoulders, arms, and rib cage are used to propel the body in a spinning anti-clockwise pattern through a series of "dips and breaks." Other instruments used in this dance are the *shakkas*—a type of rattle—and the grater. The spectator crowd is characterized by loud singing along with drumming and dancing.

Another Jamaican folk dance that has great historical significance is *Bruckins*. This dance was created in the nineteenth century to celebrate emancipation from centuries of slavery. The dance involves the dipping of the body using the feet, moving the arms in a repeated upward motion, and "a wheeling and turning of the body." This dance is performed to the rhythm of drums.

European musical influence on Jamaican music is often underestimated. A European dance that had an influential impact on the development of Jamaican folk music is the *quadrille*. In order to provide entertainment for their masters, slaves were regularly taught to play European instruments at social dances held by the Jamaican gentility (Lwein, 1976). The *quadrille* is a French derived dance that was favored by the English settlers of the nineteenth century. It is performed by four couples to music played by a fiddle, fife, guitar, drum, banjo and *rhumba* box—a large box shaped *mbira*, usually sat on while played with the fingers. For their own pleasure, the slaves steadily modified the dance (Logan and Whylie, 1982).

Mento *Music*

By the late nineteenth century, Jamaican migrant workers were finding themselves in many places across the Caribbean and Central America working on projects such as the construction of the Panama Canal. This Jamaican "Diaspora" encouraged slight Latin influences from dances like the samba, the tango, and the Afro-Cuban rumba, as well as from the calypso music of Trinidad and Tobago—the Caribbean island farthest away from Jamaica. As these migrant workers returned to the island, features of the music from the countries they had labored in and visited were added to the dominant influences that African music and European melodies already had on the on Jamaican music (Lewin, 1976).

Elements of the musical styles from these cultures are found combined in *Mento* music and dance. *Mento* music evolved mainly from

Jamaican folk music in the early twentieth century. The sound of *Mento* is acoustic and rural. The principal instruments of this type of music are similar to those that were used in the quadrille. These instruments include the banjo, guitar, rhumba box, and hand drums (Logan and Whylie, 1982). The sound of *Mento* music is unique. This distinctive sound is created by the accent placed on the fourth beat of each bar rather than on the first beat, as is the norm. The vocalization of *Mento* varies greatly in style and pitch; however, the style that is said to sound the "most Mento" is the "nasal, rural sound" possessed by the majority of *Mento* singers. Although *Mento* music was not created specifically for male artistes, they were the main performers of the music. Amongst the scores of *Mento* male performers, very few female *Mento* singers can be found (Lewin, 1976).

Mento is often confused with *calypso*, a type of music from Trinidad and Tobago. The two admittedly sound very similar but their origins are significantly different, as calypso can claim greater Spanish influence. Despite the difference also found in the musical structure of the two genres, the words *calypso* and *Mento* were, at a point in time, used synonymously in Jamaica. *Mento* artistes often followed the calypso tradition of placing the title "Count" or "Lord" before their chosen artistic name (Logan and Whylie, 1982).

Mento songs were meant to be comical. As an extremely localized form of music, the lyrics greatly satirized the everyday life of common Jamaicans. Sex was a topic featured prominently in *Mento* songs but its presence was humorously subtle. Other topics of *Mento* songs included social issues such as poor living conditions, competition between other Caribbean islands, the island of Jamaica herself, and even simple topics like Jamaican recipes and types of foods (Lewin, 1976).

Although *Mento* was Jamaica's first recorded music, it was mainly enjoyed live. *Mento* bands added to the typical sound of this music genre with instruments such as the penny whistle (fife), bamboo saxophone, and even the steel pan. *Mento* bands were often featured in hotels as tourist attractions and also performed for special occasions such as parties and weddings (Logan and Whylie, 1982).

Mento is a genre of music unlike any other produced by Jamaica in that it strongly echoed its folk "roots" while it simultaneously gave Jamaican artistes a type of music with which they could anticipate the achievement of commercial success and become globally renowned (Lewin, 1976). Stanley Motta, a businessman who founded a chain of Jamaican electrical appliance stores, was the man whose efforts helped many such artistes achieve fame.

The Growth and Spread of Mento

In the late 1940s and early '50s Jamaica did not have adequate manufacturing facilities. This problem led Motta to seek the help of an esteemed Jamaican Jazz musician, Bertie King, who lived in London. On a business trip to Jamaica in 1951, King visited Motta's small-scale studio and recorded the songs "Don't Fence Her In" and "Glamour Girl" that were sang by a group known as Robinson and the Ticklers. King then sent these tapes to London where they were manufactured by UK major label Decca through the sponsorship of a company that had earlier recorded folk music in London. This company was Emil Shallit's London-based Melodisc Company. The record was released in Jamaica in the summer of 1952 as a 10-inch 78rpm. Subsequent *Mento* discs recorded on Motta's Recording Studio (MRS) label followed this pattern of production. Other producers of *Mento* recordings included Shallit's Kalypso label, Ken Khouri's Federal label, and Baba Tuari's Indian label. The artists who were featured by these labels included Laurel Aitken, Lord Tanamo, and Count Owen (Lipstz, 1999). *Mento* music reached the height of its popularity in the early 1950s as a result of the many *Mento* records being produced at the time. Demand for the music, however, started to decline not too far after this peak.

The Decline of Mento

Many factors contributed to the gradual demise of the popularity of *Mento* music. The most significant of these factors were the introduction of electric instruments, the advent of sound systems, and the shifting political status and environment of the island. During the 1950s, a new breed of Jamaican musicians began to discount the old acoustic sounds of instruments used in *Mento* and embraced the more modern sound of electric instruments such as the keyboard and electric guitar (Lewin, 1976).

By the end of the 1940s, sound systems were starting to take over the job of live *Mento* bands. The earliest sound systems consisted of a record deck, a valve amp, and loud speakers. The use of sound systems at functions such as dances, parties, and weddings became preferred over the use of *Mento* bands. Not only were the use of these sound systems more economically convenient for party hosts, but the sound systems also played a new type of music that the Jamaican people were finding increasingly more appealing (Lipstz, 1999).

During the 1950s, Jamaica's atmosphere was alert and unsettled. Most of the islanders suffered from the deeply rooted class partitions. Unemployment was a significant problem, and it seemed that the affluent were becoming even richer while the poor continued to suffer (Barow and Dalton, 1997). By the end of World War II, Jamaica was nearing independence and her people were anticipating freedom from the British power they had come to view as exploitive and oppressive. For many, the sounds of *Mento* and folk music now appeared to be too relaxed and non-political. As their lives changed, Jamaicans started to crave music that was more compatible with the island's transformation. American R&B was the first harder-edged music of this sort that Jamaicans gravitated toward (Barow and Dalton, 1997).

This style of American music arrived in Jamaica in several ways. Transistor radios allowed Jamaicans to pick up American R&B from a few radio stations in the south of the United States. Examples of these radio stations were WNOE in New Orleans, WINZ in Miami, and WLAC in Nashville. Migrant workers returning to the island from the USA, as well as merchant sailors visiting the island carried the music with them. Finally, the most effective medium through which American R&B became popularized in Jamaica was through the sound systems that featured the music at parties and dances (Barow and Dalton, 1997).

In present day Jamaica, Jamaican folk music and *Mento* music, although not as popular as they once were, are still significant as the original definitive music of Jamaican culture. Jamaican folk songs and dances are still practiced, celebrated, performed, and taught to younger generations. *Mento* songs are still played on the radios, as well as for tourists in hotels and occasionally for functions such as weddings. Two artists that helped keep *Mento* alive when other forms of music, like ska and rock steady became prominent were Sugar Belly—an infamous bamboo saxophonist—and a group known as the Jolly Boys, who were practitioners of folk music as well as of *Mento* (Barow and Dalton, 1997). Jamaican folk music and *Mento* are significant not only in the genres that preceded them, but also in the birth of Jamaica's recording industry. Thus, these two original types of Jamaican music can never be completely erased from the island's music scene.

References

Barrow, Steve and Peter Dalton (1997). *Reggae: The Rough Guide*. London: Rough Guides, 1997.

Burnett, Michael (1982). *Jamaican Music*. Great Britain: Oxford University Press, 1982.

Lewin, Olive (1976). Biddy, Biddy Folk Music of Jamaica. *Music Educators Journal MENC: The National Association for Music Education*, 38–49.

Lipsitz, George (1999). World Cities and World Beat: Low-Wage Labor and Transnational Culture. *The Pacific Historical Review 68(2)*.

Logan, Wendell, and Marjorie Whylie (1982). Some Aspects of Religious Cult Music in Jamaica. In *The Black Perspective in Music* vol. 10, no. 1. Foundation for Research in the Afro-American Creative Arts.

Salewicz, Chris, and Adrian Boot. (2001). *Reggae Explosion: The Story of Jamaican Music*. Great Britain: Virgin.

11. The Reggae Dance of Jamaica

The influence that Jamaica has had on music in the last 40 years is undeniable. The impact that Jamaica's music and culture has had specifically on the United States is evident in symbolically evident through the Billboard charts to movies (Manuel, Bilby & Largey, 2006). American pop culture has been greatly changed by the culture of Jamaica (Chang & Chen, 1998). So how did Jamaica become so influential? What influenced Jamaican music to begin with? Why does the music inspire other cultures such as that of North America? These questions will help guide an in depth look into the history and expansion of the Jamaican musical landscape, culture and the key players involved.

Culture

Jamaica is a tropical paradise with a hot, humid climate. Much of the land is mountainous, leaving over 75 percent not suitable for farming. Because of this, the major economic base of Jamaica is services. The tropical nature of the island lends itself to tourism, which it capitalizes in by providing resorts and activities for tourists. Because of its relative closeness to the United States, a lot of Jamaica's culture and tradition is tied in with America. By examining the demographic however, this is not evident. Over 90 percent of the population comes from West Africa

11. The Reggae Dance of Jamaica 75

(Sheeler, 1957). What allows for the cultural tie to the United States is the common language of English. Now that the basic makeup of Jamaica is set, a look into the cultural history of Jamaica is needed.

For a country that is smaller than all but two U.S. states and with a population of less than 3 million, the story leading to Jamaica's unique musical style incorporates many different aspects of other nations (Sheeler, 1957). The Arawak people, the original inhabitants of the island, do not have as big of an impact as most indigenous people. In 1494, when Christopher Columbus landed on the island, he brought things with him that he was sure to give a fresh start to the culture of Jamaica: disease, war, and slavery. They conquerors of the nation were able to wipe out the entire population of the Arawak population, eventually replacing it with slaves from the African slave trade. The oppression of the Spanish was short lived, being superseded by Britain in 1655. As slaves continued pouring into the island, the slaves quickly outnumbered the masters, leading to uprisings and the freedom of some slaves. The oppression continued until the abolishment of slavery in 1834. In 1872, the capital of Jamaica moved from the interior to the coastal town of Kingston, which would later become the epicenter of Jamaican music (Sheeler, 1957).

Music

The instability and constant changing of government and leadership of the people of Jamaica dramatically affected the formation of its culture. After the abolishment of slavery, the country was faced with times of economic struggle and political volatility. The island is divided into two main parties, the Jamaica Labor Party and the People's National Party, both inspiring many songwriters.

No single genre influenced the creation of Jamaican music; it was the blending and mixing of several cultures that produced the unique sound of Jamaican music. The most influential sounds were that of the people of Jamaica (African slaves), the sounds of the southern United States (New Orleans, Florida, etc.), and the sounds of the surrounding islands. The mix of these styles produced the first authentic Jamaican music.

The population of Jamaica during the early twentieth century was mostly made up of ancestors of slaves from the African slave trade (Walters, 1990). The base of the inhabitants brought over the intense drumming style of their homeland. The different styles of African drumming mixed to form *Mento*. *Mento* songs often feature an acoustic instrument such as a guitar or banjo led by a hard drum beat. This melody is covered by light, often humorous lyrics about the everyday life and plight of the Jamaican people. *Mento* is not the only music that is attributed to the African people. The Rastafarian religion brought its own musical style into the mainstream (Chang & Chen, 1998). *Nyabinghi* or *burra* music is the most important form of Rastafarian music. The drumming, chanting, praying, and dancing common of burra was played at worship ceremonies. Along with music in worship, the native people of Jamaica used music in ceremonies for healing. Each medical herb used had "its own special rhythm that is drummed and danced as it is given to a sick person." These ceremonies mimic similar events that occurred in Africa (Chang & Chen, 1998).

Outside Influence

American music has affected almost every country in the last 70 years, and Jamaica is no exception. As Jamaica was just beginning to define its own musical style, America was in its prime, releasing its own brand new style of music. American Jazz in the 1930s and 40s was all the rage on the island. Several Jamaican jazz brands sprouted up in the late '40s in order to entertain tourists. (Chang & Chen, 1998). As music in America changed from jazz to rhythm and blues, so did the taste of the island. Because of the poverty of the population, many could not afford to purchase a radio. This poverty eventually led to the introduction of the sound system. In Kingston, mobile sound systems were created in order to play the American hits. These sound systems were the center of parties and dancing. R&B hits blasted from the speakers for almost 10 years, during the height of its popularity. Another kind of American music is responsible for the first production of original Jamaican music. In the late 1950s, the United States became a buzz with Rock and Roll. The Jamaicans craved new R&B music. Because the import of new R&B tracks from America was no longer possible, it forced the island to produce its own R&B. Because this new music was simply an imitation, and not new and different, Jamaicans eventually created their own genre.

The third and final major influence on the genres of Jamaica came from the surrounding islands. The music of Trinidad, Cuba, and Haiti have very similar musical characteristics as Jamaica, and not surprisingly, since all of the music of the Caribbean can trace its roots to African slaves and American Jazz. Often, the different genres of the islands are mistaken for each other. The different elements of each genre have been incorporated throughout the Caribbean, causing an extreme fusion of each style.

Jamaican Musical Styles

With the influences of the original genres of Jamaican music established, what styles of music did these influences create? The first genre that came from the island is known as *ska*. While the origin of the name is debated, some believe that it is simply a case of onomatopoeia, a word that mimics a sound. A genre created from many elements, ska is a fusion of *Mento*, calypso, jazz and R&B. Ska music is characterized by an emphasized drumbeat on the second and fourth bars, such as in R&B, and its placement of accented guitar and piano rhythms on the upbeats of the rhythm. To outsiders, this may sound strange, and some even believe that this placement is due to the mimic of American music over the radio, music that contained many breaks due to the weak signal on the island. Most islanders consider ska not a misunderstanding, but rather its own response to American music. *Ska* was considered fast-paced, high-energy dance music, but as the music evolved, it eventually slowed into a genre called rocksteady.

The slower paced rocksteady is identified by its strong bass line that leads the music in a syncopated fashion. What sets this music apart from others is not only the bass line, but also the accompanying vocalists. Instead of a choppy singing style associated with a fast-paced dance rhythm, rocksteady's beat allows for a stronger vocal presence. Motown-inspired singers were able to let loose and cover the richer melodies with strong, soulful voices.

The most common and widespread genre of Jamaica is arguably the style known as reggae music. The origins of the term reggae have many different theories. One theory is that it originated from a Ska hit of 1968 called "Do the Reggay." Other speculations are that it came from the word stage, Jamaican slang for prostitute or that it grew from the term *Regga*, which was a Bantu-speaking tribe from Lake Tanganyika. The expression "reggae" is sometimes used in a more wide-ranging sense to refer to most types of Jamaican music, including ska, rocksteady and dub; in this sense however, the term is more particularly used to indicate the specific genre that originated from rocksteady. Reggae is based on a cadence characterized by regular chops on the backbeat. This rhythmic section of the song is led by a rhythm guitar and a bass drum hitting on the third beat of each measure. Like rocksteady, the reggae beat is again even slower than its predecessors are. While reggae can be tied in with the religious Rastafarian movement, lyrics often deal with many other subjects including love, sexuality, and a broad social commentary.

When looking at reggae lyrics, the entire gambit of subjects can be seen but social commentary songs seem to have the biggest impact. Bob Marley's main message seemed to be one of freedom and religion. Not only do these lyrics speak to a freedom from government, standing up for your rights, but one of looking to God as a higher power. In "Stir It Up" a less serious message is seen: A more sexual message is also a backbone of the relaxed reggae genre.

Bob Marley

Reggae music became very popular not only in Jamaica but also in a short time, internationally. The strength of the reggae movement was led by Bob Marley. Marley was born to Jamaican parents, a black mother and a white father. After his father died at an early age, his mother and he moved to the capital of Jamaica, Kingston. Growing up short and biracial, Marley was forced to learn self-defense and become physically strong. He gained a reputation for his strength, leading to his nickname on all of his records, "Tuff Gong." After leaving school at 14, Marley became friends with Bunny Wailer, who eventually would become part of his group. In his free time, he would jam with local musicians. After meeting Peter Tosh, another local singer, Bob Marley recorded his first two singles. Marley then formed a group with Tosh and Wailer, becoming Bob Marley and the Wailers (Manuel, Bilby & Largey, 2006). His group gained popularity over the next several years. After getting married in 1966 and taking a short trip to America, Marley moved back to Jamaica where he became a strict Rastafarian.

Upholding Rastafarian tradition, Marley grew his trademark dreadlocks and began to partake in the religious event of smoking marijuana or *ganja* as sometimes known in Jamaica. Unlike many American teenagers who see Marley as simply a druggy, marijuana is used as a sacrament in the Rastafarian religion. The belief is that it allows a person to become closer to God. Bob Marley and the Wailers began to sell worldwide until the bands break up in 1974. After the breakup, Marley continued to use the band name, and he received his first international hit in "No Woman, No Cry." He began to tour the world, coming out with hit after hit, until cancer finally caught up with him. In 1981, Bob Marley died of cancer. His contributions to reggae music are felt long after his death. He was inducted into the Rock and Roll Hall of fame in 1994 and Time magazine listed his album *Exodus* as the best album of the twentieth century. His album *Legend* went on to sell over 12 million copies. All of these things truly show how Bob Marley took a small island genre and made it an international phenomenon.

Reggae Spinoffs

As time has progressed, so has the musical culture. While reggae is still an enormous part of the music scene, other genres have broken off into a style more conducive to sales in America. Reggae has inspired a large number of sub-genres, including the popular dancehall music (Manuel, Bilby & Largey, 2006). This style is much faster than reggae with electronic drums replacing the original drum sets. In order to have a style more encouraging to dancing, dancehall is a sped up reggae so that listeners can more easily dance to it. A deejay often "toasts" over this style. "Toasting" is a type of rapping and the lyrics tend to be bawdy.

Ragga is a subset of dancehall reggae. This subset is characterized by sampled, electronic music and corresponds to the majority of the current reggae music in production. Like all popular music, *ragga* is evolving into new forms, but it has mainly been influenced by international dance music and hip-hop. Although many consider Bob Marley and The Wailers as the only style of reggae, it is instead an evolving family of music (Manuel, Bilby & Largey, 2006). The newer styles of reggae have been produced toward the Jamaican peoples' love for dancing.

As reggae music changes, native Jamaicans have been able to use the newer dancehall styles to take over the American Billboard charts and music culture. In 1984, the Grammys added the Best Reggae Album award because of the spread of the genre. The new mix between traditional reggae and American hip-hop has been able to propel Jamaicans into popularity. Artists such as Shaggy, Sean Paul, Beenie Man, and of course, Bob Marley's sons, Ziggy and Damian, have all built a strong following in the United States through their use of the Jamaican musical culture.

Conclusion

It is without a doubt that the musical culture of the small island of Jamaica has influenced the world. Reggae music can be found in everything from the popular music of the Ivory Coast to the top of American charts and in general, in all of American popular culture including movies and clothing (Manuel, Bilby & Largey, 2006). While Jamaica's musical history is relatively short compared to most, its overall importance to the rest of the world is undeniable. The island was able to take some of the most popular elements of the twentieth century (R&B and strong percussion) and create its own blend of music. As time progresses, Jamaica's popularity and world impact will undoubtedly continue to grow.

References

Chang, O. K., and W. Chen (1998). *Reggae Routes: The Story of Jamaican Music.* Philadelphia: Temple University Press.
Freeman, B. E., and Andrea Geoghagen (1989). A Population Study in Jamaica on the Gall-Midge Asphondylia boerhaaviae: A Contribution to Spatial Dynamics. *The Journal of Animal Ecology* 58, no. 2.
Jahn, Brian, and Tom Weber (1998). *Reggae Island: Jamaican Music in the Digital Age.* Kingston: Da Capo.
Manuel, P., Bilby, K., and Largey, M. (2006). *Caribbean Currents: Caribbean Music from Rumba to Reggae,* 2d ed. Philadelphia: Temple University Press.
Mthembu-Salter, Gregory, and Peter Dalton (2000). The Loudest Island in the World. In *World Music, Vol. 2: Latin & North America, Caribbean, India, Asia and Pacific,* ed. Simon Broughton and Mark Ellingham, with James McConnachie and Orla Duane, 430–456. London: Rough Guides/Penguin.
Sheeler J. R. (1957). Population of Jamaica: An Analysis of Its Structure and Growth. *The Journal of Negro History* 24(4).
Walters, Angela (1996) How I Learned African History from Reggae. *A Journal of Opinion* 24(2): 43–45.

12. The Rumba Dance of Cuba

The rumba is a dance that rivets its image on the mind. Holding much history, it has been and is a dance of oppositions: love and hate, hostility and harmony, sensuality and prudence. Musically, it taps into the realms of technicality and improvisation. The dance and music is a marvel, leaving a lusty taste in its trail so that a natural tendency towards it never fades.

Origins of Rumba

African and Spain have shaped the music of Cuba (Haywood, 1966). The origins of the rumba stem from Africa. The steps and song of traditional rumba may have begun as remembered pieces of dance from the Ganga or Kisi people in Cuba, generalized groups of West Central African descent.

Some prospect that the Sara peoples of northern Nigeria are the founders of *rumba*. A similar dance they had is of rows of boys in front of rows of girls, approaching one another in movement and then separating. In present-day Zaire, a traditional BaKongo dance called *vane samba* appears to directly link to rumba's progenitors. A characteristic highlight occurs when the bodies of a dancing pair meet, or almost meet, at the navel. This movement mirrors the rumba's *vacunao*, a prominent feature in some forms of rumba.

The name *rumba* possibly derives from the Spanish language; the word *rumbo* translates to *route*, *rumba* translates to *heap pile*, and *rum* is of course the liquor popular in the Caribbean. Any of these words might have been used descriptively when the dance was being formed. The name has most often been claimed to be derived from the Spanish word for *carousel,* or *festival.*

Rumba developed in the 1850s and 1860s among free black slaves gathered to express their struggles with one another. Following the abolition of slavery in Cuba in 1886, poor Cubans dealt with a society still emphasizing color and class by participating in communal gatherings known as rumbas. The cathartic music and dance created eventually found its name from these meetings.

Post–1518, enslaved Africans had a continuous influence on Cuba, particularly after 1700 through 1886. During these years, "massive numbers of new arrivals kept a persistent and forceful garden of African culture growing whenever and wherever they could in the nooks and crannies" (Shephard & Beckles 457). Overwhelming colonial authority and restriction, the convention of the enslaved Afro-Cubans implicitly permeated Cuba for more than two hundred years.

Havana was the cradle for large numbers of enslaved Africans by the end of the eighteenth century. Slave barracks became kernels of anguish. Rebellion was prohibited and dangerous, so resistance was expressed in recreational music and dance.

Because revolts were feared by authorities, factionalism was tolerated and black *cabildos* were molded. *Cabildos* were homogenous African ethnic groups that operated as mutual aid societies. Unintentionally, the *cabildos* proved fundamental in the crystallization of African cultural traditions in Cuba, including language and religious practices.

With the end of slavery, poor Afro-Cubans continued to lament their frustrations of meager opportunities and depressing conditions by means of music and dance. Indigent Cubans swelled in *solares*, the crowded habituations surrounding a central courtyard, which served as rendezvous to relax, play, and dream in song, dance, and poetry.

The *solares* offered solace to those who faced racial injustice and unfair realities of political incompetence. From these courtyards, a music and dance was born. Neither completely African nor completely Spanish, but rather a layering and interfacing of both; the adoption of singing, dancing, and drumming in a unique style resulted in rumba.

Rumba's Variations

Various types evolved depending on the circumstances of particular locales. One type developed in the urban areas of Havana and Matanzas provinces and involved couple dancing. Another type, a male solo form, was produced in rural areas. The Afro-Cuban spirit of rumba grew mainly in the courtyard of the *solar,* the port district, the bars, and the sidewalks of red-light districts (Roy, 2002).

Three basic dance concepts cultivated as the rumba complex, all of which have recognizable rhythmic bases and considerably depend on pantomimed themes of seduction and competition: *columbia, yambú, guaguancó*.

Considered the oldest element of the rumba, the *columbia* was born in a hamlet near Sabanilla. Perfection of form, style, bravado, competition, and a rapid tempo are all distinguishing features. *Columbia* is danced in a series that puts all males in competition and stimulates each man to dance in solo with brilliance. The dancer first salutes the *quinto* drum and then breaks into acrobatic movements in which the feet, arms, and shoulders are stressed in a kind of rhythmic joust with the *quinto*. If with a partner, together they balance and guide one another, sometimes extemporaneously initiating new rhythms. The most accomplished dancers perform old dances balancing a glass of water or a candle on their head. Some perform the "dance of knives" with machetes. Immense inner concentration is critical to successfully showing the aptitude in musicality, stylistic structure, and creativity of which define the *columbia*.

In *yambú*, the mood and aim are danced seductively. Danced by couples to a rather slow but measured tempo, the dance maintains a sense of pure flirtation with an elegant sensuality. Charm and poise are presented in the chase, the man never making any violent gesture of capture toward the woman, as in the *guaguancó*. The couple often dances close to the ground, occasionally using a scarf to accentuate their movements.

The last-born of the rumba styles, the *guaguancó*, appeared in the first decade of the twentieth century. This slightly faster rumba is by far the most frequently performed and most popular of the rumbero cycle. The *vacunao*, or vaccination, is the goal. *Vacunao* is the term coined by the Cubans to signify the erotic pelvic thrust of the male. This gesture is not always of the hips; a hand, foot, or scarf can also symbolize the male's vaccination of the female. The woman escapes the *vacunao* by protecting her pelvic area with a covering motion and turning away, all the while sustaining the rhythm of the dance and enduring a seductive attitude. Upon observation of the *guaguancó,* one can easily note the opportunism illustrated in the choreography, the behavior of the man similar to that of a rooster chasing a hen: preening himself, puffing his chest out, strutting about, and relentlessly pursuing his potential mate. The woman, like a hen sometimes, is uninterested, tries to escape and avoid him, but is eventually attracted to him and allows him to dance nearby (Daniel, 1995).

Rumbas del tiempo de España (rumbas from the time of Spanish colonial control) or *rumbas de los viejos* (rumbas of the old people), make up a separate category in Cuba. It includes mimes of a variety of themes, always exercising rumba steps. They are said to be old stories acted out in dance form. All of mimetic rumbas are relatively slow in tempo and narrative in style. One popular dance is *Mama'buela*, the tale of a grandmother who finds her son playing in the streets when he should be in school. After many attempts to coerce him into going to school, she eventually takes pity and joins him in dancing rumba. When he makes the *vacunao* gesture, she goes into shock and faints. Dancers who perform this type of rumba are hailed as expert; they receive much praise for sharply delivering rumba's movements.

The Sounds and Feelings of Rumba

Even from the early beginnings, instruments in rumba have played a significant role. The first codified percussion instruments were wooden shipping crates of varying shapes, called *cajones*. In the time period when

Africans were enslaved, laws had been passed prohibiting the use of real drums because of the colonists' fears of slave insurrections. The colonists believed that drumming attracted crowds and incited rebellion. Therefore, the Afro-Cubans substituted boxes to satisfy their need to make music and dance. Since the beginning of the twentieth century, the instruments have evolved, and calfskin drums have superseded the *cajones*.

In rumba, the *claves*, or wooden sticks, begin the instrumentation. The rhythm feels metronomic and this usually signals the type of rumba to be danced. Following the *claves* is the largest and lowest-pitched drum, the *tumbador*, which guides the band in a sustained pitch and pattern. The second drum, *tres golpes*, is of the middle register. Requiring great skill, the *quinto* is the highest-pitched of the drum trio and the most improvisational. Completing the instrumental group is the *madruga*, a shaker, and the *cata*, a cylindrical wood or bamboo instrument played with sticks.

The *claves* and *quinto* are in 4/4 time and the other drums in 6/8 time. Over this intricate composite rhythm, a lead vocalist begins with the *diana*, a melodic fragment of nonsense syllables that is passionately or playfully sung. Following is an extended text, loosely contrived melodies and lyrics. The rumba lyrics can be about anything—love, politics, cockfights, people, etc. With the commencement of a short refrain by the chorus comes the dancing.

In all types of rumba, sounds, and visions dynamically escalate in freedom, restraint, love, and tension. The excitement weaves between not only dancers and musicians, but also engrosses the spectators. Because of the rumba's inherent intoxication, it sucks its observers into a world of sensuality and exoticism. Rumba creates a situation in which cultural boundaries are blurred and cross-cultural experiences are embraced. Louis Pérez, in *On Becoming Cuban*, draws a personal experience from a visitor to Cuba who manifests the power of rumba, even within a culturally unconditioned spectator group, to induce pleasurable feelings and behavioral expressions:

> Her slim, tense, dancer's body weaves and melts its way into the music and into the senses. A tom-tom beat in the savage, sensual music beats every trim line of her body into every tired brain.... The tourist ... is swept away by the tropic night and the tom-tom beat and the weaving bronze body; he is part of something young and strong and fierce and ageless as the jungle and unquenchable as the fiery heart of Africa [p. 201].

In a rumba performance, the explicit passion contains a mix of influences. In instrumentation, due to European influence, the highest-pitched percussion instruments play the virtuoso part. Yet the polyrhythms of the drums remain a token of African heritage. The Cuban concept of proper body orientation combines a more elongated "Spanish" and more flexed "African" structural positioning. The heavy emphasis on hip movement by both males and females displays African elements. Intricate foot movements and a lifted chest for males relate more closely to Spanish dance elements. In imitation of courtly dances of Spanish folk, females often hold their skirt edges.

What amasses in minor movements and facial expressions in rumba forges into an air of deliberation and regard. The aura is of elegance for women and a kind of glory for men. An implication of strength, courage, pride, and arrogance resonate from the anachronous male attitude and body orientation while dancing. Women contrast in the use of controlled subtlety with a mood of soft sensuousness. From both shine a paradox of liberation and constraint.

Rumba through the Years

Before the Cuban Revolution, the usual time for rumba gatherings was on Saturday evenings. The dances were spontaneous and lasted several hours. However, these days, spontaneous rumbas rarely occur. Rumbas continue to be performed on Saturdays, but they are now prepared, and at times, theatrical. Although other days can be used for performances, performance time has changed from primarily nights to afternoons. In provinces, they can be found at least once a year in each province's Culture Week or when traveling traditional groups give performances. At the national level, prepared rumba occurs at the Rumba Festival, which lasts between 1 and 2 weeks during the month of October each year.

Amateurs as well as professionals participate in dancing during these festivals. Much of the public becomes invigorated to dance. Sometimes senior couples dance, moving slowly but with experienced taste. Other times young men take center stage and are applauded for their complex exchanges with the *quinto* player. Because the *quinto* player is not familiar with the style of the dancer, much of their result depends on the kinesthetic feeling and improvisational techniques of both musician and dancer. A warm and inviting atmosphere abounds the public never ridiculing any attempt to display rumba, except for the good-humored jests at drunken soloists. When dancers exhibit their talents in animated and stunning ways, the audience cheers and often the dancer approaches the drums and salutes the drummers as is the custom.

The National Folkloric Ensemble of Cuba and the officials of the Ministry of Culture took hold of the popularity of the dance and established Rumba Saturdays in urban areas such as Havana and Matanzas. This cultural program serves as both a celebration of Rumba as a national symbol and allows foreigners an international image of Cuba. The music and dance of economically scanty Cubans, which had for years been ignored and dismissed by the dominant society, took on a new importance as a result of their "distinctively national associations, the growing anti-imperialist sentiment in the country, and an intensified search on the part of cultural critics for uniquely Cuban modalities of expression" (Moore, 1995).

By 1980, Regular Rumba Saturday was a consistent event and through dance and music. The public acknowledged the history of Cuban culture and the Revolution's new values. Rumba symbolizes an ideal that the Revolution epitomized: equality with the working masses and an identity with its Afro-Latin heritage. Having traditionally and visually represented one segment of the Cuban population, rumba has been enhanced to illustrate the nation as a whole.

The Cuban government supports the arts by paying specialists to work daily at their discipline. Professionally trained teachers from art schools are used in neighborhood cultural centers, primary schools, nursery schools, and day care centers to promote and cultivate an appreciation of dance nationally.

There are three professional folkloric companies in Cuba: Conjunto Folklórico Nacional in Havana, Folklórico de Oriente, and Cutumba in Santiago de Cuba. Conjunto Nacional represents the national heritage in dance, presenting strict conservative styles. Performances are given every other Saturday. Folklórico de Oriente is a neo-traditional company that presents traditional rumba, but leans toward contemporary stylization of classic forms. Their success is based on emphasizing the reality of culture as a constantly changing phenomenon. Cutumba, which formed as a branch of Folklórico de Oriente, presents mostly representations of the eastern provinces, particularly Haitian-Cuban forms.

Rumba and Culture

All three professional companies work with the Ministry of Culture and its educational objectives. The goals are to present folkloric material from specific regions; to identify Spanish, African, and Haitian constituents of Cuban heritage; to entertain and reeducate the Cuban public; and to familiarize international audiences with the whole conception of Cuban culture.

These companies play a major role in the sustenance of rumba. They spread the knowledge of cultural values, attitudes, history, and traditional and contemporary complexes of both music and dance.

In the nineteenth century, *Rumba* was danced predominantly by low-class black Cubans. A strong black presence had already diffused into the island; yet, as ex-slaves, Afro-Cubans were excluded from society and denied Cuban identity. In a dissertation, Robin Moore confirms the contradictions amid that time period in Cuba:

> Representatives of the Cuban middle classes tended to view Afro-Cuban artistic expression as a potential threat to national culture. At best, neo-African expression was dismissed as a "cosa de negros" (something blacks do), but, more Often, it was openly condemned as an influence that would "carry the [Cuban people] back to a barbarous phase of [cultural] prehistory" [Fornet, 1967, p. 49].

Today, the rumba remains predominantly a dance of black or dark-skinned Cubans. It has been argued that the effort of the Cuban government and its affiliated dance companies to frame Cuba's image is a futile aspiration. Critics postulate that much of Cuba has differing views and evaluations of *rumberos* and the rumba itself. Officials, white-collar workers, and light-skinned Cubans generally pay nominal respect to rumba dancers, but choose not to participate in either dancing or drumming, and tend to leave rumba events quickly and politely. The ambiguity of Cubans and their opinions of the creators and performers of rumba exist throughout the island. Nevertheless, whether or not the Cuban middle class continues to dismiss the rumba as licentious and inferior will more likely not play a part in the government's vehement attempts to enrich Cuba's national and international identity.

Rumba is the core of sensuality, unity, and well-being. Ultimately, it expresses the root of post-revolutionary Cuba and its efforts toward a nation characterized by belief in equal political, economic, social, and civil rights for all people. The breadth of ecstasy it enlightens in all is undeniable. It provokes the natural tendencies and feelings that lie passive within our bodies in a world that is preoccupied with decorum, technology, and the future. There is no refute—the rumba is Cuba, and Cuba is rumba. However, the effulgence of this music and dance spreads over all areas of the world. Its capabilities extend into aesthetic, cultural, and spiritual nourishment for any one. The rumba demands attention and collects the emotions and consequences in an explosion of sex, life, and space flowing into every voice and every movement. The rumba is a language in itself of universal meaning; born from a coalescence of oppressed cultures and rising to an international dance. Farr (2003), a native Afro-Cuban has alluded to the fact that rumba will never die. Nothing can stop it.

References

Daniel, Yvonne (1995). *Rumba: Dance and Social Change in Contemporary Cuba.* Bloomington: Indiana University Press.
Farr, Jory. *Rites of Rhythm.* New York: HarperCollins, 2003.
Haywood, Charles (1966). *Folk Songs of the World.* New York: John Day.
Moore, Robin Dale (1995). *Nationalizing Blackness: Afrocubanismo and Artistic Revolution in Havana, 1920–1935.* Diss. University of Texas at Austin, 1995. Ann Arbor: UMI. 9534899.
Pérez, Louis A., Jr. (1999). *On Becoming Cuban.* Chapel Hill: University of North Carolina Press.
Roy, Maya (2002). *Cuban Music.* (Trans. Denise Asfar and Gabriel Asfar). London: Latin America Bureau.
Shepherd, Verene A., and Hilary McD. Beckles, eds. (2000). *Caribbean Slavery in the Atlantic World.* Kingston, Jamaica: Ian Randle; Oxford: James Currey; Princeton, NJ: M. Weiner, 2000.

13. The Sun Dance of the Plains Indians

During the eighteenth and nineteenth centuries, the *Sun* Dance was the most important religious ceremony of the Plains Indians. While each tribe had small variations in their version of the Sun dance, many elements were similar throughout most tribal traditions. The annual ceremony was usually held during the summer when people from different Plains tribes gathered following their dispersal, which took place during the harsh winters. The Sun dance is a ritual of sacrifice performed by the major Plains tribes including the Arapaho, Bannock, Cheyenne, Crow, Omaha, Shoshone, and Sioux. These tribes still continue to perform the Sun dance today in a slightly modernized form. The general purpose of the Sun dance is to renew both the spirit of the participants as well as the spirit of the Earth and its resources. The dance shows that there is no true end to life, but a cycle of symbolic true deaths and rebirths (Dorsey, 1905, p. 57).

A Dance for the People

The exact reason why different tribes perform the Sun dance varies. Common motivations for the ritual include thankfulness for blessings received, the fulfillment of a promise made for a beneficial outcome in a crisis, and the desire to insure the safety of a person embarking on a dangerous task. Overall, the dance is performed to ensure the general welfare of the people. Interestingly, the Crow tribes performed the dance to seek aid in getting vengeance for tribesmen killed in battle.

Generally, each *Sun* dance has a main dancer who bears the expenses of the ceremony. The event usually involves a one-week period in which the dancer isolates himself. During this time the tribal community makes their preparations for the dance while the dancer is consumed with intense prayer. Construction of the *sun dance lodge* is accompanied by complex rituals in which a special tree is cut for use as a center pole, with the dance enclose built around it. The entrance faces east with an altar constructed in the center, usually featuring a decorated buffalo skull. The dancer must fast during the three days the dance takes place. He also must refrain from drinking water. Once it is time for the dance to begin, drummers near the east entrance of the lodge begin to chant sacred songs while the dancers enter. The other members of the tribe gather in a circle around the constructed center pole at this time. The dancer moves rhythmically back and forth from the outside of the circle to the pole in the center of the circle. The dancer blows on an eagle-bone whistle while focusing his eyes on the foot of the center pole, known as the *eagle's nest*. There are brief periods of rest once the dancer has reached physical exhaustion. At the end of the Sun dance, the lodge is abandoned and the dancer may drink water and break his or her fasting. The lodge is left the way it is for several days to remind the people of the ceremony before is it deconstructed.

History of the Sun Dance

At the birth of the Sun dance, which is thought to be during the very late seventeenth century, voluntary torture was an integral part of the climax of the dance. This was typical of the Cheyenne and Sioux tribes in particular. In these cases, dancers were pierced through the chest muscles or shoulder muscles by skewers that were tied to the top of the center pole. The dancers would continue dancing until pieces of their flesh tore away. Sometimes the tongs inserted into the dancers' bodies were attached to several buffalo skulls rather than the center pole. Because the ceremony involved self-torture, white government officials banned the Sun dance for a long time. The Indian people never really understood the white man's reasons. They saw the Sun dance as a great spiritual tradition.

Sun dance participants strive to obtain supernatural aid and personal power through their sacrifice, which will not only assure the accomplishment of desired outcomes, but will bring them a richer and more meaningful life as a member of their society. The Sun dance reaffirms tribal membership, cultural identity, and ensures that the people will prosper for another year. Following the sacred ritual, there is a renewed feeling of social harmony. As one contemporary Native American explains, the sun dance "is the ritual reenactment of the relationship the Plains people see between consecration of the human spirit and Wakan Tanka (God) as manifested as Sun, or Light, and Life-Bestower. Through purification, participation, sacrifice, and supplication, the participants act as instruments or transmitters of increased power and wholeness ... from Wakan Tanka." The purpose of the ceremony is "to integrate: to fuse the individual with his or her fellows, the community of people with that of the other kingdoms, and this larger communal group with the worlds beyond this one.... The person sheds the isolated, individual personality and is restored to conscious harmony with the universe." The community "is the bedrock of tribal life" and it "necessarily includes all beings that inhabit the tribe's universe" (Allen, 1986, pp. 61–63).

Animals of the Sun Dance

Within the Sun dance, many animals are symbolically used. For example, Sioux participants may wear the skins of rabbits on their arms and legs, for "the rabbit represents humility, because he is quiet and soft and not self-asserting a quality we must all possess when we go to the center of the world" (Brown, 1967, p. 85). The wearing of strips of rabbit fur by the Cheyenne's who build the sun dance lodge may refer back to the time when the tribe lived in the north and subsisted chiefly on rabbits. The two most persistent symbols that are present in each tribe's rendition of the dance are the eagle and the buffalo.

The eagle, a highly important sacred animal in Plains belief, plays a major role in the Sun dance. Most obviously, the bird partakes in the ritual by having his nest represented at the fork of the lodge. In Arapaho mythology, this nest symbolizes the thunderbird, or eagle, who built his nest in a cottonwood tree. Some tribes, notably the Crow and Shoshone, fasten an actual mounted golden eagle to the rafter over the entrance or near the nest. Considered "chief of all the creatures of the air," and "powerful in battle," the bird acts as "guardian protecting the people from evil." The eagle is admired for courage, swiftness, and strength. Sometimes identified as the thunderbird, he is distinguished by his extraordinarily high flight, bringing him nearer to the sun and in closer proximity to the gods' Great Mystery of benevolence than any other creature (Grinnell, 1923, p. 188).

A crow who is dancing intensely may focus on the eagle at the top of the pole. The eagle may "finally move and show itself to the person," and "may begin to dance alongside one as he 'charges' and dances back from the center pole." The eagle may then accompany that person in a vision, dancing beside him and instructing him about the medicine acquired through the vision. On the second day of the dance, a participant may see the eagle soaring above the lodge. "The eagle is alive with a beauty and strength unmatched anywhere, having been endowed with keen eyesight as well as foresight." The bird carries the Creator's messages and symbolizes forthcoming blessings (Frey, 1987, pp. 108–109, 118). In unison, each dancer constantly blows upon a whistle fashioned from an eagle's wing bone, making sounds like the cry of an eagle, keeping time with the drum. This activity symbolizes the force of prayers that rise high like eagles to reach the Great Mystery. According to Black Elk, the sound made by the whistle "is the voice of the Spotted Eagle; our Grandfather, Wakan-Tanka, always hears this, for … it is really His own voice" (Brown, 1967, p. 71). The whistle is painted with colored dots and lines to represent the remarkable perception of the eagle. The fluffy down feather at the end of the whistle is blown back and forth, representing breath and life. The plume is "taken from the breast of the eagle, for this is the place which is nearest to the heart and center of the sacred bird" (Brown, 1967,

p. 71). Under certain conditions, when a dancer suffers greatly from thirst, water may come to the eagle-bone whistle.

Because of the eagle's special capacities, his feathers have supernatural and curative functions. An observer recorded that, once, when the thirst of some Arapaho dancers became intense, a participant used an eagle feather to bring a refreshing rain. During the sun dance, a medicine man may direct his eagle-feather fan toward the bodies of people who seek healing. The feathers are first touched to the center pole and then to the patient, transmitting power from the pole to the sufferer. The sun dance leader brushes away illness with a feather. Fanning motions directed to the body may withdraw and whip away causes of sickness. Feathers are held upward toward the sky to reach the eagle so that the bird may bear the prayers for curing upward to the Creator (Frey, 1987, p. 134).

However, it is the buffalo, as the very source of life for the Plains tribes, who occupy the central role in the Sun dance. From that animal, Plains people once derived not only meat for sustenance, but skins for tipis, fur for robes, and virtually all materials for the tools and objects necessary for everyday living. Crows still commemorate the buffalo's fulfillment of their needs in former times. "Even today, Crows view the buffalo as a provider of good things for living. It represents plenty to eat, plenty to wear, and a peaceful wholesome life.'" The buffalo symbolizes the "necessities without which life would be hazardous and wearisome," and "also bestows great curing powers." In the contemporary sun dance, it still "radiates power" (Brown, 1984, pp. 307, 312). Proximity of buffalo herds as influenced by their migrations indeed determined the time and locality chosen for the great ceremonial. The preeminent status of the buffalo is illustrated by the fact that in certain tribes, the origin of the sun dance is traced to the buffalo. The inception of the ceremonial involves a visionary encounter between a person and a buffalo emissary with supernatural power. Ute and Shoshone myths, for example, reveal that the buffalo helped the individual who began the tradition, giving him instructions as to how to carry out the dance and revealing the benefits that would follow from proper performance of the ritual. For the Lakota, it was a deity in the form of a White Buffalo who brought the Sacred Pipe through which all ceremonies and rituals are empowered.

The Cheyenne sun dance was taught by the Creator to a medicine man, later known as Erect-Horns because of the buffalo horn cap he wore. He journeyed to a high peak in the company of a woman and when the couple came forth from the mountain to return home, "the whole earth seemed to become new, and there came forth buffalo that followed them" (Dorsey, 1905, p. 48).

Themes relating to the buffalo consistently occur throughout the sun dance. Historically, various ceremonies relating to the animal have taken place as a preliminary to the climactic dancing. A sacred song of the Oglala Sioux that followed certain rituals pertaining to the buffalo skull expresses the participants' desire for blessings and its association with the buffalo's power:

> *Father, be merciful to me. We want to live!*
> *This is why we are doing this.*
> *They say that a herd of buffalo is coming;*
> *Now they are here.*
> *The power of the buffalo is coming upon us.*
> *It is now here!* [Brown, 1953, p. 87].

As the Cheyenne sun dance progresses, buffalo songs change in tempo. "The rattle beat becomes slow and ponderous, as if a great herd of buffalo was moving across the prairie." A Cheyenne who was present the first time these buffalo songs were sung in the sun dance lodge related that "as they were chanted, a herd of buffalo bulls ran over the hill and down into the camp" (Powell, 1969, vol. 2, p. 658).

The great sun dance ritual establishes the tenet that there is no final death, for all living things can be renewed. Human beings, however, like all their fellow creatures, must cooperate in order to bring about universal regeneration. By feeding grass to the buffalo skull, the cycle of life is symbolically perpetuated. To appease the buffalo who gives so much to people, appreciation and good intentions must be shown, and deferential behavior is mandated. By significant acts like refraining from eating buffalo flesh after the animal has provided a vision, leaving some of the meat to propitiate the animal's spirit after a buffalo is slain, and planting a piece of sacred buffalo tongue back into the ground during the ceremonial feast (Frey, 1987, p. 121), honor is given to the spiritual presence of the buffalo. Because the animal's spirit still remains when the buffalo is killed, death is not final; eternal return is assured for both buffalo and humankind through reciprocal actions that maintain the harmony of the natural world. Thus at the close of the Sioux sun dance, Wakan-Tanka is addressed: "You have taught us our relationship with all ... beings, and for this we give thanks.... May we be continually aware of the relationship that exists between the four-legged, the two-legged, and the winged. May we all rejoice and live in peace!" (Brown, 1967, p. 98).

References

Allen, P. G. (1986). *The Sacred Hoop: Recovering the Feminine in American Indian Traditions.* Boston: Beacon.
Brown, J. E. (1967). *The Sacred Pipe.* Norman: University of Oklahoma Press.
Dorsey, G. A. (1905). *The Cheyenne: I. Ceremonial Organization.* Chicago: Field Columbian Museum Publication.
Frey, R. (1987). *The World of the Crow Indians.* Norman: University of Oklahoma Press.
Grinnell, G. B. (1923). *The Cheyenne Indians.* New Haven: Yale University Press.
Powell, P. J. (1969). *Sweet Medicine.* Norman: University of Oklahoma Press.

14. The Hula Dance of the Hula People of Hawaii

What is the Hula?

The mention of the *Hula*, for most people, brings to mind the stereotypical picture: an exotic dance based on the undulating hips, danced by scantily clad young women in grass skirts and coconut bras danced for the sole purpose of entertainment in a tropical, carefree paradise. This, however, could hardly be farther from the truth of the *Hula*.

The *Hula* is the ancient cultural dance of the Hawaiian people. It was—and to some degree still is—used for many purposes, none of which were sheer entertainment (Robert, 1926). The *Hula* was used to tell stories: passing on legends, local history, family lineage, and the understanding s of the culture. The *Hula* of the commoners was used also to praise nature and give honor to local heroes. *Hula* was also used as a sacred ritual including prayer and fasting; all to appease the god of the Hawaiian people. Essentially, the *Hula* was used in all forms of Hawaiian life. This dance, in effect, is the driving force of the Hawaiian culture. As King Kalakaua of Hawaii put it, "The *Hula* is the heartbeat of the Hawaiian people."

The Different Types of Hula

The *Hula* has been around longer than the Hawaiians have—it was brought to the islands of Hawaii with the people as they migrated there.

With a dance so old, such as *hula kahiko* (ancient hula), it is impossible not to have many different kinds of *Hula* used for reasons as varied as worship and bestowing honor.

The most religious of the *Hulas* is the *Pahu Hula*. Named for the most prominent instrument used in the dance, the *pahu drum*, this *Hula* evolved from prayer. Originally called *ha'a*, a priest would pray on bended knee with gestures to the gods (Robert, 1926). Eventually, this was done to the beat of a *pahu drum*. Other priests were added and the gestures were standardized. The whole thing was performed in unison. More music was added and it became the most sacred *Hula* of the Hawaiian people. "*Ha'a*" now refers to a style of dancing; dancing in the *ha'a* style means dancing on bended knee. The *Pahu Hula* is not open for innovation or artistic interpretation. It is performed exactly the same way every time; any deviation could compromise the prayer (Robert, 1926). Because of this restriction, the *Pahu Hula* is always taught in its entirety. The *Pahu Hula* is so sacred that there is a set of *kapu*, or restrictions, set upon the *mea hula* dancers.

The eight *kapu* are:

1. *Pikai*—the sprinkling of salt water on the *mea hulas* [= hula dancers] and a minor exorcism.
2. *Ma'i*—a *mea hula* with a menstrual period was not allowed to perform.
3. Sex—performers were forbidden to have sex outside of marriage.
4. *La'i*—all *mea hulas* must wear a *ti* (*la'i*) leaf on their person.
5. Costume—the color, style, and lei must be correct for the dance. White is never worn for the *Pahu Hula*, as it is the Hawaiian funeral color. *Hala* leis are never used as adornment, as the connotation is error.
6. Seriousness of Expression—performers are not allowed to smile, giggle, laugh, or play around. The *Pahu hula* is considered sacred and a form of prayer, therefore very devout, and must be danced in unison. It was believed that prayer performed in unison was more powerful than prayer performed by an *alaka 'i hula* (a solo dancer) and if you were not serious, you were not sincere in your prayer.
7. Eating restrictions—the *mea hulas* must fast before a performance. After the performance, the *mea hulas* may not eat from a common bowl (*poi*). Usually—even at a family party—the *mea hula's* food was prepared separately.
8. Prohibition—attendance at a funeral or contact with the dead is not allowed.

If a *mea hula* is not able to honor the *kapu*, the *kumu* (priest) takes it upon himself to make the sacrifices for the *mea hulas*.

While the *Pahu Hula* is a sacred temple dance used for worship, it is also used to honor people, nature, and animals. The *Pahu Hula* is seldom performed in public; it is usually performed in temples. Originally, only men were allowed to perform the *Pahu Hula*, but as time went on, women were allowed to perform it as well. However, men and women are not allowed to dance the *Pahu Hula* together.

Similar to the *Pahu Hula* is the *Hula Pele*. The *Hula Pele* is a *Hula* that honors the goddess *Pele*, the most prominent of the Hawaiian deities. *Pele* is the fire goddess and the goddess of the volcanoes. *Pele* is known as "she who shapes the sacred lands"; as goddess of the volcanoes, she has power over all of the Hawaiian Islands. The *Hula Pele* tends to have bombastic movements as the *mea hulas* attempt to imitate *Pele*: her intensity, her journey to Hawaii, her battles with her sister Namakaokaha'i, and her destructive lava flows.

The *Ku'i* is considered to be the "old-fashioned" *Hula* by contemporary *Hula mea hulas*. The *Ku'i* is the formal court-style *Hula* and it serves as a link between the old *Hula* from the days before the arrival of the missionaries and the new *Hula* of today. This *Hula*, like most *Hulas*, tells a story. The *mea hulas* wear a *holoku*, a long formal dress, similar to the strict Victorian dress codes of the days of the missionaries. The *mea hulas* also, contrary to the iconoclastic stereotype of the *Hula*, wear shoes.

The *Ala'apapa* or *Olapa Hula* is a secular *Hula*, formulated by commoners. The *Ala'apapa* or *Olapa Hula* did not evolve from the *Pahu Hula*, as many believe. While it may have some of the same movements as the *Pahu Hula*, it is its own artistic form. The *Ala'apapa* or *Olapa Hula* usually tells a story, and is used for entertainment, instruction, honor, the passing down of history and traditions, or anything else besides worship.

The Instruments of the Hula

Every *Hula* is danced to different music—the music must be correct for the type of *Hula* performed and the story told just as the costumes must always be correct for the particular *Hula*. In order to create all the different kinds of music and beats needed for all the various *Hulas* that exist, there must be many different kinds of instruments (Robert, 1926). All of the *Hula* instruments are made from items from nature.

Some of the most important instruments used for the *Hula* are the drums, as they form the backbone of the *Hula* by providing the beat that drives the *Hula*. The most prominent type of drum is the *ipu*, or gourd drum. The various types of *ipus* include the *ipu heke* (a gourd drum with a top section), the *ipu heke 'ole* (a single gourd drum without a top section), the *ipu hula* (a dance drum made of two gourds sewn together), and the *ipu uai* (a moveable gourd drum). However, there are other drums, including the *pahu* (a drum made from the trunk of a coconut tree with a shark-skin covering), and the *puniu* (a drum made from half a coconut shell with a covering made from the skin of the Kala fish), that are often used as well.

To accompany the drums of the *Hula*, there are other instruments. Wind instruments are varied from the *hano* (a nose flute), the *hokeo kani*, to the *hokiokio*, the *ipu hoehoe* (gourd whistles), the *pu la'i* (a ti leaf whistle), and the *pu* (a large triton conch shell). Other instruments are used to be both audibly and visually stimulating and are played by the *mea hula*(s). These instruments include *uli uli* (a decorated gourd rattle), the *papa hehi* (a footboard that the *mea hula* dances on, thus creating music), the *kala'au* (dancing sticks that were struck together then rolled along each other, creating a clacking sound), and the *ili ili* (small, smooth, black stones that are struck together to make a clicking sound; these are sometimes referred to as "Hawaiian castanets").

The History of the Hula

The true origins of the *Hula* are shrouded in myth and legend (Barrere, Kelly & Pukui, 1997). However, the island of Molokai, the fifth largest of the Hawaiian Islands and the island with the largest population of people of Hawaiian descent (thus giving it the title of the "Most Hawaiian" of the Hawaiian Islands), is credited with the birth of the *Hula*. Other accounts say that the *Hula* migrated to the Hawaiian Islands with the people.

The most accepted myth about the birth of the *Hula* begins with the goddess Laka, the goddess of the *Hula*. Legend has it that she gave birth to the *Hula* at Puu Nana, a sacred hill at Kaana, on the island of Molokai (Barrere, Kelly & Pukui, 1997). From there, it is said that Laka traveled from island to island teaching the *Hula* to all those who wanted to learn. It is rumored that Laka's remains are hidden beneath Puu Nana.

Another myth about the beginnings of the *Hula* is that of Hi'iaka; Hi'iaka was another sister of Pele. The myth goes that Hi'iaka danced to appease her fiery sister, Pele, and the dance that resulted was the *Hula* (Barrere, Kelly & Pukui, 1997).

Part of the evolution of the *Hula* to where it is now is due to La'a-mai-Kahiki. On one of his voyages to the Hawaiian Islands from Kahiki, he brought with him a *pahu* drum. When he got off his canoe, he struck his *pahu* and the islanders were so enchanted with the sound that they followed La'a-mai-Kahiki wherever he went. La'a-mai-Kahiki was a patron of the *Hula* and introduced new forms of it to the Hawaiians.

However, in 1778, Captain Cook landed on the island of Kaua'i, bringing with him the ideals of the Euro-American world (Bechwith, 1970). These ideals changed the *Hula* forever. American Protestant missionaries appeared in 1820, intent on converting the Hawaiians to Christianity and the Western way of life. What the missionaries saw of the *Hula*—seminude *mea hulas* (Hula dancers) with undulating hips—was considered lewd, heathen, primitive, and overly sensual. The missionaries accepted the Hawaiian language in order to preach but they banned the *Hula*, not knowing that it held a prominent place in the culture of the people whose land they were invading. The Hawaiian monarchs alternately cherished and crushed the *Hula* and other aspects crucial to the Hawaiian culture. The ideals of Western culture flourished in Hawaii as the people grew impatient with the *kapu* and other restrictions of the ancient religion.

In 1818, Queen Ka'ahumanu became a Christian and ordered all *heiau* (sacred temple sites) and sacred images destroyed. With this, the formal *Hula* rituals were also destroyed. In this single move, the *Hula* was forced underground. The *Hula*—as well as all other forms of glorifying and worshipping the Hawaiian deities—was taught and performed in secret on remote areas of the islands. Some families continued in the old *Hula* traditions, keeping them in the family. Many of these families have founded some of the top *halaus* (schools of *Hula*) which can be found not only on the Hawaiian Islands but around the mainland of the United States as well.

When the *Hula* was forced underground, it became exploited by white entrepreneurs—that which was forbidden was of course that which was sought after. The Hawaiians were glad to take part, as this exploitation provided them with the chance they needed to perform their sacred dance, even if it was viewed as being done solely for the purpose of entertainment.

14. The Hula Dance of the Hula People of Hawaii

In the 1830s, King Kamehameha III issued an edict guaranteeing religious freedom and tried to reestablish the *Hula* as a central part of the Hawaiian culture. Right around this time, the missionaries finally realized that they could not successfully suppress the *Hula*, so they "compromised." The missionaries allowed the *Hula* to be performed, but they insisted that the traditional *pa'u* skirts be replaced with the more Victorian *holoku*, which had high-necks and long sleeves.

The most hope for restoring the old *Hula* came with the reign of King David Kalakaua, elected in 1874. Nicknamed the "Merry Monarch" for his love of song, dance, and revelry, King Kalakaua restored the Hawaiian culture and made the *Hula* the national symbol of the Hawaiian people. King Kalakaua is credited for declaring that *Hulas* the heartbeat of the Hawaiian people. During his reign, the *halaus* came out of hiding—*mea hulas* performed at both his coronation and his 50th birthday. After his death, however, the *Hula* returned to being a dance devoid of meaning and solely for entertainment. Due to tourism, however, the *Hula* remained a national symbol.

The Hula *Today*

Today, most *Hulas* are not sacred, but are instead secular. True to form, however, *hula 'auana* (modern-day *Hulas*) still tell stories, many having to do with the old myths and legends dealing with the Hawaiian deities.

The *Hula* is most visible in the annual *Hula* competitions. In April, one can visit the Merry Monarch Festival on the island of Hawaii, held in honor of King Kalakaua. At the Merry Monarch Festival, both men and women compete in the *Hula Kahiko* and *Hula 'Auana* and solo female *mea hulas* vie for the position of Miss Aloha Hula. In June, on the island of Oahu, one can visit the King Kamehameha Traditional Hula and Chant Festival. The King Kamehameha Festival holds competitions in *Hula Kahiko* and *Hula 'Auana* for me, women and mixed groups.

While most *hula 'auana* are secular and/or solely for entertainment, it is still possible to find traditional religious *Hulas*. Those, however, are separated from the Hawaii that is open to tourists. Because of these few dedicated *kumus* (master teachers and historians) and students, the traditional Hawaiian *Hula* will never die.

References

Barrere, D., M. Kelly & M. Pukui (1997). *Hula: Historical Perspectives*. Honolulu: Bishop Museum.
Bechwith, Martha (1970). *Hawaiian Mythology*. Honolulu: University of Hawaii Press.
Broughton, S. (1994). World Music: The Rough Guide. London: Rough Guides.
Buck, Elizabeth (1993). *Paradise Remade: The Politics of Culture and History in Hawai'i*. Philadelphia: Temple University Press.
Emerson, Nathaniel (1915). *Pele and Hiiaka*. Hawaii: Honolulu Star Bulletin.
Hopkins, J. (1982). *The Hula*. Hong Kong: Apa Productions.
International Encyclopedia of Dance, 6 vols., (1998). Edited by Selma Jeanne Cohen, et al. New York: Oxford University Press.
Kaeppler, Adrienne L. (1993). Hula Pahu: Hawaiian Drum Dances. Vol. 1. Ha'a and Hula Pahu. Honolulu: Sacred Movements.
Robert, Helen (1926). *Ancient Hawaiian Music*. Burnice P. Bishop Museum Bulletin 29. Honolulu: Bishop Museum.
Stillman, Amy Ku'uleialoha (1982). The Hula Ku'i: A Tradition in Hawaiian Music and Dance. Master's thesis, University of Hawaii, Honolulu: UHH.
Stillman, Amy Ku'uleialoha (1994). Bibliography. In *The Hula*, ed. Jerry Hopkins. Honolulu: Lee.
Stillman, Amy Ku'uleialoha (1994). Hawaiian Hula Competitions: Event, Repertoire, Performance, Tradition. *Journal of American Folklore* 103.
Stillman, Amy Ku'uleialoha (1996). Competition Hula: An Index of Mele and Halau in the King Kamehameha Hula Competition (1982-1995) and the Merrie Monarch Hula Competition (1980-1995). Typescript, University of Hawaii Library.
Takamine, Victoria Holt. The Hula 'Ala'apapa: An Analysis of Selected Dances and a Comparison with Hula Pahu. Master's thesis, University of Hawaii.
Tatar, Elizabeth (1979). Annotated Bibliography Hawaiian Music. In *Hawaiian Music and Musicians: An Illustrated History*, ed. George S. Kanahele. Honolulu: University Press of Hawaii.
Tartar, Elizabeth (1982). *Nineteenth Century Hawaiian Chant*. Pacific Anthropological Records No. 33. Honolulu: Department of Museums, Burnice P. Bishop Museum.
Tatar, Elizabeth (1993). Hula Pahu: Hawaiian Drum Dances. Vol. II. The Pahu: Sounds of Power. Museum *Bulletin in Anthropology 3*. Honolulu: Bishop Museum.

FILMS

Hawaiian Rainbow (1987).
Hula Ho'olaule'a (1960).
Hula: The First 30 Years, Merrie Monarch Festival (1994).
'Iolani Luahine: Hawaiian Dancer (1976).
Kodak Hula Show (1993).
Kumu Hula: Keepers of a Culture (1989).
Then There Were None (1995).
'Ula Noweo (1963).

15. Swing Dancing of New York

> If you play a tune and a person don't tap their feet, don't play the tune.—COUNT BASIE, 1904–1984

In a strictly segregated society, a Jewish man, Moe Gale, opened the doors of his dance hall on March 12, 1926, between the 140th and 141st Streets of Lenox Avenue in Harlem. Named the Savoy Ballroom, managed by Charles Buchanan, the dance hall was located on the second floor of the building and stretched the length of the entire block. Carpeted lounges, mirrored walls, and a spring-loaded wooden floor attracted many dancers and Big Band groups to this ballroom. Even though the ballroom was a nice place to spend the evening, the true attraction was the dancing (Wintz, 1988). Various dancers, both white and African American, were drawn to the music and innovative dancing styles that later came to be known as Swing. Although this blend of African Jazz and European dance music had been around for a few years prior to the Savoy opening, it was not until the Savoy opened that this dance form received its name. Watching the enthusiastic gyrations of the dancers on the floor, a newspaper reporter asked "Shorty George" Snowden what the dancers were doing. Searching for a name, Snowden's eyes fell on a newspaper article entitled, "Lindy Hops the Atlantic" and said, "Lindy Hop," and the name became synonymous with the dance moves displayed at the Savoy during the late 1920s and in the 1930s (Stowe, 1994).

The Birth of Swing

> The real birth of swing was in the 1920's, during the Harlem Renaissance. The Harlem Renaissance was a time of great creativity and innovation for African American writers, artists, and musicians, and swing was just one of many art forms to prosper at that time.—VISEL, HART, AND WALKENHORST, 2005

Improvisation and creation were key elements in the Savoy Ballroom. New dance moves were created every night, new forms of aerials and dips. From this encouragement of new styles and moves, as well as the general spread of swing dancing, came various forms of swing dancing, including West Coast Swing, the Carolina Shag, East Coast Swing, Balboa, and many others (Wintz, 1988). All of these other styles of swing dancing originated from the Savoy Style, known as the Lindy Hop, and evolved as time went on. West Coast Swing originated in California and is a smoother style of swing than the original Lindy Hop or Jitterbug (Stowe, 1994). There are many theories as to its origins but most involve a man named Dean Collins, who after dancing in many nightclubs in New York, including the Savoy Ballroom, moved to the city of Los Angeles to pursue a career in movies and introduced the west coast to his style of swing dancing (Bloom, 1989). Another idea behind his movements are that, due to his dancing in movies, his moves were done in a slotted form where the man danced in place while the lady travels back and forth (Stowe, 1994). Although many attribute the beginning of West Coast Swing to Collins, he regularly denied his involvement and stated that there was no other style except Swing. West Coast Swing survived the many musical and dance movements that followed and was voted California's State Dance in 1989 (Bloom, 1989).

Another form of swing dancing that evolved was the Carolina Shag, a style of Swing popular in the Carolinas emphasizing the leader's nimble feet (Wintz, 1988). The Carolina Shag, the state dance of South Carolina since 1984, originated in Myrtle Beach, drawing from African American roots, the movements of Lindy, and the enthusiasm of white teenagers in the 1940s (Stowe, 1994). The Carolina Shag is said to be a combination of the Charleston and the Collegiate Shag (Bloom, 1989). White teenagers would frequent black clubs watching the dancers and the new dance moves that evolved from the balcony, taking what they liked as their own (Stowe, 1994). During the mid-1940s, with the occurrence of World War II, music slowed down considerably and the Carolina Shag adapted to the speed of the music, having slower movements. Many events that featured Carolina Shag dancing also occurred on the beaches of South Carolina, making fast moves harder for dancers to perform. The dance met the social needs of society, giving teenagers and other dancers somewhere to dance and a dance that coincided with their dance arena, which has received the nickname "beach dancing" (Bloom, 1989). This six or eight count dance has mirrored movements. The female was expected to follow and mirror the steps of her partner occasionally. Complex moves of this dance involved couples who "develop their own personal repertoire of mirrored sequences using crosses, hooks, kicks, brushes, turns, spins, etc.," and these moves were initiated through a verbal call. The moves being what would be termed "unleadable" without such a call (Bloom, 1989). Fancy footwork from the leader, movements are meant to compliment the styling of the male leader with very few spins due to the dancing on the beach (Bloom, 1989). The Carolina Shag celebrated individualistic movements with a partner who also had his or her own personal style, both styles coming together throughout the dance in mirrored or complementary movements (Stowe, 1994).

East Coast Swing, the ballroom version of swing dancing, originated around the early 1940s as the American Society of Teachers of Dancing's denounced of the agile jiving of many forms of swing dancing (Bloom, 1989). This six-count style was much easier to learn than the West Coast Style, the Jitterbug, or the Lindy Hop, and many teachers used this as an introduction to the movements of other swing variations, teaching the essential swing rhythm (Stowe, 1994). Following in his parents footsteps, Vernon and Irene Castle, the "father and mother of modern ballroom instruction worldwide," Arthur Murray attempted to bring the ever changing and expressive form of swing into the dance studios (Bloom, 1989). Due to the individuality of many forms, many dance instructors turned to this East Coast Swing that was developed through Murray's schools a form of swing instruction (Stowe, 1994). East Coast Swing is still taught in many dance halls as a form of swing and is used as a building block for other types of swing dancing, the basics, such as triple step, touch step, and single step, being taught in these classes.

The Music and Movement of Swing

Swing music, drawing primarily from jazz rhythms, greatly influenced the dancers' rhythm and movements. Many dancers' moves being inspired by the music. Big Bands dominated the music scene during the 1930s and into the 1940s, with legends like Chick Webb, Duke Ellington, Count Basie, Dizzy Gillespie, Charlie Parker, Art Blakey, Thelonious Monk, and Benny Goodman as the forerunners of swing music (Glass, 2005). In Swing music, "the band leader and his musicians were considered the star," drawing in crowds to the venues they played and creating the inspiration for the dancers' individual moves (Glass, 2005). It all began, however, with Duke Ellington's "It Don't Mean a Thing If It Ain't Got That Swing" which was recorded in 1932. Following Ellington's lead, new bands emerged playing this new form of music, which emphasized four beats to a measure where they all and played off various instruments in the band, brass versus reeds (Wintz, 1988). Most Big Bands of that time had up to three trumpets, three trombones, three or four saxophones, and a four-piece rhythm section which included the drums.

As well as drawing from African American music, many of the movements of swing were indirectly influenced by African moves through the people who created swing and the dance styles that preceded swing. The orientation toward the earth, the importance of community, the strong use of percussion to determine the beats that moves were performed on, the competitive dance, the polyrhythmic movements, and the improvisation is all elements of swing dancing that are drawn from African dances. Many of the dance movements are low to the ground with a swiveling motion while the arms and legs perform to a different beat, possibly to the notes of a trumpet instead of the drum that the movements are usually performed on (Stowe, 1994). New moves were also displayed in the dance halls to highlight a dancer's skill and versatility (Wintz, 1988).

Swing Evolution

While swing dancing was quite popular between the two world wars, new generations were emerging with different cares and music than the generation that preceded them. New forms of music like Rock and Roll, Twist, and Disco emerged in later years and swing dancing adapted itself in order to survive (Bloom, 1989). While the dance was not as prominent as it once was, it still remained in the shadows of the more modern dances. A new entertainment tax made acquiring live big bands expensive, and with the falling prices of recorded music, many dance halls got smaller since the large stage area was not needed. The new dances had to change to accommodate what little room there was for dancing (Glass, 2005). With the introduction of American Bandstand, a prominent dance show in the 1950s, many of the original forms of swing were also pushed aside or various moves of differing styles were incorporated into one form (Bloom, 1989). New moves were shown on this program. The dances based on swing movements to the new Rock and Roll rhythm and teenagers across America tuned in to see the new moves and learn them in their living rooms (Glass, 2005). Swing began a comeback with the emergence of Frank Manning, who taught swing dancing around the world. Swing reemerged on the scene, reenergized by the "neo-swing bands and vintage fashion," like the Brian Setzer Orchestra with their popular hit "Jump, Jive and Wail," (Bloom, 1989).

Although the popularity of swing dancing declined during the 1950s, through the 1980s it still remained in the new dances that were being performed and on the side of popular culture. People still danced to swing music, playing records of the Big Bands and reminiscing of the old times. Many dancers felt the impact of the swing era during the twentieth century. Many people loved swing dancing and would do it no matter what music was played. Stowe (1994) observed that the generation was not about to leave the dance just because the music changed. Due to the spirit of the dance and of the dancers, this dance survived the changing cultural climate through the latter half of the twentieth century.

Swing dancing, while no longer in the mainstream culture, is thriving in dance halls across America and other continents including Europe. Many dance halls host weekly swing dances where not only do the older generations turn out, but younger individuals as well. Swing has bridged the gap between generations becoming a non-verbal form of passing senses of emotion, pride, freedom, and self-expression from generation to generation. Competitions are frequently held around the United States for various forms of swing dancing from West Coast to Balboa to freestyle performances. In Tampa's Zendah Grotto, individuals meet to dance into the night to recordings of both old and new swing songs, to learn new styles of swing, and just to dance. Individuals from the ages of ten to eighty-three mingle to the sounds of a brass led band, a pumping beat, and shuffling feet. While there still is a generation gap, with many of today's youth focused on only popular culture music such as rap, punk, or heavy metal; there are qualities in swing dancing that draw in a number of youths revitalizing itself in the next generation. The upbeat notes force a foot to start tapping and the body to start moving. The very nature of swing is what makes it attractive to both the elderly and the young. Smith summarizes the draw that swing possesses with: Glass, (2005), observed that swing music still inspires the freedom of improvisation, a romantic style remains in the dance culture and, most importantly, dancers still love dancing with a partner. That is why swing will continue to attract dancers throughout the next generations, because it touches the heart of humanity.

References

Bloom, Harold (1989). *Modern Critical Views: Langston Hughes.* New York: Chelsea House.
Floyd, Samuel A. Jr. (1990). *Black Music in the Harlem Renaissance: A Collection of Essays.* New York: Greenwood.
Glass, Barbara (2005). Introduction: The Africanization of American Movement. In *When the Spirit Moves,* 1999, National Afro-American Museum and Cultural Center. Retrieved November 28, 2005, http://www.savoystyle.com/african.html.
Huggins, Nathan Irvin (1995). *Voices from the Harlem Renaissance.* New York, Oxford: Oxford University Press.

Hughes, Langston (1986). *The Big Sea.* New York: Thunder's Mouth.
Hutchinson, George (1995). *The Harlem Renaissance in Black and White.* Cambridge, MA: Belknap Press of Harvard University Press.
Jeana Visel, Sarah Hart, and Elizabeth Walkenhorst (2005). It Don't Mean a Thing If It Ain't Got That Swing. Retrieved December 10, 2006, from http://www2.kenyon.edu/depts/IPHS/Projects/swing1/swingmain.htm.
Knoles, George Harmon (1955). *The Jazz Age Revisited.* Stanford, CA: Stanford University Press.
Shaw, Arnold (1987). *The Jazz Age.* New York: Oxford University Press.
Singh, Amritjit, William S. Shiver, and Stanley Brodwin (1989). *The Harlem Renaissance: Reevaluations.* New York: Garland.
Smith, Shona, The Lindy Circle. Retrieved November 30, 2005, from: http://www.lindycircle.com/history/lindy_hop/.
Stowe, David W. (1994). *Swing Changes: Big-Band Jazz in New Deal America.* Cambridge, MA: Harvard University Press.
Wintz, Cary (1988). *Black Culture and the Harlem Renaissance.* Houston, TX: Rice University Press.

16. American Jazz

If you have to ask what Jazz is, you'll never know.—LOUIS ARMSTRONG, 1901–1971

This quote from Louis Armstrong, a jazz legend, is an excellent way to summarize jazz in a nice, short, concise sentence. Jazz is an ever-changing musical style. It has taken on many different faces through the years. From its roots in blues and ragtime, jazz has bridged the gap between vernacular music and cultivated music. "Jazz developed into America's most distinctive- many would say greatest- contribution to the arts worldwide" (Kerman, p. 389). Jazz still exists today and continues to evolve and surface on the musical scene throughout the world.

Origins

Jazz ... dance music, generally syncopated, [and] played by a band eccentrically composed. The jazz drummer, a sort of one-man band, provides the characteristic feature of jazz, which is noise.— ANON: *CHAMBERS' ENCYCLOPEDIA*

In the early twentieth century, roughly around 1910, jazz came into existence by drawing heavily on two other styles of black music: blues and ragtime. "Emerging around 1900, the blues was a major influence on early jazz- and has remained a major force in American music ever since" (Kerman, p. 390). Blues is a type of musical style that focuses around loneliness, trouble, sadness, and depression. Blues originated in the African American slave population around 1900. The idea of the blues of the time was to express the oppression felt by the slaves. The structure of blues consists of a lot of repetition of lyrical structures. Stanzas consist of two lines that contain rhyming elements. Along with the repetition, many of the lines in blues are improvised as the song is unfolding. "Ragtime, a precursor of jazz, was a style of piano playing developed by black musicians playing in bars, dives, and brothels" (Kerman, p. 391). Resembling marching music at its core, ragtime is a type of music that focuses around syncopated piano playing. The idea is to allow one hand to play the rhythm of the song and the other hand to syncopate that rhythm. "Ragging" came to be known as syncopating the music. Syncopation will be explored in the next section. The improvisation from blues and the syncopation from ragtime merged together to lead to the development of jazz.

Characteristics of Jazz

Jazz is not actually a type of music, but rather, jazz is a way of performing music. Jazz is "a special, highly charged way of performing that music" (Kerman, p. 390). As stated above, jazz is based around two key factors, syncopation and improvisation. The first key feature of jazz is improvisation. It focuses on individuals rocking out on their instrument with no actual music to tell them what notes to play. This is set off by short interludes or breaks in the music. The second key feature of jazz is syncopation. Syncopation is defined as being offbeat in the rhythm of the music by accenting particular beats. In jazz, syncopation has two rhythmic levels. Level one, played by the percussion, piano, string bass, and other instruments of this type, forcefully drives home the beat and the meter of the piece. This level lays down the baseline that drives the music forward. The second rhythmic level of syncopation, played by trumpet, clarinet, trombone, saxophone, and piano, generates the melody of the piece. These two rhythmic levels constantly syncopate one another throughout the piece of jazz music. In addition to this type of syncopation, another type of syncopation in jazz is beat syncopation. This type of syncopation makes the music "swing" by moving the beats just slightly in front of metrical points in the music. This type of syncopation developed from jazz and had strong roots in African American drumming.

Types of Jazz

Originating in the south, New Orleans came to be known as the first important center of jazz music. Often "pure" jazz is called New Orleans jazz or Dixieland jazz. This is the area where jazz developed and began to gather popularity. The name Dixieland jazz came from The Dixieland Jazz Band of which Louis Armstrong, a jazz legend, was a member. Early jazz in New Orleans was for a black audience; it was informal, low budget, and a rather casual art form. Most jazz bands of the time consisted of six to eight players. Early jazz embraced all the above-mentioned attributes of jazz. Since jazz was growing in popularity and bands were forming and growing, improvisation became somewhat more complicated. Jazz bands would "jam," or collectively improvise, the music together. The members of the band would take turns rocking out on their instruments. The musicians seemed to develop an additional sense allowing them to fit in well with their fellow musicians.

Louis Armstrong

Louis Armstrong and recording technology helped popularize jazz. "Louis Armstrong was an all-American jazz baby, born in New Orleans, Louisiana on the Fourth of July 1900" (Bergreen, 1997, p. 14). Growing up in New Orleans, Louis began playing the trumpet. "There were many good, experienced trumpet players in town, but none of them had young Louis's possibilities" (Bergreen, p. 27). As a young musician, Louis proved his expertise with a trumpet. As he grew up, he played in seedy clubs and on riverboats. In the 1920s, he recorded many records. These records allowed jazz to leave the vernacular scene and spread out into the mainstream music industry. The Jazz Age was upon them.

The Jazz Age

The Jazz Age, roughly from 1920 until 1930, was an era in which jazz was the main focus in the music industry. Jazz had gone from being a genre that was disliked by many classically inclined audience—lovers of the symphony. They thought jazz was vulgar, sexual, and would corrupt the youth. During this time, musicians made an effort to move jazz into the concert halls. George Gershwin was the most successful musician to bring jazz, or at least a very close interpretation into the concert halls. Gershwin had successfully bridged the gap between vernacular music and mainstream music (Kerman, 2004, p. 404). The popularity that jazz was receiving began to bring about changes in jazz. White musicians and managers began entering the jazz scene leading to swing.

Swing

In the 1930s, with the entrance of white musicians and managers, large jazz bands, or swing bands began to form. Swing bands consisted of anywhere from 10 to 25 musicians. Due to the size of these bands, it was much more difficult for the members of the band to carry out improvisation within the music. The pieces played by swing bands had to be much more structured so that the large number of musicians could form a cohesive unit that played well together. Although improvisation was limited, it was not eliminated. Particular spots in the swing pieces were set aside for improvisation by select individuals. The core concepts that make jazz "jazz," were still preserved. Interestingly enough, the white swing bands; Benny Goodman, Glen Miller, and Artie Shaw, were the more commercially successful entities. However, the black swing bands, Count Basie, Duke Ellington, and Chick Webb were much better composers. With the end of World War II, so came the end of swing bands.

Bebop

With the collapse of swing came the rise of Bebop. Bebop was somewhat of a tribute to the original "pure" jazz. The musicians strived to have strong segments of improvisation in their music. Bebop incorporated three main instruments, trumpet, piano, and the saxophone. Along with the struggle to get back to improvisation, bebop also developed some crazy harmonies that pushed the boundaries of the normal music of the time. A great bebop artist was Miles Davis. He always had a curiosity about trying new things in music; a new sound, another way to do something. This viewpoint from of Miles Davis captures the soul of bebop. As time passed, rock and roll entered the scene and slowly began to push jazz into the background.

Pushing jazz into the background, rock and roll became the new major focus of the music industry. Although jazz is not the main focus, it still lives on and develops. A few other types of jazz that popped up after bebop were cool jazz, free jazz, modal jazz, Afro-Cuban jazz, and electric jazz. This just shows that jazz did not die and still lives on in today's society. The highly energetic performing style that is jazz has evolved through the ages and will continue to do so.

References

Armstrong, Louis (2006). Jazz: Famous Quotes and Quotations. Music with Ease. Retrieved November 30, 2006. http://www.musicwithease.com/jazz-quotes.html.

Bastin, Bruce (1986). *Red River Blues: The Blues Tradition in the Southeast*. Urbana: University of Illinois Press.

Bergreen, Laurence (1997). *Louis Armstrong*. New York: Broadway.

Keil, Charles (1991). *Urban Blues*. Chicago: University of Chicago Press.

Kerman, Joseph, and Gary Tomlinson (2004). *Listen*, 5th ed. Boston: Bedford/St. Martin's.

Litweiler, John (1984). *The Freedom Principle: Jazz after 1958*. New York: Da Capo.

Lomax, Alan (1993). *The Land Where the Blues Began*. New York: Pantheon.

Maultsby, Portia (1990). Africanisms in African-American Music. In *Africanisms in American Culture*, ed. Joseph E. Holloway, 185–210. Bloomington: Indiana University Press.

McCalla, J. (1982). *Jazz: A Listener's Guide*. Englewood Cliffs, NJ: Prentice Hall.

Narvaez, Peter (1993). Living Blues Journal: The Paradoxical Aesthetics of the Blues Revival. In *Transforming Tradition: Folk Music Revivals Examined*, ed. Neil Rosenberg, 241–257. Urbana: University of Illinois Press.

Palmer, Robert (1991). The Church of the Sonic Guitar. *South Atlantic Quarterly* 90(4): 649–674.

Peabody, Charles (1903). Notes on Negro Music. *Journal of American Folklore 16*: 148–152.

Rotenstein, David S. (1992). The Helena Blues: African-American Folk Music and Cultural Tourism in Helena, Arkansas. *Southern Folklore* 49(2): 133–146.

Scarborough, Dorothy (1923). The Blues as Folk-Songs. In *Coffee in the Gourd*, J. Frank Dobie, ed. *Publications of the Texas Folklore Society* 2, 52–65. Austin: Texas Folklore Society.

Shumway, David R. (1991). Rock and Roll as Cultural Practice. *South Atlantic Quarterly* 90(4): 753–770.

Southern, Eileen (1983). *The Music of Black Americans*. New York: Norton.

Spencer, Jon Michael (1991). The Diminishing Rural Residue of Folklore in City and Urban Blues, Chicago 1915–1950. *Black Music Research Journal* 12(1): 25–41.

Szwed, John F., and Morton Marks (1988). The Afro-American Transformation of European Set Dances and Dance Suites. *Dance Research Journal* 20(1): 29–36.

Titon, Jeff Todd (1993). Reconstructing the Blues: Reflections on the 1960s Blues Revival. In *Transforming Tradition: Folk Music Revivals Examined*, ed. Neil Rosenberg, 220–240. Urbana: University of Illinois Press.

Werner, O. (1984). *The Origin and Development of Jazz*. Dubuque, IA: Kendall-Hunt.

17. Popular Dances of Mexico

Understanding world music is useful in understanding a specific culture and elements of importance to that culture. World music helps people to understand certain culture's origins, politics, dances, and traditions in social and cultural contexts. Mexico is one culture in which our understanding can be aided by exploring its music. Mexico has a diverse and complex range of musical origins, traditions, and styles. Mexican music has been used as a building block for other musical styles and has also incorporated other styles. Mexico's musical history can be dated back to the ancient cultures of Mexico before the arrival of Europeans. It underwent major changes upon the arrival of Europeans. This rich musical history continues to morph and evolve still today. Mexico's music provides insight and clues about what is important to the country's culture and also individual parts of Mexico's culture. Mexico is such a vast country that different styles of music often represent different subcultures of society. Mexico has undergone a large evolution in its traditional music that enables one to gain cultural insight about the people.

History

First, some background information on Mexico is needed to understand the evolutionary history of Mexico's music better. Mexico is a very large country that covers 1,972,550 square miles of land between the United States and Central America. In a July 2006 census, the population was estimated at 107,449,525. There are three main ethnicities present in Mexico: *mestizo* (Amerindian-Spanish) which accounts for 60 percent of the population, *Amerindian*, which accounts for about 31 percent and *white* which makes up 9 percent. Spanish is the national language, but many indigenous languages are still spoken in the country. The area we know today as Mexico was conquered by the Spaniards in the sixteenth century and didn't gain its independence until 1810. The citizens had an important revolution from 1910 to 1917 when they signed their current constitution. Their present-day mainstream culture was made out of a mixture of Amerindians and Spaniards. For this reason, Mexicans have generally epitomized their political independence as "painful birth." The President of the country is Enrique Peña Nieto (2012–). Mexico is a federal republic, which means it has partially adapted the U.S. constitutional theory, civil law system, and judicial review of legislative Acts. The economy in Mexico is a free market. They have a large and diverse economy. Per capita income for the average Mexican is roughly one-fourth of the average American. This causes 40 percent of Mexico's population to tally below the poverty level (CIA: *The World Factbook*, 2006). Overall, Mexico is known as a vast country with a long tradition of multicultural influences.

Ancient Musical History

Mexico's music history began long before the country of Mexico was ever colonized. Two of the country's most advanced indigenous cultures had some of the more advanced music in the world at that time. Both the Aztecs and Mayans, through traditions passed down to modern day and archeological finds, have been shown to be very advanced in their music. The Mayans and Aztecs have many similarities in their music's origins and transformations. It is essential to understand these two culture's history in order to understand the music.

Mayan culture is believed to have begun around 2,000 BC when Mayans settled in what is present day Southern Mexico. They are most known for their advanced architecture and knowledge of astrology (Mudge, 2003). Unfortunately, it is very difficult to understand much of the origins of music, song, and dance because the Mayans left very little description of it. To the Mayan culture, music was incredibly important because it was viewed as sacred and spiritual. Mayan people believed that music was pleasing to their various divinities. Mayans used music for ceremonies, rites, rituals, magic, and religious and civil events. Similar to other types of world music that we have studied, the Mayans always used music, song, and dance together (Mudge, 2003).

Mayan Instruments

The Mayans developed a wide array of musical instruments that were essential to their music. Each instrument in Mayan culture was personalized for the musician. Musicians were always very religious men in Mayan culture. Women were never allowed to play music. They were allowed to dance, but not with the men (Mudge, 2003). They used clay, wood, rubber, bones, shells, and other things in nature to create their musical instruments. Out of these materials, the Mayans created multiple types of advanced flutes, drums, rattles, bells, and marimba-styled instruments. The Mayans had such advanced instruments that they were able to play multiple notes at the same time to create chords and intervals. It is currently known through archaeology that the Mayans used at least 19 different instruments (Mudge, 2003). Mayan music has been all but lost for the same reason their civilization was lost: the Spaniards. When the Spaniards arrived, they conquered the Mayans and attempted to Christianize them. The traditional Mayan music, song, and dance were seen as uncivilized and not allowed (Mudge, 2003). The pattern of musical development follows the exact pattern that their civilization followed. The culture advanced steadily until the arrival of Spanish influences. Although Mayan music as it was in ancient times has almost been eradicated, its elements still exist in types of Mexico's music.

The Aztecs

Another ancient culture that greatly influenced the origins of Mexican music was the Aztecs. The Aztecs arrived in present day Mexico much later than the Mayans. They didn't settle the area until around AD 1200 (Montezumas, 1998). Like the Mayans, the Aztecs have a rich musical history. They used many of the same instruments that the Mayans to the South used. The Aztecs mostly used flutes, ocarinas, conch shell trumpets, rattles, rasps, shakers, and drums in their music. The Aztecs' most important instrument was the *huehuetl*. According to pre-Hispanic legends, Huehuetl was a deity who was unable to become incarnate, so he arrived on Earth disguised as a drum. The drum is covered in an animal hide that is used to produce two different sounding percussion tones (Tulga, 2006). The major difference between the Aztec instruments and the Mayan instruments was in their tuning. Mayan instruments were tuned according to the musicians' tonal, timbre and cultural preference, but Aztec instruments were tuned to a five note pentatonic scale (Time, 1940). This is an interesting shift because Aztecs didn't allow musicians to tune their instruments to their liking. They had a sophisticated scale that instruments with a definite pitch were tuned to Aztecs also developed schools called *cuicalli* that were specifically designed to teach music (National Geographic, 2006). Aztec music was used for ballads, war songs, and dance rituals. Like the Mayan music, it is difficult to say definitively that we can know true Aztec music because none of it was ever written down by the Aztecs (Time, 1940). However, there is some documentation from explorers about the drum patterns the Aztecs used in their music (Tulga, 2006). This enables us to have at least a primitive understanding of true Aztec music. Aztec music died out in a similar fashion to most of the culture in the region. The Spaniards conquered them early in the sixteenth century and put an end to the Aztec peoples' traditional way of life. However, it appears as if the Aztec culture was declining fairly rapidly already at that point (Mexican and Aztec History, 1998). The instruments used, the fashion they were used in, and the Spanish conquests give one great insight into how Mexico's native music has been transformed into some of the styles present in modern times.

Music

When the Spaniards conquered the indigenous people of present day Mexico, they brought their music with them. This started a period in which Spanish music and instruments dominated the musical styles of the era. The main type of music that the Spaniards brought with them was religious music. The Spaniards brought Catholicism and all of its traditions to the indigenous people. Only Western singing was allowed in the region. The traditional song and dance of the Aztecs and Mayans was superseded with choir music (Mudge, 2003). Another interesting style of music that the Spaniards brought with them was bullfight music. The Moors had brought bullfighting and its music to Spain from Egypt, and the Spaniards brought it to Mexico. The Spaniards held the first bullfight in Mexico City in 1526 in honor of a Spanish emperor, Hernando Cortés (1485–1547). This was the first time that the bullfight music that is usually recognized as being Mexico's was heard in the region (Summers, 1994).

The next form of music to have a major impact on Mexico's musical past is arguably the most famous. The *Mariachi* was formed during the French intervention between 1862 and 1867 (Summers, 1994). *Mariachi* music is particularly interesting because it is the first to fuse together European instruments and Mexican instruments. It is the first of many musical fusions that we see in Mexico. A Mariachi band usually contains the European instruments of violins, trumpets, and a guitar. It is also comprised of a *vihuela* (round backed guitar), *guitarron* (bass guitar), and a Mexican folk-harp. These three instruments have European origins but have been altered to where they are purely Mexican instruments. The original origin of Mariachi is debated, but most believe that the music in its present state began in the state of Jalisco during the nineteenth century (Higgins, 1991). Mariachi musicians play what are called *Sones* in Mexico. A *Son* is a mixture of Spain's, Mexico's, and Africa's folk tradition. One of the most popular Sones is *La Negra*. Many of the Sones are specific to a certain region, but some are national. The Mariachi, like other musical traditions in Mexico and all over the world, is meant to be composed of music, song, and dance (Higgins, 1991). Mariachi music is an example of many genres of Mexican music that are national but differ by region.

The next main style of national Mexican music is the *corrido*. It is especially important to Mexicans because it is an epic ballad that documents the revolution from 1910 to 1917. It romantically described positive and negative tales from the time. It can be accompanied by a single guitarist or a variety of small ensembles. Since that time, it has had a major influence on Mexico's regional music, even though it is a national phenomenon. The new corridos are stories of things in individual regions that have had an impact on that region's people (National Geographic, 2006).

Another evolution in Mexico's music occurred when the Germans emigrated to the Texas-Mexico border. The German accordion was soon joined by the Mexican instrument, bajo sexton, which is a 12-string guitar. These two elements fused to create *Nortefla* or *Norteno* music. This type of music was formed around the turn of the twentieth century. It was actually created in Texas but was very popular with Mexicans in the North. From this Mexican style of music, another genre developed. These two instruments were accompanied by a drum-set and sometimes a saxophone. The groups using these instruments created Tex-Mex, which was an immensely popular genre during the 1940s and 1950s (National Geographic, 2006).

These three main musical traditions in Mexico do not currently make up much of the Mexican mainstream music. However, the traditional music is still used as a way to display and remember their culture. Mexico's cultural music is seen most during fiestas and holidays. The traditional music and dance are immensely important to Mexico's most important events. Their culture is preserved when they sing and dance to the gods and, celebrate national events and fiestas. Some popular performances include dances to the gods, performances for Lent, and fiesta dances. Some of the popular fiesta dances include the "Dance of the Little Old Men" (Viejitos) and "The Mexican Hat Dance" (Jarabe Tapatio). Some of the most important days of the year are when the people of Mexico unite and celebrate the "Day of the Dead" and "Cinco de Mayo." They are national festivities full of traditional song and dance (Mexican Government, 2006).

Modern Music

Popular modern music is a combination of Mexican popular groups and other countries popular music. Some of the popular Mexican music has roots in some of the traditional styles of Mexico, but, for the most part, there are entirely separate genres. Some of the most popular are *cumbia*, pop, hip-hop, and rock. Electronic music has also had a large impact on Mexico's popular music lately. As Mexico's young population increases, the traditional music of Mexico is being constrained to traditional events and activities. In the last decade, there has been an unprecedented crossover of some of Mexican recording artist into the English music industry. The blend of the authentic Latin rhythms and the European rhythms is complicated due to the fusion of bilingual texts in English and Spanish language. These include artists such as like Ariadna Miranda whose song "Equivocada" from her album *Primera fila*, which has peaked at No. 2 in the Latin Pop songs category on the Billboard charts and No. 8 on the Hot Latin Songs chart in the last three years. Others icons of Mexican popular music include Luis Miguel and Belinda Peregrín. For example, Belinda's most popular song, "Ni Freud, Ni Tu Mama," is a fusion of techno and rock 'n' roll with a large electronic influence. The only real similarity found between Belinda's music and traditional Mexican music is that it is sung in Spanish. Another popular Mexican song is "Duele" by the group Kalimba. This song, however, unlike "Ni Freud, Ni Tu Mama" and "Equivocada," exhibits more Latin influence timbres and rhythms. It encompasses some popular tradition instruments such as a violin and guitar but incorporates the piano and electronic guitars. It is a form of Latin Rock that shows some traditional influence, but clearly did not evolve from traditional Mexican music. There are artists from the United States, Australia, Brazil, and the United Kingdom in the Mexican Top 40 songs list. This shows the acceptance of all kinds of music in popular Mexican culture. Mexico's current lovers of pop culture are participating in the globalization of music while still retaining the important traditional styles handed down to them.

Conclusion

This review of Mexican music cannot possibly cover all of the styles of Mexican Music. Some of the popular styles left out include *banda, huapango balada* pop, Latin alternative, and classical. Mexico's music is incredibly regional and to understand Mexican music fully, one must study each individual region's variation of a genre. In spite of this, it is possible to examine the evolution that traditional music has undertaken as a result of cultural circumstances in order to understand the meaning behind Mexico's traditions. Mexico's music has evolved in each of its important cultural shifts. It has changed from the ancient music of the Aztecs and Mayans to the traditional music that Mexicans are so proud of today through a series of observable cultural changes. Mexico appears to be experiencing another one of those important cultural shifts today with the acceptance of world popular music. In the past, when new music has been introduced into Mexico, musicians have incorporated it to create a new form of traditional music. The same thing will most likely recur. Each type of Mexico's traditional music exhibits a cultural shift and fusion of traditional instruments and new music. The country's musicians readily create new cultural music by mixing multiple styles and genres. Even though Mexico's music is constantly changing, they hold on dearly to their national traditions. In these traditions, ritualistic music and dance are essential. Therefore, Mexico may be in danger of losing the meaning of its music. The constant evolution of Mexico's music may seem to make it difficult to understand the culture, but in reality, it is this evolution that exemplifies and defines Mexico's culture.

References

Billboard. (2006). Billboard Singles and Album Charts. *Billboard,* Nov. 20, 2006. www.billboard.com/bbcorn/chartsjsp.

Billboard. (2006). Charts All Over the World. *Billboard,* Nov. 20, 2006. www.lanet.lv/misc/charts/.

CIA. (2006). *The World Factbook*: Mexico. CIA Government Publications, Nov. 20, 2006. https://cia.gov/cial/publications/factbook/geos/mx.html.

Higgins. (1991). History of the Mariachi. Mexico, The Meeting of Two Cultures, Nov. 20, 2006. http://www.mariachi.org/history.html.

Mexican Government. (2006) History and Culture. Mexican Embassy, Nov. 20, 2006. http: //www. mexican-embassy.dk/history.html.

Montezumas. (1998). Mexican and Aztec History. Montezumas Australia, Nov. 20, 2006. http://www.montezumas.corn.au/aztec.htm.

Mudge, M. (2003). Uncovering the Endangered Musical Traditions of the Ancient Mayans of the Yucatan Peninsula. Western Michigan Homepage, 1–11. Nov. 27, 2006. http://homepages.wmich.edu/~s0mudge/Page2.htm.

National Geographic. (2006). Mexico. National Geographic World Music, Nov. 27, 2006. http://worldmusic.nationalgeographic.com/worldmusic/view/page.b.

Summers, J. (1994). The Music of Mexico. *Mexico Living and Travel Update Journal,* 1 3. Nov. 27, 2006. http://www.mexconnect.com/mex/musicmex.html.

Time. (1940). Aztec Music Reconstructed. *Time Magazine,* 1–2. Nov. 27, 2006. http://www.timecorn/time/magazine/printout/0,8816,884120,00.html.

Tulga, P. (2006). Aztec Drum Rhythms: Making Music with Syllables and Fractions. *Music Through the Curriculum,* 1–5. Nov. 27, 2006. http://www.philtulga.com/Aztec%20Music.html.

18. The Slave Dances of North America

In the year 1619, Captain John Smith, a resident in the New World, observed that about the last of August came a Dutch man-of-wane that sold him "twenty Negars" (Craven, 1972). This marked the arrival of the first Africans to the English colonies in the Americas. These Africans were brought here as slaves, specifically to work as laborers and servants. However, the Englishmen didn't expect that these same slaves would do anything else besides work their fields and take care of their houses. They never anticipated that these slaves and the customs they brought with them would shape the musical history of the Americas forever.

18. The Slave Dances of North America

Origins of African American Music

In order to understand why African slave music could have this sort of dramatic effect on the Americas, it is necessary to look at the origins of African American music. It is necessary to look at West Africa, the origin of almost all of the early slaves. Eileen Southern, a professor of Afro-American Studies at Harvard, writes in her book, *The Music of Black Americans*, that "one of the most striking features of African life was the importance given to music and the dance, and travelers seldom failed to comment upon this" (Southern, 1997, p. 4). She continues, "For almost every activity in the life of the individual or the community there was an appropriate music; it was an integral part of life from the hour of birth to beyond the grave," (Southern, 1997, p. 5). Every event was celebrated in public dances, which were accompanied by music, depending on the situation. All dances divided the assembly into four different groups: the married men, the married women, the young men, and the maidens (Southern, 1997) Africans used the music for religious rites, war, hunting, victory celebrations and for homage to the king. However, the "large part of the music making in African took place on a less formal, highly socialized level that brought together members of the community in either selective groups or as a whole to share in common experiences" (Southern, 1997, p. 7). It is important to understand that the soul of music came from the combination of music, drama, and dance, and he writes in his book, Black American Music, that this "became expertly woven in the language and customs of the people" (Roach , 1992, p. 7).

When Africans came to the colonies, they came in chains and were separated from their families and their communities. They only had their traditions from the motherland and passed these traditions down to their children. Given the importance of music and dance in Africa, it is now possible to believe that this same reflection would be seen among the slaves in the colonies. However, although it is true that African slave trade to America began in 1619, there are few descriptions and/or written occurrences of African musical activity before 1800 (Burnim, 2006). This is due to not only the small population growth before 1800; it was also because more slaves were being transported to the West Indies, where it was far more profitable. As the islands grew, planters and their slaves moved, mostly to the mainland.

Slave Music

Music was the primary, and sometimes the only communication for slaves, much like their African ancestors. Their songs recorded the circumstances of daily life just as a person would use a biography or a diary. They used their music to comment on their problems and keep the memory of the few amusements they were allowed. They voiced their hopes and their despairs. Their music was often used to remind them of their "humanity in an environment that constantly denied their humanness" (Southern, 1997, p. 157). While there were definitive songs as Europeans would recognize them, often with a specific, identifiable tune and words, sometimes the songs were merely cries in the field. These cries could be a cry for water, food, to help, to identify one's location, or just a cry of sorrow or happiness. It was common practice as well to for slaves to be forced to sing and dance. Africans were forced to dance on the deck during their air breaks and they were also often whipped into singing and dancing before being placed on the auction block.

Singing accompanied all the work a slave did as well whether it was picking cotton, harvesting cane sugar, or any of the small odd jobs like mending a fence or cooking a meal. This music served two functions for the most part, one being to overcome the monotony of the work and the other to coordinate the movements of the job at hand, lift the spirits of the indefatigable workers, enable the slower workers to keep pace, and ward off fatigue. In fact, planters encouraged the singing to get the maximum amount of work out of the gang. The song leaders sometimes were excused from labor or given rewards or incentives to devote attention and energy to the singing. Lone workers however, had no need to coordinate their efforts or work movements with others, so their songs could take on their own personal feeling. The mood of the moment defined the tempo, text, and the melody. "The slaves distinguished among song types according to the function of the songs, as in African tradition, and were concerned that their activities be accompanied by appropriate songs. There were few hard and fast rules; often it was merely a matter of adjusting the tempo" (Southern, 1997, p. 165).

Dance

The favored recreational activity for these African Americans (the term is used loosely, as the majority of these slaves were still from Africa), was dancing. Recreational dance and music occurred on Sundays but was limited after 1739 when the clergy complained that Africans were tarnishing the Lord's Day with their celebrations. More generous landlords also allowed Saturday evenings for this dancing. It would seem that many slaveholders realized the importance of giving their workers a break from the grind of daily labor. Holidays were also set aside as days that landlords typically exempted their slaves from labor. These holidays included New Year's Day, Easter, and Christmas. As with weekend breaks, the slaveholder ultimately decided which days the slaves would take as holiday break. Recreational music almost always included a fiddler. The slaveholders would even provide the fiddler to the workers. The pride in their dances came from the fact that they emphasized vigor and vitality. White men were astonished to see that instead of resting, African Americans would spend an entire night of wild and fast dancing. Holiday dances generally lasted the all night. Enervated musicians were sometimes relieved or the slaves would go to a style of dancing called "pattin' juba," which will be described later.

The sites of these dances were also a place of social gathering. Stories that often included songs in the narrative were often told. Slaves' stories were about the adventures of animals and the adventures of their biblical heroes, but they could not be about themselves. It is theorized that some hundreds of folktales were in circulation about Brer Rabbit and his friends but only the Charles Gals survives today.

Another use of their music is for the entertainment of the masters. Slaves frequently were called in to sing for their masters for various reasons. Some only sang a song to "dispel the tedium of the moment" (Southern, 1997, p. 175). Others were called in simply because the masters had an appreciation for their music. Many owners placed the value of a slave on his ability to improvise in a song. It is worth restating the enormous value slaveholders placed on a good fiddler. Fiddlers had entry into places no other slave could go into and here often exempted from a day of hard word. There are accounts of the wives of owners crying when the master released his prized fiddler.

Meaning

Thus far it has been discussed that the music of African and African American (there is a difference in this time period) slaves had many uses. However, what did it actually mean to them? White men in this time period misinterpreted the singing and dancing as uncaring, that slaves thought blacked the normal human response to oppression, loss of loved ones, and deprivation of freedom. Whites saw the blacks as cheerful and contented, merrily working with their music. However, obviously, they were way off. Frederick Douglass explained that slaves sang the most when they were the unhappy. Frederick Douglas, in his autobiography, writes,

> I did not, when a slave, understand the deep meanings of those rude, and apparently incoherent songs. They told a tale which was then altogether beyond my feeble comprehension; there were tones loud, long and deep, breathing the prayer and complaint of souls boiling over with bitter anguish. Every tone was a testimony against slavery, and a prayer to God for deliverance from chains [Douglass, *My Bondage*, 43–84].

Evolution

Slave songs have always remained just that—the songs of the slaves; however, this music would eventually change the music history of this continent forever. The progress of slave music came from the fact that African Americans took their music to church. The traditional hymns of Western Europeans began to fuse with traditional African singing and eventually led to the birth of secular folk music. This folk music would eventually go under further change and evolve in to what we call early Blues music.

The very first Africans in the Americas followed closely to their African musical roots. The characteristics of the music still included a multipart rhythmic structures, repetitive choruses with the lead singer, scales of four to seven steps, and the call and response style of alternating phrases. Vocal music remained dominant throughout the seventeenth and eighteenth centuries. However, economic constraints started to wither in the colonies and the people could afford to purchase instruments for their homes. They purchased violins, oboes, guitars, flues, fortepianos, and harmonicas, which, as you have already seen, found their way to the slaves.

Instruments

The most common plantation instruments were the fiddle and the banjo. A few slaves were able to purchase instruments from money they earned in their free time, others were gifts from their masters, and most were homemade. Fiddles were made from a knife, pine boards, and guts from a cow that were cut into strips, dried, and treated. A banjo could be made from a gourd by stretching a thin skin over the opening, adding strings made from the gut, and raising the strings on a bridge. Other than string instruments, the slaves used anything they could find to make musical sound. Old iron pieces, jawbones, wood and sticks, flutes were made from all different sorts of materials, and panpipes were made from canes of sugar.

In the South, laws prohibited slaves from using drums, horns or loud instruments that may call or give sign or notice to one another. Slaveholders knew of the African tradition for the talking instruments and tried to eliminate this source of secret communication. This, compiled with the fact that drums were used in a slave uprising in 1739, were the main reasons for this outlawing of the central instrument in African music and dancing. The Africans quickly found substitutes for these however. They used simple hand clapping, foot stomping, and a technique called "patting juba" to fill the large void left by the drum.

Festivals

Slave festivals and dances, allowed by the holders, were characterized by African traditions. Black northerners carried out elections to elect their own "governors." The holiday, 'Lection Day Festival, was carried out in May or June. Slaves were given about a half a week to elect their rulers and celebrate. The events included a parade in which the best musicians were given the honor of playing. This was followed by a ceremony that consisted of dancing, games, and music.

Pinkster Celebrations were originally celebrations for Pentecost Sunday for the Anglican Church. They turned into a full week celebration often featuring traditional Congo dances. The events attracted large amounts of white spectators to see the "Carnival of Africans." The leading spirit of the dancing played the master drums and called the dances. He was accompanied by banjos, fiddles, drums, and the "hollow drum." The week ended up being a full week of intense dancing which ended with the Sabbath Day. A popular dance in Louisiana and the surrounding territory was *La Calinda*. Two drums of unequal length open at each end and covered with skin were the two main instruments that kept the beat of the dance, which was never described. The drums were accompanied by a guitar-like instrument with four strings, called a banza. Other African style dances were the chica, bamboula, the coonjine or counjaille, and the Congo dance. These dances were prohibited by most evangelical religions, but the French and Spanish governments had allowed these dances before the Louisiana Purchase in 1803.

Corn shucking was a community event in which a planter invited workers from neighboring plantations to come on a certain day. Gangs of workers would march to the location, singing the entire way, choose sides and then choose a leader. Each team would then compete, the workers responding in chorus to the shouts of their leader. When all the corn had been shucked and the winning team recognized, a feast and dance began.

Conclusion

It should come as no surprise that the music of the first and early slaves should resemble much of that from West Africa. Given that songs were an important tradition in their culture before they were forced into labor in the Americas, it is only reasonable to believe that their dances and music would remain an important part of their lives, specifically because that had no other remembrance of their homeland. What is interesting, however, is the response of the white men; the white men were enamored with of these slaves and their music. There are even accounts of them joining the dances, and singing, and playing along with them. White men paid to have their slaves trained in a music instrument once music schools started popping up all over America. What is also interesting, however, is seeing how quickly African Americans took to Anglo American religions and how quickly they transformed their own music into the folk, blues, jazz, and ragtime that were soon to come. You would not expect a cultural group who clung so closely to the only remnants of their traditions to change so easily.

References

Allen, William Francis, Charles Pickard Ware & Lucy McKim Garrison (1867). *Slave Songs of the United States.* New York: A. Simpson & Co.
Burnim, Mellonee V., and Portia K. Maulsby (2006). *African American Music.* New York: Routledge.
Craven, Wesley (1972). A New Edition of the Works of John Smith. *The William and Mary Quarterly 29*(3).
Roach, Hildred Black (1992). *American Music.* Malabar, FL: Krieger.

Southern, Eileen (1997). *The Music of Black Americans: A History*. New York: W.W. Norton.

Southern, Eileen, and Josephine Wright (2000). *Iconography of Music in African-American Culture*. New York: Garland.

19. The Tango of Argentina

The Origins of Tango

Buenos Aires is a South American port city that saw a huge influx of immigrants in the late 1800s and early 1900s. These immigrants were mainly poor people seeking a new way of life. Few women and families immigrated to Buenos Aires. However, there were many young men that crossed the Atlantic to Buenos Aires looking to make their fortunes there (Denniston, 2005). These trends in immigration led to the development of a large lower class made up of mostly males. Buenos Aires also played host to many sailors on a daily basis as they stopped through the port town on their shipping routes. The environment of Buenos Aires adjusted to the kinds of people that settled there. With the sailors came the development of brothels (prostitution houses), bars, and gambling casinos. These places entertained the soldiers during their stay in Buenos Aires. It is in this setting that the Tango originated and slowly began to spread to other parts of the world (Brown, 2005).

There were also big housing areas called *conventillos* (Brown, 2005) that developed for the poor immigrants. The *conventillos* were long open areas with rooms, kitchens, and shared bathrooms at the end. They had large common areas where their tenants would dance and enjoy themselves. It took a little while for the Tango to reach the residents of these *conventillos* but when it finally did, it became immensely popular and spread quickly to other people.

In the early 1800s, all dancing among couples was done with the man and woman standing directly opposite each other. There was little or no physical contact between partners, only the occasional touch of the hands (Ferrer, 1960). The first dance to break this barrier was the Viennese Waltz in the 1830s (Denniston, 2005). The Waltz used a closed hold with the woman's right hand in the man's left and the man's right arm around the woman's waist. This is what we consider the standard hold today.

At that time, the close hold was still considered scandalous. It was a while before the Waltz became accepted. The Polka followed the Waltz in 1840. The Tango, the third dance to use this scandalous close hold (Denniston, 2005), followed the Polka in the 1880s. The acceptance of the Tango was very difficult because the Tango was a much more intimate dance than either the Waltz or the Polka. The Tango involved more than just a close hold. The torsos of the dancers touched, as did their faces.

The word "tango" has no clear origin. Some think it stems from the Latin verb "tangere," which means "to touch." Others say it comes from the Nigeria/Congo region of Africa, where the word "tamgu" means "to dance" (Brown, 2005). The origins of the dance and music of the Tango are as varied as the origins of the word.

The Tango is a fusion of many different styles of dancing brought to Buenos Aires by the immigrants who settled there. There are African influences from the *candombe* rhythms that the African slaves beat on their drums. The *Milonga* music, which combined Indian rhythms with the music of the Spanish, also influenced the Tango (showgate). The Tango was a blend of European, African, and Native American music (Brown, 2005).

Sounds and Movements of the Tango

The Tango music is played on a variety of instruments. The three main instruments are the flute, the violin, and the guitar. The bandoneón joined this trio at the end of the nineteenth century (Ferrer, 1960). The bandoneón is a free-reed German instrument similar to the accordion. It is played by holding the instrument with both hands and pushing in or pulling out the main part of the instrument while pressing buttons on either side (Bandoneón). After the bandoneón became a popular instrument of the Tango, Vicente Greco formed the standard tango sextet. Born in Buenos Aires, in the candombe neighborhood of Concepción, Vicente Greco, a self-taught musician is credited for codifying the tango. This sextet consisted of a piano, a double bass, two violins, and two bandoneóns (Ferrer, 1960).

The Tango began as the dance of the Cyprian and the Pandar. The dancers acted out these roles in the dance. Because the dance was based on the life of a prostitute, it was very sexual in nature. It was danced in the brothels of Buenos Aires with the prostitutes who made their livings there. Sometimes it even involved a duel between two men, often ending in the symbolic death of one of them (Ferrer, 1960).

Dancing the Tango well was very important for men. It was a way to show their status and to impress women (Ferrer, 1960). However, they could not practice with a woman while they were learning. The prostitutes were too expensive to dance with very often. Other women would only dance with an excellent partner. There were so few of them compared to the number of men that there was no reason for them to waste their night dancing with a bad partner (Denniston, 2005). Because of this, men were forced to learn from other men. They would also dance with other men as they were learning to improve their skills (Ferrer, 1960).

The Tango gradually evolved into the "dance of sorrow." It speaks of frustrated love, fatalities, and destinies engulfed in pain (Mafud, 1966). It became popular among the lonely, low class immigrants seeking to escape from their feelings. From the lower class, it gradually spread up the social ladder up into the higher classes and eventually spread to other parts of the world.

The Golden Age of Tango

As the Tango rose up the social ladder, it softened slightly. It was at this time that the Tango began to spread to other regions of the world (Mafud, 1966). The Tango invaded Paris in the early 1900s. From Paris it spread to other European capitals such as London and Berlin (Brown, 2005). The Tango then made its way back across the Atlantic Ocean to hit New York.

Back in Argentina, the Tango went through a period of decline after a military coup overthrew the Hipólito Yrigoyen government and ended the citizen's right to vote in 1930 (Mafud, 1966). When the citizens of Argentina regained many of their political freedoms in the late 1930s, they brought the Tango back up with them. The Tango became a part of everyday life and a symbol of national pride (Brown, 2005). Musicians began writing new music and lyrics for the Tango (Mafud, 1966). Upper class intellectuals took an interest in the Tango and under their influence, the Tango took on a more romantic air.

The Tango reached the height of its popularity in 1946 when Juan Peron and his wife Evita came to power. This was in the middle of the Golden Age of Tango, which lasted from about 1935 to 1952. The end of the Golden Age of Tango coincided with Evita's death in 1952. At this time, the Tango began a long descent from the spotlight (Brown, 2005). Rock and roll music invaded Argentina, and the Tango faded from the glory it had known under the reign of Juan Peron. Next to rock and roll, the Tango seemed somehow out of place (Mafud, 1966).

There was a large revival of the Tango in the 1980s. It began with the fall of the military dictatorship in 1983 (Denniston, 2005). People wanted to learn the Tango because they were proud to be Argentine again, and the rest of the world identified the Tango with Argentina. It was mainly young, new dancers who participated in this Renaissance. Dancers from the Golden Age had been pulled around too many times by the government to start dancing again so soon (Denniston, 2005). This led to the development of a new kind of Tango, full of complex choreography.

The opening of Luis Bravo's musical *Forever Tango* in 1994 reflected the world's newly discovered fascination with the Tango. After all, it was not just in Argentina that this revival occurred. It occurred all over the world. People in America, London, and other parts of Europe were also showing an interest to dance the Tango. *Forever Tango* ran for a year on Broadway and went on tour in North America and in Europe. *Forever Tango* features the music and dancing of the Tango with an all Argentine cast and an onstage orchestra that includes the bandoneón (Brown, 2005).

Variations of the Tango

There are many different types of Tango dancing. These types include Argentine Tango, Tango Liso, Tango Nuevo, Show Tango, Salon Tango, and Ballroom Tango. Each specific style of Tango has slight variations from the Tango that was created in Argentina at the end of the nineteenth century. However, they all have the same general characteristics. All of the versions are very passionate dances that make use of long gliding steps.

The Argentine Tango developed in Argentina and Uruguay. It was influenced by versions of the Tango that came back to South America from Europe and North America. The Argentine Tango relies very heavily on improvisation. The dancers are taught certain sequences of steps, but they are free to modify and rearrange these steps to form new ones (Brown, 2005).

This Tango is danced counterclockwise around the outside of the dance floor. While there is no specific rule against cutting across the middle of the floor, it is not custom to do so. Cutting across the floor is frowned upon. Couples are allowed to go at their own pace on the dance floor, provided they do not inconvenience the other couples around them (Brown, 2005). They should dance at such a pace that they do not run into the couple in front of them and also do not hold up the many couples behind them.

The Argentine Tango is danced in a very close embrace, with the chests of the dancers and sometimes even the heads touching. The feet are kept further apart, giving the couple the appearance of an upside-down "V." In each step that the dancers take, their feet stay close to the floor. As they dance around the floor, their ankles and knees often brush together.

There are a four main dance pattern moves in the Argentine Tango. In the *gancho*, one dancer, usually the woman hooks her leg around her partner's leg. The *parada* occurs when the leader puts his foot against his partner's foot. In a third move, the *arrastre*, the leader drags the follower's foot. The final move is called *sacada*. There are several different kinds of *sacada*. The *sacada* is when the leader steps into the follower's dancing space, thus displacing the movement of her feet.

The Ballroom Tango has developed from a simplified version of the Tango that first visited America and Europe. It was adapted to fit in with ballroom standards of dancing and judging. The movements became more staccato, or jerky, and the characteristic head snaps not present in the Argentine version of the Tango were added. The English Ballroom Tango developed as a highly competitive dance while the American version developed mainly as a social dance.

There are many differences between the Argentine and Ballroom Tangos. First of all, in the Argentine Tango, it is acceptable for the man to step on the same foot as the woman. This is called a "crossed" or "uneven" walk. In Ballroom Tango, this is not the correct way to dance. Second, the posture of the dancers varies in these types of Tango. In Argentine Tango, the woman remains upright on her axis or may even lean in to her partner. In Ballroom Tango, the woman shies away from the man when he pushes toward her. Third, the music that the Argentine Tango is danced to is much more varied than the music that Ballroom Tango is danced (Brown, 2005). This allows dancers of the Argentine Tango to dance the Tango all night, without becoming bored.

Another difference between the Argentine Tango and Ballroom Tango is the way the feet move with the body. In Argentine Tango, the movement of the body is supported by the feet. This means that, as the body leans and twists in different ways, the feet follow and move to allow the body to continue that motion. In Ballroom Tango however, the feet move first and the body follows. One final difference is that, because there is so much improvisation in the Argentine Tango, it is constantly changing and evolving. Ballroom Tango, on the other hand, has been standardized. Therefore, it has remained the same for many years (Brown, 2005).

The Tango's Prominence

The Tango has been featured in many movies today. *Moulin Rouge* is a movie in the musical genre that was released in 2001. One of the dance numbers in *Moulin Rouge* is a tango. In the movie *Chicago*, which is also a musical, there is a tango called the "Cell Block Tango" that is danced in the jail cells. The Tango also features prominently in other movies such as *Shall We Dance, Mr. & Mrs. Smith, Assassination Tango,* and *Scent of a Woman.*

Tango generally represents more than just a dance—it is a way of life of people of Argentina. It is, as it were, the heart of the Argentine people. Each good period in their history is marked by the Tango. It is a show of their pride, their power, and their passion.

References

Borges, Jorge Luis (1930). *Evaristo Carriego*. Buenos Aires: M. Gleizer.
Borges, Jorge Luis, and Silvina Bullrich (1968). *El compadrito*. Buenos Aires: Emece Editores.
Brown, S. (2005). A History of Argentine Tango and the Evolution of Its Styles. Retrieved November 15, 2005 from http://www.tejastango.com/evolution.html.
Canton, Dario (1968). "El mundo de los tangos de Gardel." *Revista Latinoamericana de Sociología*, IV:183–197.
Denniston, Christine (2005). The Hidden History of Tango. Retrieved November 28, 2005, from http://www.history-of-tango.com/index.html.
Ferrer, Horacio (1960). *El tango: su historia y su evolución*. Buenos Aires: Coleccibn La Siringa.
Germani, Gino (1955). *Estructura social de la Argentina*. Buenos Aires: Raigal.
Germani, Gino (1962). *Política y sociedad en una epoca de transición*. Buenos Aires: Editorial Paidds.
Hernandez, Jose (1939). *Martin Fierro*. Buenos Aires: Editorial Losada.
Lara, Tomas de (1961). *El tema del tango en la literatura argentina*. Buenos Aires: Ediciónes Culturales Argentinas.
Mafud, Julio (1966). *La sociológica del tango*. Buenos Aires: Editorial Américalee.

Rossi, Vicente (1926). *Cosas de negros*. Buenos Aires: Libreria Hachette (reprint 1958).

Sábato, Ernesto (1965). *El tango: discusión y Clave*, 2d ed. Buenos Aires: Biblioteca Clásica y Contemporanea.

Scobie, James R. (1964). *Argentina: A City and a Nation*. New York: Oxford University Press.

Sebreli, Juan José (1966). *Buenos Aires, vida cotidiana y alienación*, 9th ed. Buenos Aires: Ediciónes Siglo Veinte.

Vega, Carlos (1936). *Danzas y canciones argentinas*. Buenos Aires: G. Ricordi y Cia.

Vilarino, Idea (1965). *Las letras del tango*. Buenos Aires: Editorial Schapire.

20. The Chacarera Dance of Argentina

In the world, there are different types of music. For example, in Africa, music is used in rituals while in America; music is primarily used for entertainment. Music around the world has been shaped by the many people who live in those countries. An example of this cultural mixing of music can be seen in Argentina. Argentina was originally inhabited by Indians but during the nineteenth and twentieth centuries, Argentina's population grew rapidly as thousands of immigrants arrived from Europe. While most Argentines are of Spanish or Italian descent, the families of others came from Germany, Switzerland, the former Yugoslavia, and Ukraine. The native Indian population of Mapuches, Collas, Tobas, Matacos, and Chiriguanos today amounts to no more than 1 percent of the total population.

With this mix of cultures, Argentina, over the last 2 centuries, has both socially and culturally changed. One of the ways that Argentina has changed culturally is in its music. Modem music, folk music, and tango music are three of the types of music in Argentina that have changed during the past two centuries.

Modem music in Argentina includes Rock and Roll, Argentine punk, Buenos Aires Hardcore, and Cumbia villera. Rock and Roll in Argentina started in the mid–1960s. Musicians started to compose songs and lyrics that were relevant to social and musical themes. What kick started the movement for Rock and Roll was the British invasion. The main groups from the British invasion were the Beatles and the Rolling Stones. In Argentina, the Rolling Stones had more popularity. During this time period most of the Argentine rock groups recycled hits from English rock and roll to recreate their own style. Rock and roll bands in Argentina are rare and unique today, because they only sing in Spanish. By only singing in Spanish, these bands do not attain globular popularity since they are not played in English speaking countries like the United States, the United Kingdom, or Europe. However, if a person were to translate the lyrics they would most resemble the lyrics that English rock artist use.

Punk

As in England, Argentine punk developed as a way to protest the politics of the country and to broadcast the controversial ideas about the government. Punk gained popularity while Argentina was under a dictatorship. In the first few years of the Argentina punk movement, the music was poorly documented. This was because it took place in an underground scene. The punk movement had a political take on the government and at it was seen as heroic and had an almost mythical status (Cofen & Jermyn, 2002).

Buenos Aires Hardcore

Buenos Aires Hardcore is the name of the movement that gathered the hardcore bands that started to play in the Buenos Aires area in the late 1980s (Buenos Aires Hardcore, p. 1). Most of these bands were influenced from the New York Hardcore scene. These bands often mixed punk, metal, and hip-hop (Buenos Aires Hardcore, p. 1). However, some bands offered a style far different from the violent New York Hardcore style (Cofen & Jermyn, 2002).

Cumbia

Cumbia was traditionally music that was found in Columbia. The music was and still can be heard with a full array of African percussion. The dance that goes along with the music is highly flirtatious. The dance is usually a couple's dance (Cofen & Jermyn, 2002). During the dance, the men wear a red handkerchief around their necks, while the women wear long skirts. The women hold a candle that follows the men around in a romantic pursuit. In the political circles, Cumbia is considered a vulgar, lower class musical form by the government. When Cumbia entered Argentina, it became very popular with the villas miseria (shantytowns) around Buenos Aires, who transformed the Cumbia into Cumbia villera. The music today is written around cumbia beats and lyrics that go deep into themes of crime and drug abuse. Most artists can be spotted by the way that they look. Cumbia villera artist have long hair and have a bad-boy attitude. What catapulted Cumbia villera into the spot light was when football stars from these areas claimed their allegiance to the music (Cofen & Jermyn, 2002).

Folk Music

Folk music in Argentina is composed of Andean music, Chacarera, and Chamame. A type of folk music found in Argentina is Andean music. Andean music is usually called "Inca Music," but this is incorrect because it was established before the Inca's were even in Argentina (A Short History of Andean Music, p. 1). Andean music in Argentina today is from centuries of cultural and ethnic mixing (Cofen & Jermyn, 2002). The start of the change of Andean music began with the Spanish conquest of the Andean Highlands and the Incas. During the Spanish occupation, a change in music began because of the introduction of new instruments (Cofen & Jermyn, 2002). One of the new instruments the Spaniards brought was the Spanish guitar. This new instrument led the native to make new instruments to be played with their favorite types of music. One instrument that was made and was used in Andean music was a *charango*. This instrument looked looks like a lute (Cofen & Jermyn, 2002). In today's society, Andean music is in demand. In 1952, the government established a folklore department (Rossi, 973). This led to Andean music being broadcasted on radio stations.

Chacarera is another type of folk music from Argentina. This music originated in northwest Argentina. The name is derived from the main instrument that is played, the Chacarera. Chacarera is usually played with a guitar, violin, accordion, and bombo leguero (Rossi, 1973). This music is best danced by couples loosely dancing on their own, with rounds and turns. The origin of the dance is unknown, but the name "chakra" means farm, which fits since the dance was usually performed in rural areas (Rossi, 1973). The chacarera took until the twentieth century to make its way all the way to Buenos Aires and, although it was welcomed because of its tradition, it could not compete with the tango (Rossi, 1973).

Another type of folk music is Chamame. Chamame is from the Argentina Mesopotamia. When the Spanish came, they made reductions in the Jesuit population (Rossi, 1973). This started a growth in culture in this area and the growth continued until the Jesuit's were expelled by the Spanish in the late eighteenth century. Yapeyu in Corrientes became known as the centre of the musical culture. This is the birth place of Chamame. Chamame then started to mix with the local instruments, such as the Spanish guitar, the violin, and the accordion (Rossi, 1973). Chamame is considered the Corrientes' Polka because the name Chamame was used in 1931 when recordings were being made. The mix of all these instruments gives us what we today call Chamame.

Tango

One of the universal and well known types of all of Argentina's music is the tango. The Tango is Argentina's national music and dance (Dala, 2001). The tango throughout the years has risen and fallen in popularity, but always seems to return to favor and be danced even more passionately. The tango was born in Buenos Aires during the nineteenth century. During this time, Buenos Aires was considered a melting pot of ethnic groups and cultures. Different ethnic groups from around Europe and Africa were all living together with nature in the same villages as well as urban centers and sharing different aspects of their lives, especially music. Towards the end of the nineteenth century, the blending of these various music and dances gave way to what we know today as the tango. In the early years of the tango, it was not accepted by the upper classes. This was because it was the favorite music of those bent on social upheavals such as thuggery and other crimes associated with gangsters and brothels. The tango only became fashionable in Argentina after it became popular in France (Dala, 2001). When Argentine middle and upper class realized that the tango had become popular in Paris, then the most fashionable city in the world, they quickly forgot about its origins in brothels and started to tango (Dala, 2001).

The tango, in the beginning, was only instrumental (Dala, 2001, p.101). The instruments used were the piano, the violin, the guitar, and the flute. The tango is also often played with a kind of large accordion called a *bandoneon* (Dala, 2001 p.101). These bandoneons were imported from Germany but are no longer made, so the old ones are carefully maintained (Dala, 2001, p.101). As the Tango gained popularity, dance steps and words were added to the music. The first item added to tango music was dancing. In the nineteenth century, the tango was a solo dance performed by a single woman (Rossi, 973). The Adualisian tango was the next form of the tango. This was a tango between one or two couples walking together using castanets (Tango History, p. 1). It soon became immoral because of its flirtations music (Rossi, 973). The tango then went through an evolution, and it became ballroom tango. This form of tango originated in the lower classes of Buenos Aires (Tango History, p. 1). Clothing worn was full skirts for the women and gauchos with high boots and spurs for the men (Tango History, p. 1). Ballroom tango was mainly performed between a couple holding each other tightly and gliding together in long elegant steps, occasionally pausing in dramatic poses (Cultures of the World Argentina, p. 97). Today, the tango is danced across the world from Argentina to New York to Paris, performed in various styles.

The last major component of the tango was introduced in 1910 when lyrics were added to the music (Dala, 2001). Tango songs were a mixture of love and of longing. One of the best tango singers of all times was Carlos Gardel. Carlos was a French immigrant who came to Buenos Aires as a boy. At a young age, he was making a living by doing odd jobs during the day and at night entertaining his neighbors with his passionate love songs. Carlos Gardel's first success came with his partner Jose Razzano (Dala, 2001). When Razzano lost his voice, Gardel went solo and took a step toward becoming a star. Gardel got his big break in 1917, when he recorded the song "Mi Noche Triste" (My Sad Night) (Dala, 2001). This song jump-started his career, which allowed him to perform all over the world and to act in seven films. Gardel's life ended tragically in a plane crash in 1935 (Dala, 2001). Gardel's body was returned to Buenos Aires where thousands of fans mourned his death (Dala, 2001).

Evita

Since Argentina is steeped in music, it seems only fitting that one of their beloved leaders be immortalized in a musical. *Evita*, written by Andrew Lloyd Weber, is an award winning musical and film. *Evita* was based on the real life of Eva Peron, who was an actress, had her own radio show, and married Juan Peron. Juan Peron became president of Argentina with Eva's help. Eva used her position to improve the position of woman and the poor. Unfortunately, she died very young of cancer. On her tomb in Buenos Aires, it bears the inscription, "Don't Cry for me, Argentina, I am with you" (Dala, 2001). Weber used these immortal words for one of his most passionate songs in his musical.

Conclusion

Argentina is a different society today than it was then. Its music has changed because of conquest and because of immigration. This can be seen in the Argentine music, folk music, modern music, and the Tango. Argentine music has been influenced by British invaders and Spanish Conquistadors but Argentines have influenced the world with their very own tango. The tango can be danced in ballrooms or seen on TV's *Dancing with the Stars*.

References

Andean Nation (2000). A Short History of Andean Folk Music. Retrieved November 21, 2006, from www.andeannation.com.
Cofen, Ethel C., and Leslie Jermyn (2002). *Cultures of the World: Argentina*. New York: Benchmark.
Dala, Anita (2001). *Nations of the World Argentina*. Austin, TX: Raintree Steck-Vaughn.
Frank, Nicole (2000). *Countries of the World: Argentina*. Milwaukee, WI: Gareth Stevens.
Rossi, Nick (1973). "Music of Argentina." *Music Educators Journal* 59(5), 51–53.

21. The Capoeira Dance of Brazil

Capoeira is a unique art form that combines opposites like fighting and dancing, violence and aesthetics, and game and death. While it is unclear as to where the name *capoeira* comes from, it is well-known throughout the world as a fight-dance that uses the beauty and efficiency of animal movements for combat. There are differing theories as to where the name originated. Some attest that it is derived from the name of an aggressive bird called "Odontophorus capoeira spix" while others think it is a word describing the destroying potential of the art that originated from the Tupi-Guarani people (an aborigine tribe of Brazil), meaning a forest that has been completely cut down.

The History of Capoeira

The history of capoeira is rich and the dance is thought to be almost 500 years old, but there are different ideas as to how it officially originated. The first of these theories is that the dance developed in Africa as a courtship dance in the Bantu tradition of Angola used by men trying to attract young women. The second basic theory of its development is that it originated around 1538—the beginning of an era where about 18 million slaves were brought to Brazil. The idea was that the art began on the ships that brought slaves from Africa to South America and was refined in the Brazilian fields. Since slaves were not allowed to fight, but song and dance was tolerated by the guards, they masked this fighting form as a type of dance.

The rhythm and the movements for capoeira were in the minds and bodies of the African slaves. They felt as if this were the only thing the slave-drivers couldn't take from them. It gave the slaves a chance to prepare for resistance against those who they crossed paths with, such as the slave-drivers. As a fast and effective way of fighting, capoeira was traditionally performed in circles known as *rodas*, which were formed by the slaves. As soon as a guard came too close to the circle, the fight turned into a dance that was tolerated. Working under inhumane conditions in the fields, the slaves had only two choices: death through exhaustion and torture, or escape to the forest. In the 1690s, many slaves were able to escape the awful conditions of the fields. These slaves were known as Maroons and they founded villages called *quilombos*, where they were better able to organize resistance against adversaries. Aside from the direct use of weapons, capoeira was the main tool that the Africans used against the slave-drivers. The Maroons would even combine the use of weapons with the art of capoeira, and it was common for them to practice with razors between their toes or knives in their hands to make this a more effective method of protection (Stephens & Delamont, 2006). Survivors of ambushes with Maroons that involved hand-to-hand combat described scenes of mayhem, stating that "the Maroons appeared from nowhere, striking them with blows from angles that they could not fathom." As a result of the quick and direct manner with which Maroons executed capoeira, those under attack would often attempt to flee as quickly as possible (Hall & Jefferson, 1976).

The Repression of the Capoeira

When the Portuguese king Dom Jao VI, who was fleeing Napoleon Bonaparte's invasion of Portugal, arrived with his court in Brazil in 1808, the laws affecting capoeira began to change. Around 1814, capoeira and other forms of African cultural expression suffered repression and were banned in some places by slave masters and overseers. Deadly interactions were occurring sporadically between slaves, the colonists and even between the slaves themselves. There was no tolerance for capoeira's existence and those found practicing capoeira were often punished with a slashed Achilles' tendon, knee, or even throat. The official ban was a severe issue for the slaves, who were confined to perform the art in private locations, and capoeira became known quietly as an "underground art form." With the signing of the Golden Law in 1888, which banned slavery in Brazil, the slaves had a tough time assimilating themselves with the existing socio-economic order. The master of capoeira, known as the *capoeirista,* was highly criminalized by society. In Rio de Janiero, criminal gangs began to sprawl, which terrorized the population. In 1890, during the transition from the Brazilian Empire to the Brazilian republic, these gangs were often used by both monarchists and republicans to pressure and break up rallies of adversaries. It was rather common to see weapons such as clubs, daggers, or switchblades used with capoeira to create more damage (Hall & Jefferson, 1976).

In Bahia, Brazil, capoeira had developed into a more ritualized fight-dance game, and the *berimbau* was introduced as a chief instrument used to command the *rodas*. The sessions of capoeira always took place in hidden locations as the dance was re-outlawed, this time officially in 1892 by the first constitution of the Brazilian Republic. During the time of *carnival,* tough capoeira fighters would lead gangs through the streets of Recife and if two gangs crossed paths, fighting and bloodshed would typically ensue. Of all the known capoeira gang leaders, Nascimiento Grande was the most feared and notorious. Some say that he was killed during police persecution in the early 1900s, while others say that he migrated from Recife to Rio de Janiero and died there of old age. Another notorious *capoerista* was Manduca da Praia who always dressed in an extremely elegant style. It is said that he owned a fish store and lived comfortably. He held tremendous power, and it is said that he controlled elections in the area he lived in, helping to absolve him from a rumored twenty-seven criminal cases (Hall & Jefferson, 1976). Successful *capoeristas* were able to lead gangs and generate substantial power, sometimes giving them street credibility as small-scale dictators.

Capoeira in the Mainstream

Due to its forbidden practice, capoeira was not popularized in the mainstream until the mid-part of the 1900s. The two central figures responsible for its popularity growth in Brazil were Mestre Bimba and Mestre Pastinha. They are the most prominent figures of capoeira today and their roles in its history are so important that they are considered the "mythical ancestors" of all capoeira players.

In 1932, Mestre Bimba, whose real name was Manuel dos Reis Machado, opened the first capoeira academy in Salvador, Brazil. He started teaching what he called "the regional fight from Bahia," and this eventually became known as *Capoeira Regional*, a faster and more aggressive form than the traditional *Capoeira Angola*. This feat was made possible by nationalistic policies of President Getulio Vargas, who wanted to promote capoeira as a Brazilian sport. Although Bimba opened his school in 1932, official recognition didn't come about until 1937, when it was technically registered. On July 9, 1937, the police turned up at Bimba's school, and he was told to go with them. Bimba was taken to the governor's palace where he was asked to perform the fight-dance with several of his pupils. The performance was a tremendous success and with Bimba convincing the government of the cultural importance of capoeira, it became legalized in enclosed areas that were registered with the police. A new era for capoeira began with the opening of Bimba's academy. The game was taught to the children of the upper classes of Salvador, Brazil. Mestre Bimba remained active in capoeira his whole life and was even planning to give a capoeira demonstration on the day he died, February 5, 1974 (Hall & Jefferson, 1976).

In 1941, Mestre Pastinha, whose official name was Vincente Ferreira Pastinha, opened his Capoeira Angola School. This marked the first time that capoeira was to be taught and practiced openly in a formal setting. He became known as the "Philosopher of Capoeira" because of the many adages that he used. Unfortunately, government authorities confiscated his academy in efforts to reform the *Largo do Pelourinho*, a city-square in Salvador. Although he was promised a new academy, the government never came through. Deeply saddened by this, he confined himself to living in a small room until his death in 1981 at the age of 92 (Hall & Jefferson, 1976).

The influences of Mestre Bimba and Mestre Pastinha were monumental in modernizing and spreading the awareness and popularity of capoeira throughout Brazil. Through their efforts, capoeira was accepted by the masses, and has grown tremendously over the past five decades. In 1974, it was recognized at the national sport of Brazil, calling for the creation of a National Federation of Capoeira in order to unite the sprawling emergences throughout the country (Hall & Jefferson, 1976).

The Elements of Capoeira

In its modern form, capoeira blends a variety of elements to create a unique art form that is both entertaining and acrobatic. More formalized performances generally begin with musicians playing the chief instrument and symbol of capoeira, known as the *berimbau*. This instrument directs the speed and style of the performance through distinctive rhythms. As the chief instrument used in capoeira, the *berimbau* is customarily played by the *mestre*, or *senior capoeirista*. The *berimbau* is made up of a long wooden bow called a *verga*, bent by a steel wire known as *arame* that runs from one end to the other. A hollow gourd called a *cabaça* is attached near the bottom with strong twine, and a thin stick known as a *baqueta*, or informally called a "wacker stick," is used to strike the wire to make a sound. The pitch of the sound is regulated by a coin called a *dobrão*, which is pressed against the wire at different levels ("Berimbau")

There are three distinct types of *berimbaus*, which all differ in tone, size, and musical role. The first type, known as the *gunga*, is a lower-toned *berimbau* marked by a large *cabaça*, a thinner *verga* and a loose *arame*. It generally plays a base rhythm for the performance. The second type of *berimbau*, known as the *médio*, is a medium-toned instrument that generally plays a harmonious rhythm. It is marked by a medium-sized *cabaça*, a thicker *verga* and tighter *arame*. The main rhythm of capoeira is usually played by the third type of *berimbau*, called the *viola*. This is a high-toned *berimbau* marked by a small *cabaça*, a thick *verga*, and a tight *arame*. The variations in tones are determined by the levels of pressure of the *dobrão* against the *arame*. An open tone is generated by not touching the *dobrão* to the *arame*. It the *dobrão* is pressed firmly against the *arame*, a closed tone is generated, and if the *arame* is touched lightly by the *dobrão*, it creates a buzz tone. These tones help to dictate the sound of the *berimbau*, which dictates the movement of the performers ("Berimbau").

The typical performance of capoeira today usually begins with musicians playing instruments such as the *berimbau*, the *atabaque*, (a type of conga drum), the *pandeiro* (tambourine), and *agogo* (bell). The musicians are based at the foot of a circle known as the *roda*. The *roda* is made up of participants who customarily crouch down while musicians and players may be singing a song in Portuguese. Players enter the game from the *pe'da roda* (foot of the circle), usually marking their entrance with something spectacular such as a cartwheel. Once they are in the middle, the two players interact with a series of jumps, kicks, flips, hand and headstands, and other ritualistic moves. Games can be friendly or dangerous with the music playing a major role in dictating the feel. Specifically, the rhythm being played and content of the lyrics ("Berimbau").

The Capoeira Today

Although capoeira no longer acts as a means of resisting oppression, *mestres* still want players to remember the game's original intentions ("Liberation in Motion"). Its popularity has blossomed to all parts of the world and the dance has been assimilated into many cultures with strong acceptance. In Brazil, capoeira is now second in terms of popularity only to soccer amongst all sports. There are no gender-specific roles or boundaries for performers, which has helped to popularize the dance further. The informal nature of the dance allows it to be performed in any type of location. Awareness is being promoted through the teaching of capoeira and schools can be found in every U.S. state as well as each continent, with the exception of Antarctica. The most concentrated display of capoeira in the world can be found in the *favelas*, or slums, of Brazil. It is here that people feel the strongest connection with the cultural symbolism of the dance. It is an art form that grew out of poverty and united people throughout its development. In general, life is difficult for those living in the *favelas*, as they are poverty stricken and lack the luxuries that others take for granted. Capoeira unites individuals on a cultural level and serves as a link between generations; a vehicle to communicate Brazil's history through successive generations.

It is interesting to contemplate the future of capoeira. The dance has evolved from a method of protection to a unique form art that blends martial art with the grace of dance. The ability to perform capoeira anywhere can almost ensure its survival, but there are certain elements to the dance, which may evolve over an extended period of time. Some of these elements include the instruments, movements, and costume. The importance of the *berimbau* in capoeira's performance is highly unlikely to diminish, but the inclusion of brass instruments seems like a possible prospect if performers want to emphasize particular isolated moves. Drums will forever remain an integral part of capoeira as it is essential to maintain a rhythm for the performers to move to, but the particular types may vary to some degree as preference patterns change. There are no formal costumes for performing capoeira; rather, the attire that people are dressed in may dictate whether or not they decide to perform. Traditionally, elaborate costumes have been used to direct more attention to the performers. Examples of these include martial arts attire and the use of bright colors. In the ensuing years, a more formalized costume may develop as the general preferences of individuals blend together to formulate a standard. Through time, new movements may develop as they already have, and people will build in the future upon what is considered spectacular now. One can only speculate what may happen to capoeira in the distant future, but it is evident that the turmoil capoeira has had to endure throughout its history will make it an art form that is incapable of being forgotten.

References

Barley, N. (1983) *The Innocent Anthropologist: Notes From a Mud Hut*. London: Penguin.
Douglas, M. (1966) *Purity and Danger*. London: Routledge & Kegan Paul.
Ezzy, D. (2001). A Simulacrum of Workplace Community: Individualism and Engineered Culture. *Sociology* 35(3), 631–650.
Geertz, C. (1977) *The Interpretation of Cultures*. New York: Basic.
Hall, S., and Jefferson, T. (1976) *Resistance Through Rituals: Youth Subcultures in Post-War Britain*. London: Hutchinson.
Hockey, J., J. Katz and N. Small (2001). *Grief, Mourning and Death Ritual*. Buckingham: Open University Press.
Manning, P. (1989) Ritual Talk. *Sociology* 23, 365–385.
Sanders, B. (2005) In the Club: Ecstasy Use and Supply in a London Nightclub. *Sociology* 39(2), 241–258.

Scheper-Hughes, N. (1992) *Death Without Weeping*. Berkeley: University of California Press.

Stephens, N., and S. Delamont (2006) Balancing the Berimbau: Embodied Ethnographic Understanding. *Qualitative Inquiry*.

Turner, V. (1967) Betwixt and between: The Liminal Period in rites de passage." In *The Forest of Symbols: Aspects of Ndembu Ritual*, 93–111. Ithaca: Cornell University Press.

22. Brazilian Music and Dances

Unlike any other country in South America, Brazil has continually defined itself culturally through its music. "In Brazil, perhaps more than in any other Latin American nation, popular music has traditionally been a potent cultural force" (Moreno, 1982). Through music, Brazilians are able to convey their feeling concerning government, love, and society. Although many musical genres have evolved through Brazil's history following their 1822 liberation from Portugal, this essay will focus on those styles critical to the development of culture in Brazil, namely Choro, Samba, and Bossa Nova.

History

In order to understand the music of Brazil, one must first understand the conditions under which this great nation was forged. Brazil was first discovered by Portugal in 1522 by Portuguese explorers looking for the New World. Soon after they arrived, the Portuguese began establishing colonies where an unprecedented fusion of cultures would occur. In 1822, following the Portuguese crown's fleeing of Portugal in order to avoid confrontation with Napoleon, Brazil was able to declare its national independence. In its wake, Brazil was forced to embrace the cultures of three distinct groups. The first group was that of the Europeans. While Portugal was colonizing Brazil, hundreds of immigrants from Europe crossed the Atlantic in hopes finding opportunity in the New World. The second group was the indigenous groups in Brazil. Prior to the arrival of the Portuguese, hundreds of tribes of indigenous people populated Brazil's immense landscape. The third group was that of the African slaves who were brought over in the slave trade that dominated a good portion of the nineteenth century. This may be the most important group, seeing as no popular Brazilian music lacks elements of African culture in it. Essentially, to understand Brazilian music, one must view Brazil as a giant cultural melting pot in which three cultures melted and reformed into musical genres and dances. Behague (1973) has observed that in the Brazilian context of popular music ... the groups involved are not racially homogenous, yet the meanings associated with their music are distinct to those groups. This seems to be the result of a class social organization rather than of racial subdivisions. The music of Brazil is equally influenced by all faucets of ethnicity in Brazil and each category of music is then categorized by social class. This essay seeks to explore each category of music and the social class that influenced its development.

Choro

The first style of music associated with Brazilian culture was *Choro*. "In principal, all Brazilian instrumental music, which contain at least some elements of Brazilian character, may be considered *Choro*" (Garcia, 1997). Choro is less of a musical statement and more of a style. Defining Choro is more difficult than it seems, and to understand Choro best one would be best suited to view it as a musical cultural icon and base. "Choro is a general term with divergent meanings. The word may designate an instrumental ensemble, the music played by this instrumental group, or certain popular dance forms.... David Appleby suggests that it comes from the Portuguese verb chorar, to cry or weep.... Choro is derived from the melancholy character of the music" (Garcia, 1997, p.57). For the purposes of this paper, we will define Choro as the founding musical style of all Brazilian musical genres. Choro was a Brazilian reaction to its youth as a nation, and most will agree that originally Choro was a way of giving European musical styles a unique Brazilian flare.

The Choro, which emerged around 1870 less as a distinct musical genre and more as a local way of performing the European dance tunes in vogue at the time, especially the polka (Reily, 2000). Choro was developed in the first Brazilian capital of Rio de Janeiro. This is fitting, seeing as Rio was Brazil's central melting pot for its distinctive cultures. The Choro ensemble's roots can be traced to about 1870 in Rio de Janeiro ...

over time, these forms came to be played in a more "Brazilian" manner: a fusion of the diverse elements taken from Portuguese, indigenous, and African cultures, all of which became a part of the local musical landscape (Garcia, 1997). In addition, many view Choro as a reaction to the political landscape in Brazil during the nineteenth century. "The Choro evolved during a period of intense political and social change.... Music was a unifying force during these troubled times, helping to establish a national identity" (Garcia, 1997, p. 59). Choro was Brazil's first groundbreaking cultural ambassador. In a time in which Brazilians were searching for their identity in a society fused together through so many diverse cultures, Choro helped to bridge the gaps that could have been detrimental to Brazil's development as a nation.

Choro as a musical genre is incredibly difficult to define because it encompasses so many modern Brazilian musical genres. In general, Choro refers to the musical ensemble of a wood and string trio, a pianist, and a guitarist. While these are the instruments used to develop the sound, Choro is characterized by its rhythm. Rhythm is the most important element in defining the Choro. Rhythmic freedom has become a principal characteristic of Brazilian popular music in general, and is highly influenced by the indigenous instruments and dance forms (Garcia, 1997). The specific rhythm that is being referred to is the distinctive ABACA tonal structure associated with Choro and all Brazilian forms of music. Although Choro itself was a musical phenomenon, this musical style only scratched the surface of what would follow.

Samba

Samba is considered a descendent of Choro, and is the most popular global form of Brazilian music. The Samba is the most internationally known form of Brazilian popular music. Rhythmically it is from the same mold as the Choro, combining the characteristics of the polka with African rhythmic figures and complexity.... The Samba was an important part of Choro during its heyday and was then the Choro's successor as the most popular Brazilian music form (Garcia, 1997). Tracing the roots of Samba does not take one far away from the roots of Choro. In fact, Choro and Samba were born in the same city and influenced by the same groups of people. The urban Samba originally emerged from the slums of the turn-of-the-century Rio de Janeiro. Its beginnings lay in the rhythmic drumbeats that traditionally accompanied African religious ceremonies brought to Brazil by the African slaves (Raphael, 1990). Samba was a creation of Choro and the next building block in understanding Brazilian music today.

The Samba does not go untouched by the social classes as mentioned earlier. In fact, the majority of the Brazilian middle and upper classes despised the Samba because they felt it was a symbol of the poor. The evolution of Samba constituted a process that was largely alien to the urban middle class in Brazil. The "respectable" middle class had considered the Samba a lowly, primitive musical form and interested itself more in the European and North American traditions (Moreno, 1982). Even though the upper crust of Brazil did not like the Samba or its origins, there is no denying the unbelievably catchy tune of the Samba. Whether they liked it or not, eventually the upper class would grow to love the Samba. During the course of the 1920s, members of the larger society developed an appreciation for the Samba (Raphael, 1990). The Samba today is responsible for the most important cultural event in Brazil, which is Carnival.

Carnival

During one part of the year, usually during summer, the Samba schools in Rio put on the most fascinating show on the face of the planet, *Carnival*. This event would not even exist if not for the cultural assimilation of Samba. In the 1920s the Samba emerged as a sophisticated urban form, undergoing almost continuous change to the present. It became associated with the celebration of Carnival and its driving two-beat rhythm seems to compel the entire country to dance (Garcia, 1997). In no other country in the world has a musical genre encompassed its society quite like Samba. The Brazilian society literally puts itself on hold for four days during February when the entire country celebrates the art and music of Samba. In terms of importance to society, no other icon has done more for equality and national identity than that of the Samba.

Bossa Nova

The next stage of development in Brazilian music is that of *Bossa Nova*. Given the critical role of popular music in the national culture, it would be difficult to overemphasize the significance of Bossa Nova in the formation of contemporary Brazilian society (Moreno, 1982). Bossa Nova

22. Brazilian Music and Dances

seemed destined to re-define the Brazilian music scene as it allowed for the mixing of Brazilian genres, namely Samba. As a variation of Samba, Bossa Nova, meaning "new way," is essentially a form of Afro-Brazilian Samba and has its roots in the music brought to Brazil by African slaves (Moreno, 1982). This new Samba was incredibly popular also because it allowed Brazilian musicians to fuse the music of their culture with the music of other cultures, namely American jazz. The final refinement and successful amalgamation of American jazz and Brazilian Samba resulted in Bossa Nova.... Bossa Nova's main appeal, therefore, was that it combined a prestigious foreign element, American jazz, with a traditional Brazilian form Samba (Moreno, 1982). Bossa Nova is incredibly unique because it offered a solution to Brazilians who still felt Samba was too primitive for their refined tastes. The fusion of American jazz and Brazilian samba was a combination that proved to be unstoppable, and most forms of contemporary Brazilian music still revolve around the sounds of Bossa Nova.

The sound of Bossa Nova is unique and, like the Samba, is grounded in the different rhythmic structures. Its innovative harmonic structure included dissonant tones and frequent key changes; its melodies and bass lines were enriched with chromatic notes; its rhythms were complicated, unexpected and yet typically Brazilian (Moreno, 1982). Brazilian musical tones and rhythms were forever changed by Bossa Nova and the elements that characterized its beat have been forever engrained in the sound of Brazilian music today. The Bossa Nova phenomenon no doubt revolutionized the Brazilian popular music scene (Behague, 1973). Although music is the most important part of Brazilian culture as a whole, specific dances like *Capoeira* have also come to define the cultural melting pot known as Brazil.

Copoeira

When the African slaves arrived in Brazil, they brought with them much more than their physical bodies. They brought with them their cultures, traditions, and art forms. Among these art forms, the Brazilian martial art/music style *Capoeira* was among the most prominent and controversial. For the reader unfamiliar with the sport of Capoeira, let me characterize it as an acrobatic, Afro-Brazilian martial game, played in a circle with musical accompaniment, in which two players try to take each other down, or otherwise dominate each other, while demonstrating mastery of movement (Lewis, 1995).

The Brazilian art form of Capoeira was controversial because in the nineteenth century, elite Brazilians believed that the African slaves were using Capoeira as a means of training to overthrow their masters. Seeing as though this is a game centralized around choreographed fighting, it is not hard to believe that this would have been a highly scrutinized art form. Today, youth in the slums of Brazil have used Capoeira as a way of discouraging others youth from engaging in otherwise prominent forms of petty street crime. Capoeira schools, which are formed by masters, are often attended by Brazilians who do not have as much as their counterparts. They use the art form to channel their frustrations and find worth in a life that for some would seem not worth living.

In terms of Capoeira itself, the process and act is a remarkable sight for all. To describe this act better, one should imagine *Capoeira* in two parts. The first part is that of the fighters themselves. Symbolically, there are usually two fighters who are attempting to defeat each other. The second component is that of the roda, or circle, that encompasses the fighters. Within the roda, there are individuals who are playing music in a call and respond manner, and other students. In *Capoeira* some players take up instruments and sing around the edge of the ring, creating a musical environment for the actions of the two players involved in physical contest inside. Singing is seen as absolutely necessary to the action by many players, and in some styles no physical play can occur without a sung invocation (Lewis, 1995). As seen through this quotation, the concerns of many that Capoeira was a hidden martial arts form and not a musical creation was unfounded. In fact, as previously stated, the music in Capoeira is just as important to the act as the actual fighters in the ring themselves.

Conclusion

Brazilian music is one of the unique phenomena in our history as a musical global society. After studying the musical histories of so many other cultures, it is hard to find another culture in which music has played such a critical role in defining itself and people. Through music, Brazil was able to integrate three completely different groups of people successfully. What may be even more impressive, Brazil is a country that actually declared a national holiday so that they could honor their music and traditions. Through Samba, Choro, and Bossa Nova, Brazilian music has taken the global musical stage by storm. There would be no reason to assume that as time evolves, so will the musical styles of Samba. Given the success of Bossa Nova, one can only sit and wait for the next hot musical style to emerge from the melting pot of cultures and genres in Brazil; a country at the forefront of musical innovation and culture.

References

Behague, Gerard (1973). *Ethnomusicology* 17(2), May, 209–233.
Garcia, Thomas (1997). *Luso-Brazilian Review* 34(1), Summer, 57–66.
Lewis, Lowell (1995). Anthropologies of the Body. *Cultural Anthropology* 10(2), May, 221–243.
Moreno, Albrecht (1982). *Latin American Research Review* 17(2), 129–141.
Raphael, Alison (1990). *Latin American Music Review /Revista de Musica Latinoamericana* 11(1), Spring-Summer, 73–83.
Reily, Ana Suzel (2000). Brazilian Musics, Brazilian Identities. British Journal of Ethnomusicology 9(1), 1–10.

PART III: ASIA

23. The Odissi, a Classical Indian Dance

A country rich in history and tradition, India is home to a variety of dance rituals. There are only six recognized types of classical Indian dance but many modern dances exist as well. Much of India's culture is defined by these classical dances along with the modern dances. While scholars must establish if a dance is classic or not, modern Indian dancing mainly comes from Bollywood movies. The attire is specific for each Indian dance, and traditional costumes, jewelry and make-up are all important aspects of Indian dancing. The Odissi dance is probably the oldest classical Indian dance, originating from the coastal town of Odissa and performed as a religious act of passion.

The Elements of Indian Dance

In order to be considered classical form, the dances must include specific elements that have been present in Indian dance for as long as there have been records. The three main elements are *nritta*, *nritya*, and *natya*; together these elements define what Indian dance is. The nritta is the pure dance, without expression or anything abstract added to it (Khokar, 1984). The nritya is the nritta plus *abhinaya,* which are looks of feeling. *Abhinaya* is expressed by *rasa*, feeling, and *bhava*, disposition. There are numerous *rasas*, one for almost every different type of feeling. The *nritya* is often expressed by *mudras*, the combination of palm, finger, and wrist positions. Generally, the *mudras* accompany the ballad being chanted by the dancer and help express the story being told (Coomaraswamy, 1936). Only a few types of *mudras* exist: the one-hand *mudra* and the two-hand *mudra.* Less than thirty varieties exist in the one-hand category, but there are more in the two-hand category. The positions do not have one particular meaning, but the *mudra* must match the facial expression. The *mudras* also have a symbolic meaning to Shiva Nataraja, the "lord of the dance" in the Hindu religion (Coomaraswamy, 1936). The *natya* is the act of telling a story or topic. *Natyas* are similar to fables and folklores of American tradition. The majority of *natyas* come from old Indian stories and traditions (Khokar, 1984).

Classical Indian Dances

Perhaps the most famous Indian classical dance is the *Bharata Natyam*. This dance developed in Tamilnuada, in the lower region of India. A solo dance, the Bharata natyam is usually performed as an act of adoration to the gods, in particular to Shiva Natyam. The dance has specific dancers, *devadesis*, females who are bound to the Lord Shiva and to Hinduism (Kinsley, 1993). *Devadesis* no longer exist today, but in classical times, they would spend months and even years learning the dance before dancing in public. Most *devadesis* performed in public until health issues, such as sickness or old age, became too great of a concern to perform the dance properly. In order for *devadesis* to stop performing the dance in public, they had to seek permission to have their *tudus* removed. *Tudus* are studs in the ears of the *devadesis*, and once they were removed by a formal procedure, the *devadesis* were allowed to leave the life of public performance (Kinsley, 1993).

The *Odissi* dance is one of the recognized classical dance forms. It originated in the town of Orissa, located on the Bay of Bengal. Orissa is a coastal region, and had an agriculturally based economy. In classical times, the Indian people of Orissa constructed magnificent temples to praise their gods. Each temple was built with prayer and adorned by the skills of masters in craftsmanship, sculptors, and architects (Coomaraswamy, 1936). Each temple was considered a gift to the gods; mainly they were built in order to ensure a prosperous agricultural season. This religious rite was, and is, extremely passionate and sensuous. The Odissi dance was born during the "enchanted millennium of classical art," a time period in which the creation of the arts flourished in India (Kinsley, 1993).

Today, the Odissi dance is still performed as a part of a religious ceremony. However, more often, the Odissi performance is done as a celebration of a "reinvented tradition and heritage." The performance of the Odissi dance is not done solely for religious purposes. It is performed mainly to teach about the history of Indian and Hindu culture, not continue it. The performance is a preservation technique for the Indian society (Kinsley, 1993). Children learn about the dance and the majority of other Indian classical dances by seeing them in performance, not by actually performing them. However, young people do take part in a number of dances, but not always the traditional ones. Modernized versions of classical dances, along with new dances inspired by popular Indian musicals, are taught to children. In Indian culture, all movies are actually musicals, showing the importance of music and dance to the society. From the time they are very young, the music from their religious ceremonies, along with music from movies, are a vital aspect of Indian children's lives (Coomaraswamy, 1936).

At first, scholars were not accepting of the dance; however, when its origin was traced to sculptures in the Ranigumpha caves in Udaygirig, the historical name for Orissa, it became more widely accepted. The sculptures go back to the second century, making the Odissi dance the oldest known classical dance form of India (Kinsley, 1993). Because the original form of the dance could not be found, the Mahari and Achariya people adapted the existing form of the Odissi dance from the Bharata Natyam and the sculptures on the walls of the Ranigumpha caves. The first record of the Odissi dance being performed is found in the manuscripts from Lord Jagannath, performed as a ritual for the pleasure of the lord. Because of the deep roots and traditions of the Odissi dance, it is now acknowledged as a classical dance form. It is a restrained, rhythmic, and real portrayal of a dance recital, becoming the center of art and culture during classical times. The dance is now well established, showing the love, delight and intense passion the Indians have for their gods (Khokar, 1984).

Elements of the Odissi Dance

The Odissi dance begins with a prayer to the gods and a thanksgiving to mother earth, known as the God Vigneshwara. In the Hindu culture, the God Vigneshwara is the god who removes all obstacles from the Hindus lives. After the invocation the viewers of the dance are brought into the world of miming, and with music, they make moves similar to those found in the *Ranigumpha* caves. The introduction to the dance then continues with *nritta*, pure dance, often maintaining a delicate balance between acting and dancing. There is no expression or meaning behind the dance movements. The prelude ends with the *shloga*, a citation either in Sanskrit or Orissi.

Secondly, the *pallavi*, branching from the *jateeswaram* from the Baharata Natyam, this section of the dance is meant to put the spectators in the proper religious mood for the dance. It generally is based on the Gita Govinda, a Hindu tale about the love between Lord Krishna and cowherdess Radha (Kinsley, 1993). The *pallavi* is extremely evocative, filled with sculpturesque stances. At this point, Odissi becomes an expressional dance and the lyrical tone becomes intertwined with extremely fast dance sequences. These sequences contain stances based on the ancient cave drawings. During this part of the dance, the movements become fast paced and intricate. The end of the *pallavi* leads to the *moksha*, the climax of the Odissi dance. This portion comes from the *tillana* from the Bharata Natyam, literally translated to mean salvation or liberation. At this point of the dance, the true religious background of the dance is evident. The spirituality is clear as the audience watches the dancer become lost in the dance. Most dancers describe this feeling as becoming one with the dance; they do not think about what they are doing, it just happens. Most Indians feel the gods take over the physical body, using it to convey the message of faith to the audience (Kinsley, 1993).

The Music of India

Odissi is a combination of *lasya*, femininity, and *tandava*. The dancer must be able to alternate between different dance styles throughout the dance. The music accompanying the dance is a mixture of *Hindustani* and *Carnatic* styles. Hindustani music comes from North India and stems from both Hindu and Muslim musicians. Most Hindustani music begins with an improvised introduction followed by a previously composed piece. This portion is often a short segment played in a continuous cycle and there are particular improvisation aspects to it as well, just with a pre-composed basis. This characteristic makes Hindustani music similar to American jazz music. Carnatic music, the classical music of Southern India, is one of the oldest music traditions in the world. Similar to Hindustani music because of the improvised themes, Carnatic music is monophonic, meaning one-toned. Unlike American music, which can have a variety of tones that may be considered romantic, joyful, ecstatic, depressing, etc., *Carnatic* music is generally only played in one tone, making it easily recognizable. In Carnatic music, there are more than seventy basic tones, providing for a variety of melodic movement.

Clothing of the Odissi Dance

Traditional Indian clothing is worn while performing the Odissi dance. Indian clothing is famous for being exquisite. The embroidery is what sets Indian clothing apart from all other traditional clothing; intricate designs make each individual outfit unique. Often times, particular outfits bear a level of significance to the wearer, signifying a special event or time in their life. Because the dance is a solo dance, and almost always danced by women, their clothing is the most important. Men's clothing is often worn for comfort and nothing else. Fashion and appearance are not as important for men as it is for women in Indian culture. Men typically wear trousers, *lunges* or pajamas, and shirts, *dhotis* and *Kutras*. Women most commonly wear the *sari*, which is the most flattering clothing for all body types. It is worn by draping it around the waist and then wrapping the end over the shoulder. Generally the *sari* reveals the midriff and is worn with the *choli*, a tight-fitting blouse. The sleeves go up to the woman's elbow or upper arm; the *chili* can button in either the front or the back and usually emphasizes the woman's breasts. The *sari* and the *chili* can be made of cotton, silk or synthetic material. The common people usually have clothing made out of cotton while silk is worn by the upper classes and royalty. In some parts of India, an article of clothing called the *ghagra* is worn with the *choli* instead of the *sari*. The *ghagra* is a skirt-like article with pleats sewn in, which reaches the ankles (Kinsley, 1993). A combination outfit, the *salwar-kameez*, is another common costume worn by women. The *salwar* is a rectangular cloth, drawn at the waist and tapering to the ankles. The *kameez* is similar to a long shirt or dress, worn over the *salwar*. Usually the *kameez* has long sleeves, slits up the sides, and buttons up the front. Instead of a *salwar*, women can wear a *churidar*, a tighter version of the *salwar*, with the *kameez*. The *dupatta* is often worn with the *salwar-kameez* and the *ghagra-choli*, used to cover the chest and head (Khokar, 1984).

Jewelry is a vital aspect of Indian costuming. Gold is the most common metal worn. Gold is often combined with precious gems and beads to accentuate the clothing. Women usually receive gold ornaments as part of their dowry on their wedding day, symbolizing economic status. Most often, the jewelry is worn against the skin. The nose pin, similar to the nose ring, is a symbol of purity and marriage in Indian culture although, as time evolves, unmarried women now also wear nose rings or pins. Necklaces are a very popular piece of jewelry and can be made out of everything from glass beads to gold and diamonds. The *mangalasutra* is the most significant necklace, traditionally worn as a symbol of a wedded woman. Women wear the *mangalasutra* from the day of their wedding until their husband dies. Bangles are worn on the wrist and are believed to be a protective barrier women have over their husbands. Ear ornaments, studs, and rings are extremely popular. Most girls have their ears pierced at least once by the time they turn one year of age. Other significant ornaments include finger rings, toe rings and anklets. Finger rings can be worn by all women of all ages and classes. Toe rings and anklets, however, are only worn by married women. These ornaments are typically made of silver because gold is considered a "pure" metal and not supposed to be worn on the feet. Only royal Indian families are permitted to wear gold on their feet. The *mangatika*, or *tikli*, is traditionally worn as an ornament on women's heads. It is a small pendant on the end of a chain, attached to the hair, worn in the parting of the hair. Historically in India, married women wore the *mangatika*, but today even married women rarely wear it (Kinsley, 1993).

Traditionally, Indians wear specific make-up in everyday life and while performing dances. *Kajal* is similar to eyeliner and is first worn when a child is six days old. It is worn on the eyes, as well as in a black dot in the middle of the child's forehead. This dot is supposed to mar the child's beauty, and this lack of perfection is said to protect the child from evil. As the child gets older, the mother no longer applies *kajal* to the forehead, but it is still worn on the female's eyes. After getting married, Indian women wear a *sindoor*, a dot on the forehead, symbolic of their married status. The *sindoor* offers power and protection for the husband, and is applied by the husband as a part of the wedding ceremony (Kinsley, 1993).

Conclusion

The classical Indian dance the *Odissi*, originated in the second century during classical Indian times. The Odissi has deeply religious roots, first performed as an act of adoration for the Lord Vigneshwara, and portrays the story of the love Lord Krishna had for cowherdess Radha. To perform this dance, the dancers must maintain an extraordinary level of skill, exemplified by the rapid, intricate dance sequences. Indians perform the Odissi dance today on specific occasions for religious purposes, but otherwise, it is only performed as sort of an exhibition. The Odissi dance, one of the oldest known Indian dances, is an important part of Indian culture. Watching a performance of the Odissi dance is like watching a dance recital, tender and vigorous, yet intensely erotic and devotional, making it a unique experience for all. The Odissi dance is continuous a source of inspiration for the Indian people, and it transcends all the limits of communication between the gods and their people. The Odissi dance is for all people extending across the barriers of classes and meant for all times.

References

Clooney, Francis X. (1998). *Hindu Wisdom for All God's Children*. New York: Orbis.
Coomaraswamy, Ananda (1936). *The Mirror of Gesture*. New York: E. Weyhe.
Devi, Ragini (1972). *Dance Dialects of India*. Delhi: Vikas.
Ellfeldt, Lois (1976). *Dance, from Magic to Art*. Dubuque, IA: Wm. C. Brown.
Ghosh, Manmohan G. *Natyasastra Translation*. Calcutta: Royal Asiatic Society of Bengal, 1950.
Hanna, Judith Lynne (1988). *Dance, Sex and Gender*. Chicago and London: University of Chicago Press.
Hanna, Judith Lynne (1988). *Dance and Stress: Resistance, Reduction and Euphoria*. New York: AMS, 1988.
Jansen, Eva Rudy (1993). *The Book of Hindu Imagery: The Gods and Their Symbols*. Diever, Holland: Binkey Kok.
Jones, Clifford (1980). *Kathakali: Epic Dance-Drama of India*. Monographs on Asian, Music, Dance and Theatre in Asia, VII. New York: Asia Society.
Khokar, Mohan (1984). *Traditions of Indian Classical Dance*. New Delhi: Clarion.
Kinsley, David R. (1993). *Hinduism: A Cultural Perspective*. Englewood Cliffs, NJ: Prentice Hall.
Kirk, James A. (1972). *Stories of the Hindus*. New York: Macmillan.
Knott, Kim (1998). *Hinduism: A Very Short Introduction*. New York: Oxford University Press.
Majumdar, D.N. (1961). *Races and Cultures of India*. New York: Asia House.
Ortner, Sherry B., and Harriet Whitehead, eds. (1981). *Sexual Meanings: The Cultural Construction of Gender and Sexuality*. New York: Cambridge University Press.
Parthasarathy, R. (1992). *The Tale of an Anklet, An Epic of South India, The Cilappatikaram of Ilanko Atikal* (Translated, with an Introduction and Postscript). New York: Columbia University Press.
Rangacharya, Adya. (1992). *Introduction to Bharata's Natya-Sastra*. Bombay: Popular Prakashan.

24. The Bharata Natyam and Kathak Dances of India

Origins of Classical Indian Dance

According to Hindu mythology, there was no dance until the end of the Golden Age. During the hundreds of thousands of years of the Golden Age, virtue was present everywhere and morality was at its peak. It is said that, after the Golden Age, the gods became restless and, led by Indra, appealed to Brahma, the creator, for a pleasant way to spend their time. They asked that the pastime be appealing to all the senses and should be allowed in all castes and classes (Khokar, 1979). In response to their pleas, Brahma created a technique of theatre that portrayed *Vedas*, or eternal truths. He enlisted the help of Bharata, a trusted sage, in performing his techniques (Khokar, 1979). With the help and advice of Lord Shiva, dance was added to the technique. As a result, Bharata wrote the *Natya Sastra* outlining all the aspects of Indian classical dance (Khoka, 1979). The *Natya Sastra* is the oldest known text on Indian dance and was written by Bharata between 200 BC and AD 200. It is there that the formal rules and techniques of Indian dance were laid out and expounded upon. They are still followed today (Mathur, 2005). Whether or not one takes the story of Bharata, Brahma, and Lord Shiva literally, the creation of the *Natya Sastra* demonstrates that Indian dance has been held in high regard since the beginning of Hindu civilization.

Dance played a key role in Hindu religion and devotion and, in so doing, formed the tradition of *Devadasis*, also known as temple dancing girls. These girls were given much respect and status and their sole responsibility was to dance and perform for the temple god (Kishore, 2005). In addition, *devadasis* were in reality married to the temple god and served him not only as worshipers, but as wives. Dancing as an Indian art form was born and nurtured in temples and is considered a form of devotional expression. Today, all classical Indian dancing begins with a prayer and any dance that does not is considered vulgar. Some even go so far as to state:

> dancing is vulgar in which the actress does not begin with a prayer, and those who look upon the dancing of such a vulgar actress will have no children, and will be reborn in animal wombs.—Abhinaya Darpana of Nandikeshvara [Kishore, 2005, p. 3].

Technique

Indian dance can be placed into two categories: *nritya* and *nritta*. *Nritya* is dance with miming and gesticulation set to words in a song. It is also known as *abhinaya*, which is Sanskrit for *abhi* meaning "towards," and *ni*, meaning "to carry" (Dhananjayan). This type of dance seeks to portray emotions through body language, especially facial expressions, eye movements, and hand gestures known as *mudras* (Mathur). *Nritya* as expression can be put into four categories: *angika, vachikabhinaya, aharyabhinaya*, and *satvikabhinaya*. The first, *angika*, refers to any physical movement used to convey meaning, including *mudras* and poses. The second, *vachikabhinaya*, refers to any vocal and verbal expression given through the song accompanying the dance. The third, *aharyabhinaya*, is the mood expressed by the environment through make-up, costumes, and sets. The fourth, *satvikabhinaya*, refers to psychological expression given especially through the dancer's eyes and overall character (Matu, 2005).

On the other hand, *nritta* is considered pure dancing in which all movements and gestures do not convey any mood or meaning. This type of dance's emphasis is on aesthetic beauty and the statuesque poses and stances in the dance are considered vital. Not only does the *nritta* involve many symbolic poses but it also communicates the song's *tala*, or rhythm (Vatsyayan, 1995).

Indian dance embraces the ideal of balance and perfect vertical movement. Dance reflects the movement of human forms under the influence of gravity. It is because of this value that Indian dance lacks quick leaps and gliding movements commonly seen in Western ballet. In Indian dance, the dancer attempts not to cover or eliminate space by large and leaping movements, but to achieve a space beyond time by creating a consummate scoundrel pose within the *tala* (Vatsyayan, 1995).

Bharata Natyam

This dance developed in Tamil Nadu is considered the oldest classical Indian dance (Mathur, 2005). The Bharata Natyam is a deeply spiritual dance and is connected to the *devadasis* institution of temple dancers. Because of the connection to the *devadasis*, the dance was considered a sacred offering. Anciently, it was performed in front of an image of the temple deity as part of a ritual inside the temple and was even performed outside on religious celebrations. In Bharata Natyam, both pure dance and expression have equal value (Khokar, 1979). Expression (*Nritya*) is seen in the dancer's interpretation of a song. The dancer's face shows emotions in response to both the words of the song and the feeling of the music. All aspects of the face are used to express a number of different emotions including the eyes, eyebrows, mouth, lips, and cheeks. More concrete images and ideas are communicated with other parts of the body such as the hands and feet. The dominant emotion in Bharata Natyam is devotional love for the deity (Khokar, 1979).

In earlier days, Bharata Natyam was both a solo and group dance. The solo form that it now takes was developed around the nineteenth century and is credited to four brothers from Tanjore: Chinnayya, Ponnayya, Vadivelu, and Sivanandam. The dance as it is today is considered a narration given by the dancer and is divided into six distinct parts.

The first part is the *alarippu*. The word *alarippu* literally means "bud blossoming," perhaps because it is the literal unfolding of the dance to follow (Jeyaseelan, 2005). It is an invocation, or prayer, invoking the blessing of the gods for a successful dance. This is performed merely to the rhythm of the drum and is considered pure dance (*nritta*) without expression or meaning. The basic movements begin with the dancer in consummate scoundrel balance in a standing position and continue with movements of the shoulders, neck, and arms. All movements and positions of the limbs are in their simplest form and can be considered a "warm-up" for the rest of the dance (Vatsyayan, 2005).

The second part is the *jatisvaram*, also categorized as *nritta*. In this section of the dance, the dancer's movements are guided by the music accompanying the dance. The word "*jatisvaram*" comes from the title of a musical score that has three separate movements made unique by the absence of any poetry. It is this score that the dancer follows. As the melodic line varies within the metrical beat, the dancer introduces different rhythmic patterns of dance. Within these variations, however, the first beats of each new melodic line and rhythmic pattern correspond perfectly with the end of each dance sequence (Vatsyayan, 2005). The *jatisvaram* allows the dancer to perform as much pure dance as possible and allows for a variety of artistic creation and demonstration of the performer's talents (Vatsyayan, 2005). It is known for complex footwork, captivating poses and body movements (Jeyaseelan, 2005).

The third part is the *sabdam*. This is where the dancer first introduces expression and miming. The expression is made to be easy to interpret and very literal (Vatsyayan, 1995). The song that this part is set to usually has a devotional, heroic, or love theme and commonly sings the praises of a god or tells a myth (Jeyaseelan, 2005). The *sabdam* is a short section of the Bharata Natyam that serves primarily as a transition between the pure dance of the *jatisvaram* and the highly expressional dance of the upcoming *varnam* (Vatsyayan, 1995).

The fourth part is the *varnam*. This is the climax of the dance and the most intricate and elaborate of the performance. It is in this section that the dancer's talent and skill reaches their full potential (Jeyaseelan, 2005). It provides the dancer with the best opportunity to improvise and express the theme of the dance. The dancer begins with an introduction that must be exactly coordinated between dancer, singer, and drummer. After that, the rest of the *varnam* alternates between expressional dance and intricate footwork and movement set to variations of the rhythm, or *tala*. The start of each pure dance sequence is precluded by a stamping of the feet to the time cycle (Vatsyayan, 1995). The subject of the song that the dance expresses is usually the god Vishnu or Shiva and it describes his many characteristics and virtues. The song tells of the worshiper's love and devotion for the god and expresses a yearning for his presence. In turn, the dance communicates at this point the strongest sense of faith and idolization of a human for something beyond himself. The dancer is allowed considerable freedom of interpretation during the *varnam*. Gestures can be literal and follow the words of the song exclusively or merely convey an overall meaning or feeling. Indeed, without creative freedom it would be impossible for the *varnam* to be as appealing and obtain the complexity for which it is so well known (Vatsyayan, 1995).

The fifth part is the *padam*. The *padam* serves to soften the mood and tempo after the high energy *varnam* (Jeyaseelan). It is a time for relaxation that can last up to an hour. During this part of the dance, the dancer performs several small separate numbers known individually as "*padams*," hence the name of this portion of the dance. Each *padam* is an expressional dance set to a lyrical song (Vatsyayan, 1995). Most *padams* explain the love life and adventures of Hindu deities, especially Krishna and Kartikeya (Khokar, 1979). The general theme of the *padam* is usually the longing of a woman for her lover and is symbolic of a human's longing for the divine. Therefore, the dance can be interpreted on two levels: the literal and the symbolic. This part of Bharata Natyam is only taught by *gurus*, or master dance teachers, once a dancer has reached a sufficient level of maturity to perform and understand the double meaning (Vatsyayan, 1995).

The sixth part is the *tillana*. This is considered a dynamic example of pure dance. The dancer performs more statuesque poses here than in any other part of the dance. Multiple tempos are used and dance movements go from the center of the body's vertical axis to the diagonal, and even the triangular. The end of the *tillana* is the grand finale of the dance and ends at a fast tempo with sudden cessation of movement or a quick exit by the dancer.

In recent years, there has been one addition to Bharata Natyam's grand finale. It is becoming more common to follow the *tillana* with a *sloka*, which is a slow, rhythmic chanting of a benediction. This chanting is solemn, reverent, and attempts to bring the deity to a sufficiently phlegmatic and peaceful mood. It is traditionally chanted in Sanskrit language and literature (Vatsyayan, 1995).

Costume

Regardless of the theme or story the dancer is performing, there is traditionally no variation in the costume worn. This includes both the dress that is worn and jewelry worn on various parts of the body. The *devadasi* dress worn during the dance is comprised of well-fitted *pyjamas* underneath a long *sari* of silk or brocade. One end of the *sari* comes up between the legs in the front and is tucked in the back. The other end reaches across the chest and over the shoulder. The blouse worn is short with short sleeves and is traditionally very vibrantly colored. As for makeup, the eyes are outlined with kohl while the palms of the hand and the soles of the feet are painted red. Many different types of jewelry are used including necklaces, earrings, head pendants, nose rings, finger rings, bangles, and ankle bells. The ankle bells can contain up to 100 bells on each leg and serve a dual purpose of both ornament and a rhythm keeper (Khokar, 1979).

Bharata Natyam is often considered the most graceful, traditional, and religious of all the Indian classical dances. As such, it takes many years of extensive training and practice to learn and perfect (Jeyasellan, 2005). Indeed, Bharata Natyam dancers are never considered amateurs because of their many years of exacting training and practice (Kishore, 2005).

Kathak

The name "Kathak" comes from the word *katha*, which literally means "story." The Kathaks were a group of story tellers throughout different temples in North India. They originally merely told their stories orally but eventually added miming and expression, creating a dance form called "Kathak." It is by nature an extremely expressional dance since its purpose is to convey the meaning of a story (Khokar, 1979). As it was taken from Hindu temples into both Hindu and Muslim courts, emphasis on the religious aspect of the dance shifted focus to a view of the dance as a highly stylized form of entertainment. In Hindu courts, the pure dance aspect of the dance was cherished and valued more than anything else. As a result, it became more of a dazzling display for the eyes and less of a portrayal of a story. However, in the Muslim courts, emphasis was placed on how the dance could portray emotions and stories from everyday life. Hence, the Muslim school of Kathak focuses more on the expressional (*nryita*) part of the dance (Khokar, 1979).

From the time of its development, Kathak has been a dance intended for performance before a small audience. This has made all of the techniques and expressions within the dance necessarily more intense and elaborate. In a traditional Kathak performance, the audience is seated on the floor in a circle around the dancer or to the side of him. No specific music is required for the dance, and the music consists of the *tabla*, which are drums, and the *sarangi*, which is a string instrument. These two instruments plus the ankle bells called *ghunghroos* on the feet of the dancer, are the main source of music and rhythm for the dance. The dancer signals to the *sarangi* player to begin playing a line of music in the *tala*, or beat, and after it has been played a few times, the dancer begins. The dance movements consist of imposing stances, gliding movements of the wrist and neck, and quick darting eye movements (Khokar, 1979).

Since timing and rhythm is the key factor in Kathak, the most important movement is the footwork. The ankle bells strapped to the dancer's feet control the rhythm and movement of the dance. The most basic footwork in Kathak is called *tatkar* and involves striking the feet flat in a small space. *Tatkar* can be in done in single, double, and quadruple speeds. More advanced dancers can exceed the quadruple speeds. When the feet are in a slow speed, the hands stay in front of the body near the torso (Khokar, 1979).

In addition to footwork, Kathak also contains *Gat-Bhava*. During *Gat-Bhava*, the dancer takes the story he wishes to tell and interprets it through different body movements, especially facial expressions and hand motions. Typically, the dancer takes a simple theme such as Krishna playing a flute and expresses it in multiple ways.

Kathak dancers are generally expected to be able to improvise. A good dancer has to be alert and ready to create different expressions that fit within changing time variations. Dancers are also expected to bring new interpretations to old themes that they have perhaps performed in the past (Khokar, 1979).

Costume

Costume and make-up is not very important to Kathak. In the beginning of its development, male dancers dressed very simply with a colored drape for the legs called *dhoti* and the addition of some jewelry. After the introduction of Kathak to both the Hindu and Muslim court, dancers came to wear close-fitting *churidar pyjamas,* a long coat, and a hat or turban. Female dancers wore similar costumes. For make-up, men, used merely kohl to outline the eyes, while women wore face paint with black unguent on the eyes and betel-leaf to make the lips red (Khokar, 1979). Kathak is unique in that it is the only classical Indian dance that has links to Muslim culture and is the only dance to feature North Indian music.

Conclusion

Both Bharata Natyam and Kathak are ancient stylized forms of dancing. They both have purpose and meaning that drives the dancers. There is criticism of Indian dance as an art form because has too many rules to be truly creative and therefore truly art. However, although both of these dances are highly stylized and have set rules, each provides multiple opportunities for dancers to improvise and express themselves both as a dancer and a communicator of a story. Both dances require not only many years of hard work to be performed but a certain degree of artistic talent in order for them to succeed. Bharata Natyam and Kathak deserve much respect and admiration as performance art in its truest form.

References

Antze, Remary Jeanes (1992). Teacher, Student, Lineage. *Parabola* (Fall) Retrieved from EBSCO Host, October 18, 2000.
Bibliographic Guide to Dance. (1995). New York: G.K. Hall.
Dhananjayan, V.P. (2005). A Dancer on Dance. Retrieved October 23, 2005, from www.india-heritage.org.
Gray, J.E.B. (1961). *Indian Tales and Legends*. Oxford: Oxford University Press.

Jeyaseelan, Drioshan (2005). Classical Indian Dance. Retrieved on November 9, 2005, from www.fortunecity.com/Victorian/parkwood/388/dance.html.
Kendamath, C.G. (1986). *Indian Music and Dance: A Select Bibliography*. Varanasi: Indian Bibliographic Centre.
Khokar, Mohan (1979). *Traditions of Indian Classical Dance*. New Delhi: Clarion.
Kishore, B.R. (2005). Dances of India: An Encounter with Reality through Dance. Retrieved October 30, 2005, from www.4to40.com/discoverindia/index.asp?article=discoverindia_dancesofindia1.
Londhe, Veena (1992). *Hand Book of Indian Classical Dance Terminology*. Bombay: Nalanda Dance Research Centre.
Massey, Reginald, and Rina Singha (1967). *Indian Dances: Their History and Growth*. New York: George Braziller.
Mathur, Asharani (2005). India Heritage: Performing Arts. Retrieved November 7, 2005, from www.indiaheritage.com/perform/dance.htm.
Matu, Sangeeta (2005). Dances of India. Retrieved August 26, 1999, from http://www.angelfire.com/ma2.bharatanatyam/bn.html.
Nair, Savitiry (1993). Hands that Speak Volumes. *UNESCO Courier*, September. Retrieved from EBSCO Host, October 18, 2000.
Van Zile, Judy (1973). *Dance in India: An Annotated Guide to Source Material*. Providence: Asian Music.
Vatsyayan, Kapila (1974). *Indian Classical Dance*. Calcutta: Hooghly.
Vatsyayan, Kapila (1995). The Future of Dance Scholarship in India. *Dance Chronicle 18*(3): 485–90.

25. The Kundiman, Sinulog and Tinikling Dances of the Philippines

For centuries, music and dance has remained prevalent in the Filipino culture and has molded the Filipino national identity. While the Philippines house a diverse socio-cultural heritage such as from America and Spain, many musical and dance traditions such as the *Tinikling* and *Sinulog* dances have been preserved, and thus have endured the test of time. The *Tinikling* dance is regarded as one of the most popular dances in the Philippines and is also noted as the Filipino national dance. The *Sinulog* dance, while more traditional, is considered by many historians as channel between past and present (Ness, 1992). The *Kundiman* dance is another form of Filipino dance that remained impervious to western influence.

History of the Philippines

Comprised of approximately seven thousand islands, the Philippines carry a diversity of cultures, religions, and lifestyles within each island. More than one hundred Malay languages and dialects have evolved in the chain of islands. Even though the Philippines have been dominated by Spanish rule for three centuries, Spain was unable to create a unified society. Family relationships and ethnic and regional fidelities were an important part of life. The economic system was dependent on plantation agriculture, tenant farming, and sugar harvesting. The Filipino musical tradition is rich and has many regional variations that can be traced to Spanish and Western influences. Lullabies are among the oldest songs in Filipino history and were primarily representations of life. Songs were sometimes about sorrow, work, love, war, or marriage (Lockard, 1998). While each region had a unique music tradition, the Western bearing had an overpowering effect in the way that music and dance had developed. The Philippines was exposed to new instruments such as the violin, the guitar, and the piano. Soon the Spanish and Filipino cultures had merged and the newly introduced instruments became a part of the Filipino music. New dances had also evolved due to the Spanish hold over the Philippines. The Sinulog dance of Cebu City is Spanish influenced and celebrates Christianity and the Spanish revered saint, Santo Paz. Other dances have emerged as a result of the Spanish domination, while retaining their Filipino identities.

The Kundiman Dance

The *Kundiman* dance, for example, glorifies the Philippines and expresses the Filipinos' patriotism and love for their country. The *Kundiman* is an emotion-filled dance that laments the Spanish oppression and squelching of Filipino national ideas and positions. As the dance evolved, metaphorical applications about slavery and national heroes were tied with the dance, but soon the *kundiman* became more associated with sentiments of love and relationships. The *kundiman* is a song that conveys the grief and sadness of a troubled young man or woman over their lover. The song is played in a minor key and is written in triple time (Lockard, 1998). While there are many suggested theories as to how the *kundiman* originated, one underlying theory remains. The term *kundiman* is a shortened expression of the phrase "if it were not so." The song and dance's original patriotic form resulted in an expression of love for a woman who symbolized the Philippines. While the song was masked as a song intended for a young girl, Jocelynang Baliwag, a popular revolutionary called the song "*Kundiman of the Revolution,*" because it was really a song about liberating the enslaved people of the country.

The *kundiman* was dominant between the 1800s and the 1930s during which it went through many transformations. While the *kundiman* originally began as a declaration of love, the song and dance was then infused with Western dance forms such as the waltz, the fandango, and the danza. The song then changed from extemporaneous lyrical writing to poetic verses by poets such as Jose Corazon de Jesus, Jesus Balmori, and Deogracias A. Rosario. The songs, however, still maintained themes of love, sorrow, and heartbreak. The final change took place in the early twentieth century as a result of the American cohabitation. Composers of the song were frequently influenced by the academe and musicians such as Nicanor Abelardo and Francisco Santiago who changed the status of the song and transformed it into an art song. Santiago was a major contributor in changing the *kundiman*'s style and delivery. He changed the folk song and divided it into three parts. "*Anak Dalita,*" which translates to "Child of Woe," was Santiago's first *kundiman*. Abelardo later composed more *kundimans*, which were inspired by the works of Santiago. His more notable works include "*Mutya ng Pasig*" (Muse of Pasig), "*Kundiman Ng Luha*" (Kundiman of Tears: "Let Fall Your Perfumed Handkerchief/ To Wipe Away My Heart's Tears"), and "*Nasaan Ka Irog*" (Where are You, My Love). The love songs were mainly featured in plays, films, and musicals and were used by sarswela composers. The *kundiman* created by Abelardo, "*Bituing Marikit*" (Beautiful Star), was used by Sarswela writer Servando de los Angeles (Ness, 167). The song lamented the pains of a distraught lover begging for the light from his beloved. The song was used as a title song in a 1937 film. Currently, the song is associated more with passion filled emotions and sentiments rather than literary musical forms.

History's Effect on Filipino Music and Dance

Between 1898 and 1946, the Philippines came under the control of the United States. National sentiments were strong and remained a part of the songs written by writers and poets. In 1898, the Spanish-American War was fought and America had become a primary participant in the war. When the Americans defeated the Spanish, they announced that it was their obligation to change the Philippines and to civilize and inspire the Filipinos. While the revolution had ended, the United States was free to do whatever they wished to do with the Philippines. During the "benevolent assimilation," which was the American colonization, the Americans had taken over the education and public welfare and developed a land ownership system where powerful landowners were allowed to control the land of poor peasant tenants (Lockard, 1998). Under the United States rule, the Philippines underwent several changes in their culture and customs.

During the Revolution, Filipino music expressed sentiments of love for the country and a fundamental nostalgia for the country. At the time, the folk songs that were created expressed the interest in peasant work, moral behavior, and daily life. *"Ing Bangkeru,"* (The Boatman) is a song that praises the peasant's disposition and character. Other songs addressed concerns with maintaining national identity and pride. The ballad *"Ang Paghihimagsik,"* for instance, is a song about a peasant's long fight for independence and freedom.

As portions of the Spanish and American cultures infiltrated the Philippines, problems and concerns arose over the country's national identity. Many nationalists believed that the American command over the Philippines had disrupted the country's attempts of being a truly independent nation. Filipinos had vacillating feelings about the United States and they continued to go through stages of love for the United States and then love for the Philippines. The country's identity problems continued, and in 1988, Senator Leticia Ramos Shahani summoned for an official study of the problems associated with Filipino culture. The problem of developing a national identity from a diversity of other languages and cultures was never completely determined. According to Lockard (1998), a cultural researcher culturally, the Filipinos are not a nation yet. Neither is there a language with which they can successfully communicate. The [national] government and culture do not coincide). Despite the conflicting feelings towards America, America was a significant part of Filipino culture and established a strong base in films, music, TV programs, and popular literature.

The Sinulog Dance

Sinulog is another popular form of dance that evolved throughout the span of many decades. It is a dance that originated from Cebu City

25. Kundiman, Sinulog, Tinikling (Philippines)

and is a theatrical ritual that was noted as emanating from a masculine style of tradition. The dance expressed the social and religious contexts of Cebu City and was a tradition of religious reverence. The dance was performed in honor of the religious figure Santo Nino. Danced to the sound of drums, the dance movements involve two forward steps and one backward step. The movement mimics the current (which translates to *Sulog*) of the Cebu's Pahina River. *Sinulog* is a dance that has pagan roots and was already performed in the fourteenth century by natives to glorify and respect the wooden idols. In 1521, Portuguese navigator Magellan came to Cebu and introduced Christianity. As a baptismal gift to Rajah Humabon's wife, Hara Amihan, Magellan presented her with the Santo Nino, which is the image of the child Jesus. Christianization of the islands, however, was not fully established until forty-four years later when Miguel Lopez de Legaspi landed in Cebu on April 28, 1565. He assailed the villages and made his conquest. During that time between the Spanish Conquest, the natives of Cebu continued to dance the *Sinulog* but this time as a sign of devotion for the Santo Nino. Throughout the course of time since 1521, the *Sinulog* was a simple ritual dance performed by all villagers and was danced near the Santo Nino church. Villagers would dance by candlelight and would make sacrificial offerings either to the wooden idols or to Santo Nino. The dance would be performed on the third Sunday of January and children would don elaborate costumes called *Moro-Moro*. In the beginning, when the *Sinulog* had been performed, the ritual was not deemed as a major event in Cebu. However, in 1980, David S. Odilao, Jr., the regional director of Sports and Youth Development, arranged the first *Sinulog* parade. Children were taught how to dance the *Sinulog* to the beating of the drums, and they performed the dance around the Basilica. While the parade began as a small event, the people of Cebu then decided to make the *Sinulog* into a major festival.

Many natives of Cebu regard the *tindera sinulog* (another form of the *sinulog*) as the original dance form. *Tindera* referred to the street vendors who sold candles to visitors and family members on the Basilica. It is recognized as the "true, authentic" version because the dance form does not require elaborate preparation such as a particular type of music or a unique costume (Ness, 68). The performer also did not need to have any inherent skill when dancing the *tindera sinulog*. The dance was very simple and did not have any extensive movement. The dance was a native custom that developed in Cebu City. The choreography of the *tindera sinulog* did not have any outward influences. It was in fact deemed as being pure and much localized. The dance was an expression of the natives' daily habits and practices. Moreover, the *tindera sinulog* was a result of the city's most prominent structural tendencies (Ness, 91). Because the dance emulated the people's ideas and values, it served as a means of maintaining the Filipino national identity.

While the *tindera sinulog* was viewed as a ritual act, it was still a social dance. The dance held two services to the people. It functioned either as a *pagpasalamat*, which was an act of thanksgiving, or a *gihangyo*, which was a special entreaty. The dance had served as an act of reverence to the Santo Nino and was considered a sacrificial offering. While the *tindera sinulog* was deemed a religious act, it was not performed concurrently with prayer and it did not serve as a channel to enter an entranced state of mind. Instead, it was just viewed as another form of prayer. The *tindera sinulog* had three separate stages that began the introductory rite. During this stage, the *tindera* would stand straight in a solid manner and would outstretch his/her arms while holding candles. The dancer would then face the Santo Nino statue and hold the candles toward the image. In this stage, the *tindera* would remain still and recite prayers to the Santo Nino. The prayers were usually dedicated to a family member or loved one. This initial stage of performance indicates that the *tindera sinulog* was a very intimate ritualistic form of dance where the dancer would voice prayers to the Santo Nino. The prayers and entreaties usually differed within age and gender groups. Normally, males would ask for safety and refuge from evil spirits, while young couples implored for a long-lasting relationship or marriage. Wives sometimes called for help in sorting out marital problems, and mothers asked for health and good fortune for their children. The dance was usually performed in celebration of the living; it was not typically performed for the deceased (Ness, 133).

The second phase of the *tindera sinulog* involved more movement, but still maintained the same general style of dance as the first phase. The second stage of the *tindera sinulog* had a more abstruse, transcendental form of motion. This time the dancer focused more on his/her abilities to connect emotionally with the Santo Nino instead of concentrating on his/her own prayers and intentions. The energy, facial expressions, and hand gestures changed. The dance movements heavily emphasized the emotions of the performer. The *kasubo*, which was a sad dance, had a downward and languid movement and was accompanied by a slow rhythm. The *kasaya* dance, which was a joyful dance, had more upward and energetic movements and was performed to a quick beat. This middle stage was known as the *pahinongdan* or *magendorsar* phase, which meant "dedication" or "endorsement." The candle that was used in the dance was a symbol of the thoughts and emotions of the dancer. The intermediate phase differed from the initial and final phase because the movements were not practiced in advance, and were therefore more spontaneous. If the dance was rehearsed, it was thought that the dance would lose its sense of genuineness.

The last stage of the *tindera sinulog* reverted back to the static position. Prayers were often recited again to the Santo Nino and reflected the first stage of the performance. As the ritual ended, the dancers each bowed before the statue of the Santo Nino, which signified a form of respect to the image and signaled the end of the ritual.

The *Sinulog* has many masculine and feminine styles. In each form, the movements are identified with impromptu, unconstrained body gestures. The movements that were noted as customary in men were not considered natural for women. The masculine style of *sinulog* featured more animated and high-powered movements, whereas the feminine style was more reserved and subdued. Jumping and arm gestures that simulated fighting movements such as sword fighting, stick fighting, or spear throwing was common in the masculine form of *sinulog*. Two different styles of dance practices emerged from the *Sinulog*, and they include a healing dance and a war dance. Inside the Santo Nino church, the masculine style was performed during fiesta time when the *sinulog* was at the apex of the religious ceremony. Howling and loud shrieking was typical when performing the masculine form of *sinulog*. Occasionally, women partook in the ritual as well. Women would wear white handkerchiefs on their heads and they would wave the handkerchiefs in the air and tear them to pieces. When the dancing in the church subsided, each participant of the dance would go in front of the Santo Nino statue and kiss its foot. People danced the *sinulog* to honor the Santo Nino. After completing the dance, men and women felt more enlightened and peaceful because the dance was an assurance that their family and homes would be blessed.

In 1984, a small group of performers gathered to perform a sacred act. In this ceremony, a peasant farmer by the name of Iklot vowed to train young boys to dance the *sinulog*. Iklot's *sinulog* has similarities to a Spanish dance that was performed in by boy choristers. In Seville, choristers performed the dance as a means to cure and alleviate the pain among the ill. It was also danced to revere the Virgin Mary and the Corpus Christi. In some aspects, the *sinulog* resembles the Seville chorister dancing in its delivery and function.

The Tinikling Dance

Tinikling, another popular form of dance in the Philippines, is the most common dance and is considered the Philippines' national dance. The dance originated from the Visayan province of Leyte and is also referred to as the "Bamboo dance" because bamboo shoots are an important feature of the performance. The movements resemble the swiftness and vitality of a bird called the *Tikling*. The birds frolic and play with one another, running over branches and escaping the farmer's bamboo traps. The villagers of Leyte deem the movements of the *Tikling* as unique. Dancers imitate the birds' movements by dancing in between the bamboo poles. Swift movements accompany the dance because the performers are trying to avoid getting their feet trapped in the bamboo poles.

The dance emerged several decades ago and started when the Spaniards had control over the country. Natives relinquished their control of the land and were under the encomienda system, which was an economic system that dealt with the agriculture settlements and large land operations. Indigenous people of the land worked in patty fields for the Spaniards. At the time, the bamboo poles had thorns protruding from the side and as punishment for working too slow, the bamboo poles would be slapped against the workers' feet. The workers tried to dodge this brutal form of punishment by jumping when the pairs of sticks were separated from each other. The punishment turned into a never-ending cycle of fierce treatment because as the workers' feet were becoming more bruised, their ability to work deteriorated as well. Performing at a slower pace, the workers would then be punished again for their unsatisfactory job performance. As the workers were receiving their punishment, it is noted that from a distance, the natives looked like the heron. The natives were condemned to this form of treatment for nearly four hundred years. The constant abuse then developed into a dance.

The *Tinikling* is danced to the accompaniment of plucked strings with staccato beats and maintained with double swaying balances. Presently, the *Tinikling* is danced on special occasions such as at Barrio festivals, birthdays, graduation days, or fiestas. Four bamboo sticks are used in the dance while two to four people control the movement of the poles. The bamboo is hit on the ground three or four times and then is brought up and hit together. Typically the dance is performed by two girls and two boys during their adolescent stage. As the first couple performs the dance, the second couple operates the tapping of the bamboo sticks. When the first couple makes a mistake, the couples alternate and change positions. The dance continues and becomes trickier each time as the bamboo sticks are tapped at a faster pace. *Tinikling* holds many similarities to jumping rope, but instead of using rope, the performers use bamboo poles.

While the Philippines encountered several problems concerning their national identity, it is evident that, in spite of the Spanish and American rule, the country was still able to maintain its sense of individuality. Certain aspects of Spanish and American culture were borrowed and became a part of the Filipino identity. America has an important hold over the Philippines and has shaped much of the country's development in terms of a social and cultural perspective. Overall, the *Kundiman*, the *Sinulog*, and the *Tinikling* reflect the people's devout love and honor for their country. While the dances have evolved in accordance to the changing of times, they still maintain national sentiments.

References

Alzona, E. (1932). *A History of Education in the Philippines from 1565 to 1930*. Manila: University of the Philippines Press.
Banas, R. C. (1969). *Filipino Music and Theater*. Quezon City: Manlapaz.
Bessa, Della G. (2005). Our Signature Love Song. Filipino Heritage. Software. October 14, 2005, http://www.filipinoheritage.com/history/signature_lovesong.htm.
Bustamante, Rosalina E. (2005). Filipino Traditions in Music, Dance, and Drama: Polyphony. 1983. Software. October 17, 2005, http://collections.ic.gc.ca/polyphony/theatre_art4.html#top.
Cadar, U. (1980). Handog: Context and Style in the Vocal Music of the Maranao in Mindanao, Philippines. Ph. D. dissertation. University of Washington.
Carlinawan and Jhun (2001). Tradition. November 19, 2001. Software. October 14, 2005. http://www.wellesley.edu/Activities/homepage/filipina/philippines/tradition/tradition.html.
Dioquino, C. (1996). Education. In *CCP Encyclopedia of Philippine Art*, vol. VI. Manila: Cultural Center of the Philippines.
Guevara, L. L. (1971). References to Music in Periodicals (1862–1918) at the Filipiniana, National Library. Master's Thesis. University of the Philippines College of Music.
Lockard, Craig A. (1998). *Dance of Life: Popular Music and Politics in Southeast Asia*. Honolulu: University of Hawai'i Press.
Ness, Sally Ann. (1992). *Body, Movement, and Culture*. Philadelphia: University of Pennsylvania Press.
Parker, Horatio, et al. (1924). *The Progressive Music Series*. New York: Silver Burdett.
Parker, Horatio, et al. (1925) *The Progressive Music Series*. Phil. Edition. Compiled by Norberto Romualdez. New York: Silver Burdett.

Trimillis, R. (1972). *Tradition and Repertoire in the Cultivated Music of the Tausug of Sulu*. Philippines: University of Hawaii.

26. The Santacruzan Dance of the Philippines

Music is considered the universal form of art due to its appeal and acceptance. Nonetheless, this does not indicate that music is without individual character. Each culture has its own type of music that embodies the total experience, the collective consciousness, and the norms of its peoples. Therefore, music is the collective expression of the musical genius of people of a particular culture. One great example is music of the Philippines known for its unique blending of two great musical traditions from the West and the East. However, similar to most nations, the Philippines throughout time has witnessed evolution of music expressed in different forms and stylistic nuances (Maceda, 1971).

Types of Music

Filipino musicians have produced countless forms of music that could be categorized into three distinct repertoires; western influenced art Asiatic, westernized oral traditions, semi classical music and popular music (Maceda, 1971). The first category is referred to as indigenous people music, practiced predominantly by Muslim communities in Mindanao namely the Negritos. The Negritos are one of the most primitive tribes in the Philippines. Indigenous music in the Philippines literally describes the life of ordinary men such as farmers, hunters, and gatherers. This type of music before the colonial era was mainly functional. The ancient Filipinos have music for nearly every event such as birth, graduation ceremonies, courtship, and death. (Maceda, 1971).

To understand indigenous Filipino music, one must appreciate the instruments used, which generally group into the aerophones and wind instruments, chordophones or stringed instruments, and idiophones. Best examples of wind instruments are the bamboo flutes, which could be found all over the island. The flute found in the north is called *paldong* or *kaldong*, and in the south, it's named *palendag* and *palalu*, and has holes on one side and fourth hole on the opposite side for the thumb. Chordophones are also found in numerous places in the Philippines. This includes bamboo zither, the Spanish guitar, and bamboo violins and lutes (Maceda, 1971). Lastly, and perhaps the greatest indigenous musical instrument, is the idiophone. The most famous that has been around since the early civilization in the Philippines are the Jew's harp, suspended beams, bamboo buzzer, percussion sticks, and gongs. (Maceda, 1971).

Folk Songs

Many Filipinos in today's world remember Philippine "folk songs," the second category of musical forms, introduced by Spanish colonial power and later modified and then taken into ownership by local artist and musicians. This folk music is found in the religious and para-liturgical repertoires of countryside Christian communities as well as in various forms of entertainment and rites of passage such as marriage and funeral ceremonies (Dioquiono, 1982). However, the most important occasion during which they used folk music is during Santacruzan (may flower devotions to the Virgin Mary). A Santacruzan is generally a religious-historical beauty pageant. It is a dance whose origins go back to the 3rd century, which starts at dawn amidst sounds of songs, which depict the finding of the Holy Cross by Queen Helena, mother of Constantine the Great. The occasion is normally held during the month of May but may be experienced during other seasons throughout the Philippines.

This is an important event because Philippines are predominantly Christian. About 95 percent of the people are Christians, about 4 percent are Muslims, and the remainder are Buddhists, animists, or nonbelievers. As a child growing up, participating in this event is almost as normal as being baptized for a Christian; everyone must experience it once in their life time. It was also a tradition for a young person to participate in such specific activity like Alay (Flower offering) during Christmas Eve not only to show respect to God, but also the elders of the community.

Contemporary Music

Lastly, the newest form of the Philippine music is found in the urban communities and has been accepted by most of the population in the last 100 years. This type of music consists of the standard Western art music forms such as chamber music, symphonic music, opera, serswela and contemporary music styles, as well as the latest popular music- Latin American, jazz, country, rock, folk, and rap. However, due to the Filipino's creative nature, they have developed their own repertoire for three distinct musical ensembles: the band, the rondalla and the chorus. The Philippine band repertoire, which consists of marches, overtures and symphonic poems, is performed during military and civic parades. Unfortunately, because this contemporary music originated elsewhere, like the rondalla, which was introduced by Spain, it is difficult for most Filipinos to claim it as their own. However, there is one type of music in which Filipinos take pride and that is vocal music. Choral music became popular during the 1950s with the advent of the recording industry. One type of choral music is *kundiman*, which is a type of love song that is used in the cinema and radio. Its lyrics depict love, usually portraying the forlorn pleadings of a lover willing to sacrifice everything on behalf of his beloved (Maceda, 1971).

Another popular type of choral music is *Harana*, which is a form of courtship music. During Harana, the male would sing love songs and express how he felt about the female through his lyrics. The main instrument used to play the contemporary Harana music is the guitar (Maceda, 1998). This tradition shows what kind of culture Filipinos had before the Spaniards and the Americans arrived in the Philippines.

Foreign Influence

Historians believe that the most modern aspects of the Philippine cultural life only evolved under the foreign rule of Spain and the United States. Indeed it is true that these two cultures had major effects on Filipinos, but earlier contact with other cultures had been made before the sixteenth century, which was the time when the first Spanish ship landed in the Philippines. Malayan people are one of the indigenous tribes in the Philippines, and they were introduced to Islamic traditions through contact with Chinese and Indian traders during the fourteenth century. Two centuries years later, the Spanish imposed a foreign culture based in

Catholicism. As a result, countless lowland peoples were acculturated through religious conversion; however, the Muslims in the southern part of the island, and many upland tribal groups, maintained cultural independence. Among those who were converted to Catholicism became the educated elite who began to seek and establish the modern music of the Filipino.

Because of these foreign cultures, the Philippines became one of the most westernized nations in Southeast Asia. However, the most perturbing part about this evolution was that even after their independence in 1946, most Filipino artists were still a profound caricature of the Europe and the American cultures. Fortunately, there are a few Filipino artists, such as Jose Rizal, who helped shaped a sense of national identity. Artists started engaging in research on the indigenous people that preceded them.

Today's Music

Music in the Philippines is as diverse and rich as its culture. Trends, styles and its revolution are as unique as the country's geography, which is actually juxtaposed to these very factors. In the past ten years, mainstream music in the Philippines has expanded more than ever. A lot of this could be attributed to the media and Internet revolution. Information nowadays travels at the speed of a mouse click.

Piracy is a major problem that fazes entertainment companies, but at the same time, the public has benefited from this in a sense that various genres are more accessible to even the common folk, as opposed to America, where everything is regulated and marketed by big companies more interested in sales than developing the masses appreciation for different types of music. New artists and different types of music are easier introduced to the public because there, the fear of financial losses does not exist due to the violation of intellectual property rights and marketing and advertising fees being waived. This is not to say that piracy is acceptable, it's just a fact that affects the industry in the country. Therefore, instead of having two or three predominant music types like Pop, Hip-Hop, and Rock like in America; in the Philippines, everything is played. Radio station formats are harder to decipher because of the eclectic play lists they have to put out based on the masses' interest. There is practically a market for everything. However, they still have the traditional pop music masses that prefer to go with what they see and hear on TV and the radio, but instead of it being a majority like 10 years ago, it's merely a fraction of them.

Hip-Hop

Rap and Hip Hop have enjoyed a significant growth in the country. Turntables are now sold in stores together with guitars and keyboards—something that was hard to imagine 10 years ago being that the Philippines is a conservative country. Filipino-American artists such as Mix Master Mike (the DJ for Beastie boys) and DJ QBert (regarded as the best scratch DJ in the world) have also helped in educating Filipinos about the Hip-Hop culture. They have been holding yearly gigs in the country since 2000. Many African American rappers have also toured the country. The rapper NORE at one time purchased his own estate by the beach somewhere around the southern islands of the country. The Black Eyed Peas, through front man William James Adams, have also helped push the genre by releasing songs about his homeland. Proof of which could be seen in various spoofs by locals of the song "Bebot" over YouTube.

Rock

Rock music has also branched out into different sub-cultures. Bands no longer have to conform to record labels and have exercised their artistic freedom. Alternative Rock, Rap Metal, and Heavy Metal are only a few of the new types of rock music enjoying new-found success within the past five years. This has also opened the doors for many American bands such as Incubus, Rage Against the Machine, Pearl Jam, and Foo Fighters among others to perform in the country. The one genre that hasn't experienced popularity in the Philippines is Country, probably due to the lack of connection in the lives of the population.

Other Styles

It's not only the American influence that has caught in on the country; a lot of European acts have also made their way into the public's consciousness. An influx of house, techno, rave and *electronica* has created a craze all over the islands. People now appreciate instrumentals and electronic beats with the absence of spoken word. By the turn of the century, open rave parties that grossed thousands were a common scene. Popular foreign DJs such as BT, Chicane, and bands like Hell's Kitchen and Cream now hold annual events in the country (Dioquiono, 1982).

Conclusion

It is indeed true that Filipinos embrace countless genres of music; unfortunately, it is very disturbing that much of the population knows the foreign music more so than their own. However, Filipinos are not to blame because, throughout the majority of their country, they were under the control of other cultures. As a result, it almost became a habit for the people of the island to accept whatever was given to them.

Ten years ago, all people would listen to was what was on the shelves of music stores and what they heard on the radio. Today, it seems that a person's imagination and interest has no limit. Music has been a big part of Filipino culture. It offers an anesthetic of sorts to its people. In a country plagued by poverty and violence, I for one would attest that any fellow needs every distraction they can get.

References

Aquino, Francisca S. (1926). *Philippine Folk Dances*. Master's Thesis, University of the Philippines.
Astraquilo, Corbelita (1962). *A Study and Evaluation of the Development of Vocal Art Music in the Philippines during the First Half of the Twentieth Century*. Ph.D. Diss., Indiana University.
Atabug, Alejandra C. (1971). *Rationale and Design for an Interdisciplinary Music and Visual Arts Course in Philippine Liberal Arts Colleges*. Ph.D. Diss., University of Michigan.
Banas, Raymundo C. (1969). *Pilipino Music and Theater*. Quezon City: Manlapaz.
Barton, Roy Franklin (1949). *The Kalingas, Their Institutions and Custom Law*. Chicago: University of Chicago Press.
Benedict, Laura (1916). A Study of Bagabo Ceremonial, Magic and Myth. *Annals of the New York Academy of Science* XXV, 1–308.
Billiet, Frandsco, and Francis Lambrecht (1970). *Studies on Kalinga Ullalim and Fugaw Orthography*. Baguio City: Catholic School Press.
Blair, Emma H., and James A. Robertson, eds. (1903). *Philippine Islands*, 1493–1898, vols. I–LV. Cleveland: Arthur E. Clark.
Borromeo, Maurida (1971). *Gaddang Songs as a Material for Teaching Music*. Master's Thesis, University of the Philippines.
Bowring, John (1859). *A Visit to the Philippine Islands*. London: Smith, Elder, and Co.
Buenaflor, Sampaguita S. (1962). *A Study of Ballads in Negros Occidental*. M.S. Thesis, University of Negros Occidental.

Dioquiono, Corazon D. (1982). Musicology of the Philippines. *Acta Musicologica* 54(1/2), 124–147.

Guerra, Juan A. (1878). *De Manila a Tayabas*. Manila: Est. Tip. de C. Miralles.

Maceda, José (1971). Means of Preservation and Diffusion of Traditional Music: The Philippine Situation. *Asian Music* 2(1).

Maceda, José (1998). *Gongs and Bamboo: A Panorama of Philippine Music Instruments*. Quezon City: University of the Philippines Press.

27. The Dances of the Khalkas People of Mongolia

The Mongols played a very important role in world history. They created the second largest empire in the world, ruling over 13.8 million square miles and more than 100 million people. Mongolia is also the nineteenth largest country in the world; however much of the land is not suitable for high living standards. This affected the Mongolians' living styles, which arguably led to their rein in Asia (Kaplonski, 2004). The Mongols were nomadic people who sought power in the thirteenth century. One could argue that their nomadic habitat was an essential component for their ability to take over China. Throughout Chinese history, we see many different dynasties influence China here and there but none greater than the Mongols. The Mongols changed China and did this in many different ways. Peasants, merchants, religion, civil life, music, and culture are all areas in which the Mongols influenced China.

Influence

The influence the Mongols had on China was very negative (Kaplonski, 2004). The Mongols brought violence and destruction to all aspects of China's civilization. They were insensitive to Chinese values and inept heads of Chinese government (Baabar & Kaplonski, 1999). How would the United States feel if Canada bombarded their way into their country and took total control? Many Chinese are not too fond of the Mongols as we've seen throughout this course and they have no reason to be. During their conquest of both North and South China, they killed many Chinese and destroyed much of their country. Through this destruction of China, the Mongols also exterminated one of the basic Chinese institutions, the civil service examinations (Baabar & Kaplonski, 1999).

The civil service examinations began around the sixth century. Here they were tested on the "six arts." These arts consisted of music, archery, horsemanship, arithmetic, writing, and the knowledge of rituals and ceremonies. However, the curriculum was expanded and became even more difficult to pass. The new examination was a conglomeration of military strategies, civil law, revenue and taxation, agriculture and geography. The select few who passed this examination would be given a seat in the administrative position. When the Mongols took over China, they banned the right for this examination.

Peasants

The Mongols were smart in their support of peasants in China. They knew that the peasants could be a valuable source to the economic growth. For the peasants who lived in northern China, they were granted tax remissions and also granaries for the storage of grain. The Mongols also initiated a rural organization that was comprised of around 50 households in hopes of many things to come (Namjim, 2000). One of these hopes was to stimulate agricultural production.

This would boost the economy considerably. One area that the Mongols thought was important was taxes. They gave the peasants a fixed system of taxation. Unlike the rest of the country, these peasants did not have to worry about the fluctuation of taxes and levies. Although it seems that the Mongols pampered the peasants, there was one area in which the Mongols did not take into account the interest of the peasants, that being labor obligations (Namjim, 2000). During the Mongols rule, the peasants took part in many projects throughout China including the extension of the Grand Canal to Daidu (present-day Beijing), the creation of a vast postal-station system, and the building of a capital city in Daidu. These new projects ironically led to the fall of the Mongol empire.

Merchants

The Chinese viewed merchants as the bottom of the social status scale. The Mongols, however, had a much more favorable attitude toward the merchants and commerce. The Mongols worked hard to increase the way merchants were perceived by society. The Mongols started an association called *Ortogh*, which ideally was an association assisted merchants who were in the business of long-distance trade (Namjim, 2000). For many years, merchants who would travel across Eurasia to trade would never make it. From natural disasters to plundering by some sort of bandit group, the trading that was supposed to happen never did. The Ortogh protected any one merchant from being put out of business if a caravan did not make it. This association increased trade across and throughout Eurasia. The freedom that was given to the merchants paid dividends in the end. Along with the merchants, physicians, scientists and artisans traveled freely throughout the Mongol domains in Eurasia, and these interchanges of knowledge and culture became important not only for the rest of the world, but for China as well.

Religion

One vast difference in the Mongols was their support of many religions. From Islam to Buddhism, the Mongols were captivated by the difference each religion possessed. The Mongols built a plethora of mosques for the Moslems. This sign of sincerity went a long way, so far that some of the financial administrators consisted of Islamic people. The Mongols were also intrigued with Buddhism, especially the Tibetan Buddhists. This brought forth an astonishing increase in the number of Buddhist monasteries across China.

One of the most important figures in Mongol history was Khubilai (Kublai) Khan. He played a large role. For one, he established an administration to govern China. He also supported agriculture, trade and crafts. This support allowed the Mongols to interact with other countries and form alliances. His support of religion was also very important. He provided funds for Buddhist monasteries, Confucian scholarships, Islamic mosques and also the Christian culture. Along with these great efforts, he was also a conqueror. He brought South China under his control in 1279. Convinced he could not do this alone, he had assistance from Chinese officials to govern some small parts of China.

The Mongols also promoted Christianity. This was unheard of for their time, but because the mother of Khubilai Khan renounced her faith in it, Christianity became a religion that was passed on (Kaplonski, 2004). With about every religion getting support from the Mongols, there was one religion that did not have their support, and that was Daoism (Jackson, 1989). During this time, Daoism and Buddhism were in a struggle against each other. Their struggles would often lead to battles between the monks of the two religions. In 1281, Khubilai Khan supported the Buddhists and imposed severe limits on Daoism. As a result of this meeting, many Daoist monasteries were changed into Buddhist monasteries.

Civil Life

The Mongols have greatly affected the civilian life in China (Kaplonski, 2004). The man that can take the most responsibility for this would be Khubilai Khan. Knowing that the current capital at Khara Khorum was not suitable to become a great empire, Khubilai Khan moved it further south to the city that is now known as Beijing. The new capital was called Daidu and became typically affiliated with the Chinese and their ways. The Mongols, however, still had their influence on the city.

Music

In many cultures, music is an integral part in expressing who the people are and what they stand for. Mongolia is not any different. Through much of the twentieth century, Mongolia was ruled under communism. This led to a forced cultural domination of the Khalkhas people of central Mongolia (Haslund-Christensen, 1971). One of the greatest elements in Mongolian music is traditional long-songs (Pegg, 2001). Contrary to what might be obvious, the long songs are called this because of the extension of each syllable in the text. The majority of these songs are sad. With rather free internal structures, its topics are mainly about homesickness, family members, praising horses and wine."' Western Mongols sing these songs unaccompanied, while Eastern Mongols use an instrument called a horse-headed fiddle to accompany this style of music (Haslund-Christensen, 1971). The horse-headed fiddled is a distinctive instrument that is only used by the Mongols. It is two-stringed and bowed just like a cello. Aside from this, the best known genre the Mongols are known for is throat-singing (Pegg, 2001).

Throat singing is when the singer attempts to manipulate the harmonic resonance as air travels through the lungs. The only other countries this type of throat-singing can be found are Switzerland and Canada. The two well-known throat singers in Mongolia include Gerelsogt and Sundui (Haslund-Christensen, 1971). These remarkable performers could generate two notes at once, one being higher pitched than the other.

Culture

The Mongols affected Chinese culture in many ways. Language, theater, painting and rituals are all areas in which the Mongols patronized China. Khubilai Khan announced that the "Square Script" would be the new written language in 1269. This change was passed from the top down. Although very difficult to impose on the population, the new language made its way on to paper money, the official seal and passports. Another way the Mongols affected their culture was through theater and painting. During the Yuan Dynasty, Chinese theater exploded and became very popular. The Mongols aided this trend by building a theater in the capital. Painting also flourished under Mongolian rule. Khubilai Khan granted a court position to one of the greatest painters of all time, strictly because of his work. His name was Zhao Mengfu, part of the Yuan Dynasty, and he along with his wife, were given special privileges based on his work.

As illustrated before, the Mongol empire did fall at some point. The collapse began when they thought it was necessary to try to take over Japan in 1274 and 1281. The Mongols gave the Japanese a proposal to submit to them and their refusal to do so caused the strike on Japan in 1274. This expedition failed miserably due in large part to weather. The determined Mongols weren't going to allow one failed mission to restrict their reign. Therefore, in the summer of 1281, the Mongols struck their second attack on the Japanese. This attack was much larger than the first, but was once again defeated by the weather. From this mission we get the word *kamikaze*, which meant "divine wind." The reasoning behind this was the Japanese felt that the typhoon that destroyed the Mongols was no accident. They were convinced that the Japanese islands were protected and could never be invaded by aggressive outside forces. Furthermore, expeditions such as these weighed heavily upon the Mongol rulers in China. In 1292, they went into a Southeast Asian archipelago of Java to siege the country, but this time they were more successful. Although they were actually able to reach their destination, their inability to adapt to the weather and the infectious diseases forced them to withdrawal within a year. These unsuccessful invasions weakened the empire. In the year 1340, a flood erupted that changed the course of the Yellow River.

This caused many people to become homeless and forced them to return to Mongolia. In 1368, the Ming dynasty, a native Chinese dynasty, took back control of China.

Conclusion

The Mongols influenced China through peasants, merchants, religion, civil life, and culture. This was aided by their emperor Khubilai Khan. The question that arises is, where would China be today without the Mongols? The problem we have with history is that it becomes very difficult to predict where a country would have been if something were to happened differently. It is safe to say that the Mongols contributed to the rise in China and its prestige. The Mongols were the second largest empire in all of world history.

References

Baabar & C. Kaplonski (1999). *History of Mongolia*. Ulaanbaatar: Monsudar.
Bawden, Charles (1968). *The Modern History of Mongolia*. New York: Praeger.
Bos, E., My T. Vu, E. Massiah, and R.A. Bulatao (1994) *World Population Projections, 1994–95 Edition: Estimates and Projections with Related Demographic Statistics*. Washington, D.C., Baltimore, London: World Bank, Johns Hopkins University Press.
Christian, David (1998). *A History of Russia, Central Asia and Mongolia*. Oxford: Blackwell.
Halperin, Charles J. (1985). *Russia and the Golden Horde: The Mongol Impact on Medieval Russian History*. Bloomington: Indiana University Press.
Haslund-Christensen, Henning (1971). *The Music of the Mongols: Eastern Mongolia*. New York: Da Capo.
Jackson, Peter (1989). Mongol Imperialism: The Policies of the Grand Qan Möngke in China, Russia, and the Islamic Lands. *Bulletin of the School of Oriental and African Studies 52*(3).
Kaplonski, C. (2004). *Truth, History and Politics in Mongolia: The Memory of Heroes*. London, New York: Routledge Curzon.
Middleton, Nick (1995). *The Last Disco in Outer Mongolia*. London: Phoenix.
Namjim, Tumurin (2000). *The Economy of Mongolia from Traditional Times to the Present*. Edited by William Rozycki. Bloomington, IN: Mongolia Society.
National Geographic (2007). Mongolia. Retrieved November 10, 2007, from http://worldmusic.nationalgeographic.com/worldmusic/view/page.basic/country/content.country/mongolia_541.
Pegg, Carole (2001). *Mongolian Music, Dance & Oral Narrative Performing Diverse Identities*. Seattle: University of Washington Press.
Sanders, Alan J. K (2003). *Historical Dictionary of Mongolia*, 2d ed. Asian/Oceanian Historical Dictionaries. Lanham, MD: Scarecrow.

Soucek, Svatopluk (2000). *A History of Inner Asia.* Cambridge, New York: Cambridge University Press.

28. The Dances of China

Background

The country of China is rich in culture and history. Its culture has developed since before the time of recorded history. Even though China has been fairly secluded to other peoples and cultures, it has been able to develop on its own and along the way pick up influences from beyond its borders.

China, with the capitol Beijing, is home to one of the largest national populations in the world. The population of China totals to around 1.3 billion people, a fifth of the total world population (Bos et al. 1994). This is around four times the population of the United States, though China takes up slightly less space than that of the United States. China has about the same diversity in land use as the United States. The country uses much of its land for agriculture such as rice, wheat potatoes corn and other products. However, as with the United States, there is another side to the country; the urban and industrialized part of China. This still growing aspect of China is the main reason for its place as a world super power. China is necessary for many of the world's economies. China's currency is steadily increasing in value in comparison to the U.S. dollar. The climate of China also varies depending on the location in China. It can range from sub-arctic in northern China to tropical in the southern portion of China.

Today, China maintains a near one to one ratio of men to women. Their life expectancy averages around seventy-two years. The Chinese people are made up of around 92 percent Han Chinese and 8 percent of various other Chinese ethnicities and nationalities (Bos et al. 1994). The national language is Mandarin or standard Chinese. The Chinese community is also a fairly educated people with a literacy rate around 91 percent. The country of China is officially atheist with Taoists, Buddhists, and

Christians making up around 4 percent of the population and Muslims making up about 2 percent. China is currently being run under a communist government. Currently, the government has become more lenient to allowing foreign influences into the country though what is allowed is still fairly strict. Much of American pop culture is still denied in China. China today is quite different than it used to be in the time of its dynasties.

History

In the time of the Chinese dynasties, there were constant wars between various states. China has known war throughout history, mainly civil war. China went through several different ruling dynasties as one would overthrow the other. As time went on, the country was unified by different rulers though that would not last long. Finally, in 1949, Mao Zedong was able to unite the country under the Communist Party, forming the People's Republic of China.

Musical Influences

Two things in particular have affected the music and arts of China, the first being Confucianism. Confucius was a philosopher in ancient China whose ideas have been deeply rooted in the Chinese culture. He believed that the purpose of music was to calm the passionate side of the Chinese people and get rid of restlessness and lust. Music was not a form of amusement back then as it is considered today. This belief helped the process of developing music further. This allowed for new concepts to be thought of, as well as new instruments.

The second thing to affect Chinese culture was the Cultural Revolution, which was carried out under Mao Zedong and the Communist Party. During the Cultural Revolution, many of the Chinese arts like the performing arts and literature were changed so they reflected a pro-communist view. This as well stunted the development of the arts in China and still has lasting effects. The fact that the traditional arts were altered forcibly seems wrong. The fact that it was changed, however, reflects the culture at the time and how the people of China have developed over time. Even though it has changed unnaturally, it is still the arts of China.

Music

Music and dance in China occurred quite early in history, before the birth of Christ. Traditional Chinese music uses a distinct scale that sounds very much "oriental." This scale is called the pentatonic scale, consisting of five tones. A heptatonic scale of seven tones is also used which is usually added onto the pentatonic scale.

In the early era of the Chinese society, only the royalty and dignitaries were allowed to enjoy and study music, though as time went on, it spread to the common people of China. Folk music also popped up among Chinese peasants. There songs were usually about daily life.

Instruments

The main instruments that were possessed by the Chinese people were flutes, panpipes, and various percussion instruments like drums and gongs. In the later years, lutes and other stringed instruments were introduced to the Chinese people from Central Asia. Upon arrival, Chinese composers had to modify the music to fit these instruments. This became a part of the Chinese culture over time.

Some of the main instruments are the *lute* and *pipa*, which are stringed instruments. These were not introduced until later in Chinese society. The pipa has 19 to 26 frets and has four strings. The pipa is the most expressive of the plucked-stringed instruments of China. There are many other stringed instruments that the Chinese use, such as the Erhu, the Sanxian, the Zhonghu, and the Junghu, which use bows instead of a plucking technique. The string number on those instruments can range from two to four. The zheng and guqin resemble pieces of wood with strings running longwise across. Then the strings are either plucked or hit with small hammers.

The other set of instruments used in traditional Chinese music is percussio Zheng based. These instruments include the *gong*. The *pengling* also falls under the category of percussion instruments, and resembles finger symbols. Other instruments used are basic drums.

The next type of instruments falls under woodwinds. This includes flutes. The types of flutes that are used can be the souna, the dizi, and the guan. These can be made out of bamboo and usually just have holes drilled in. Panpipes are also used made of bamboo as well. The souna is a bit more complex than the dizi, though.

In traditional Chinese music, it is quite apparent as to which instruments are being used. In the music, one can hear the distinct sound of a flute or the plucking of strings or the drawing of a bow across the string. The sound of the bamboo flute, which has an airy Pipa tone to it, plus the plucking of the strings really give traditional Chinese music its Chinese sound. However, in addition to the instruments, the scale is still also quite important in making the music sound traditionally Chinese.

Opera

Another form of Chinese music appeared in Chinese opera. The Chinese opera evolved from folk songs and dances. These were often based on legends of ancient China, though; today they are about heroes from the Communist revolution or about a historical event of the recent past. An interesting aspect of traditional Chinese opera is the elaborate make-up worn by the actors and actresses. The best known style of Chinese opera is the Beijing Opera, which is a blend of the regional operas all over China.

Dance

Another form of traditional Chinese art is dance. There are several different dances that have been performed in China for quite some time. Some of the dances are the sword dance, the ribbon dance and the fan dance. The thing that most of these dances seem to have in common is that they have a fluid motion toward them. Everything is smooth and peaceful.

Western Influence on Chinese Art

In the modern day, the arts in China have expanded. There are still the traditional art forms, but in addition, there are now western influences in China. In the New Culture Movement in the early 1900s, many Chinese musicians who had been studying in the west returned home and brought with them western styles of the arts. They performed pieces based on western classical music. The western symphony orchestras were formed in the major cities. The piano and violin were incorporated into the Chinese instrument selection, as well as the xylophone and saxophone. Jazz was integrated into traditional Chinese music also. During the Cultural Revolution however, this was all stopped for the time being though the western influence would prevail.

Another western influence that popped up in China was Chinese rock. In the 1980s, a man by the name of Cui Jian became the first Chinese rock musician. He was the first person to play the electric guitar in China. He took the route of most rock bands by becoming an activist against the government. The Chinese government became enraged by this and banned many of his concerts, but the present day situation is calm between the two. From Cui Jian, the alternative scene in China has progressed from rock to thrash metal, to punk, to presently, *nu-metal*. Nu-metal is a mix between rock, rap, and electronica. The nu-metal scene was halted by SARS epidemic but is currently steadily rising again.

Modern-Day Chinese Arts

The Chinese opera has not changed much from its traditional beginnings. It is basically the same as it was years ago. It still uses the traditional instruments of China. Chinese dance, in retrospect, has expanded just like Chinese music. Western culture has influenced Chinese dance as well as music. Modem Chinese dance has taken the form of modem dance and ballet dance. Modem dance companies usually perform eccentric and abstract performances with an underlying idea or thought. They tend to be seen as more artsy.

Ballet is a bit different. Ballet has set rules to be followed and has more of a flow. This type of dance is the traditional type of dance all over the world. The main company in China is the National Ballet of China, based in Beijing. It has been around for almost 70 years. This type of dance does not seem to take much, if any, from the Chinese culture. The National Ballet of China has worked with Russian ballets to do many western classics like "Swan Lake" and "Giselle."

Conclusion

In a sense, China is still a young country when it comes to gaining influence from other cultures. The culture that exists deep rooted in the history and the people of China. Due to the ideals and governments China has had throughout its history, it has grown minimally compared to cultures in the west. However, as time goes by, China is slowly allowing for influences by other cultures to seep in and enrich the already vibrant culture it possesses. There is no telling how much the arts of China will be able to grow.

References

Bos, E., My T. Vu, E. Massiah, and R.A. Bulatao (1994) *World Population Projections, 1994–95 Edition: Estimates and Projections with Related Demographic Statistics.* Washington, D.C., Baltimore, London: World Bank, Johns Hopkins University Press.

DeWoskin, Kenneth J. (1985). Philosophers on Music in Early China. *The World of Music* 27(1), 33–47.

Lam, Joseph S. C. (1996). Transnational Understanding of Historical Music: State Sacrificial Music from the Southern Song, China (AD 1127–1279). *The World of Music* 38(2), 69–84.

Ling, Yang (1984). "China Recovers Her Past in Folk Song: A Report." *The World of Music* 26(1), 44–50.

Ling, Yang (1985). Music and Dance Performance with China's Oldest Musical Instruments: A Report from the People's Republic of China. *The World of Music* 27(1), 91–5.

Mittler, Barbara (2003). Cultural Revolution Model Works and the Politics of Modernization in China: An Analysis of Taking Tiger Mountain by Strategy. *The World of Music* 45(2), 53–81.

Mu, Yang (1997). On Musical Instruments of the Li People of Hainan (China). *The World of Music* 39(3), 91–112.

Rees, Helen (2001). He Yi'an's Ninety Musical Years: Biography, History, and Experience in Southwest China. *The World of Music* 43(1), 43–67.

Shui-Cheng, Cheng (1979). The Role of the Traditional Musician in China. *The World of Music* 21(2), 85–95.

Tsun-Yuen, Lui (1978). Introduction to the Traditional Music of China. *The World of Music* 20(2), 36–9.

Wen-Chung, Chou (1978). A Visit to Modern China. *The World of Music* 20(2), 40–4.

29. The Shomyo Dance of Japan

Japan is one of the oldest and most unusual civilizations in the world. The culture of Japan has survived for centuries, overcoming several difficulties on the way. Japan was born through mass immigration from Asia to the Pacific Islands, which was followed by a long period of isolation. This is why Japanese culture is unique: with little or no influence from the outside world, Japan developed many distinct cultural characteristics. After an overview of Japanese culture, this essay will examine the instruments, music styles, traditional music/dance, and popular modern trends of Japanese culture.

Culture

Japanese culture is very interesting, and one of the most notable aspects is the traditional clothing. The *kimono* is the traditional clothing of Japan and once stood for all types of clothing. As the culture developed, the kimono now stands for a full-length garment. The kimono is still worn today during traditional occasions and events. In Japanese society today, they wear the western styles of clothing. They wear business suits, school uniforms, similar footwear, jeans, and t-shirts. In addition, several of the clothing items contain English slogans on them.

Japanese cuisine is exquisite and is closely related to the environment. Traditional Japanese food is highly dependent on rice and miso. Seafood dishes are a large part of their cuisine being Japan is an island. One seafood dish that is popular around the world that originates from Japan is sushi. Japan has also adapted to western influence and evolved due to ocean trade. Based on this fact, several foreign dishes can be found in Japan as well.

Another unique aspect of Japan is the way in which religion is treated as a relaxed topic. Most Japanese people do not practice one religion, but adapt several beliefs from different religions into one. The most common practiced religions are Shinto and Japanese Buddhism. The realm of religion in Japan is hard to differentiate from the many superstitions and traditions.

The architecture in Japan is also quite interesting and has gone through several changes. Traditional Japanese buildings have thin walls due to the mild climate. The overlapping slanted roofs also help to stabilize the house and help cope with the frequent summer rains. Timber is the typical building material for traditional homes. After about 1870, western influenced changed the architecture to a more modern style. Japan's excessive population has caused most buildings to rise vertically, and the average room is small compared to western living. These aspects make Japanese architecture very unique and interesting.

Instruments

The traditional music of Japan is made up of three main types of instruments: percussion, string, and wind instruments. Most of the instruments of Japanese culture were imported from China, and several were then modified. There are many different large drums in traditional Japanese music called *taiko*. Most of these drums have two membranes and are struck with sticks. The largest drum is called the *odaiko*. In Japan, there are drum groups that are very popular to foreigners, but not to the locals who see the performances often. There are also smaller drums shaped like an hourglass called a tsuzum. There are two types of the drum, the smaller *kotsuzumi* and the larger *otsuzumi*. The *kotsuzumi* is played on the right shoulder, and the musician squeezes the laces that are attached to the membrane to change the tone. The *otsuzumi* is played on the left thigh of the performer.

String instruments are also important in traditional Japanese music. One of the most unusual string instruments is the koto, a 13-string zither that is two meters long. The strings are plucked with a pick on the thumb using the first two fingers on the right hand. This instrument can be played with two people or solo.

The *shamisen* is a two to three string lute that is about 1.3 meters in length. The instrument was popular in the pleasure districts during the Edo Period. Particular styles of shamisen music in the Edo Period developed their own form of dance called nagauta, or "long song." This instrument is also typically played very stiff and without emotion. There are two musicians who have changed this trend. As the American genre of Rock 'n' Roll reached to various parts of the world through media and migration, the Tokyo-based modern artists," Yoshida Brothers" have embraced the Rock 'n' Roll approach to the *shamisen* music where they fuse in African American rhythm and blues with American country music.

A short-necked lute called the *biwa* is the last stringed instrument in traditional Japanese music. The *biwa* varies in the number of frets ranging from four to six, and the strings from three to five. A plectrum called a bachi is used to play the *biwa* while the instrument is held vertically. The *biwa* was an instrument played by blind musicians in the guise of priests.

Flutes are a major component in traditional Japanese music. Shakuhachi is the most famous flute and is made from bamboo. There are four or five finger holes on the front and one thumb hole in the back. The shakuhachi was played often by Buddhist priest and was thought to be very spiritual. Among the other Japanese there were the nokan and side-blown takebue and shinobue. These flutes were often associated with Japanese festivals.

Music

The traditional music and dance of Japan were influenced heavily by spirituality. Several of the instruments were primarily used by the Buddhist priests who found harmony and peace in playing music. Additionally, many of the musical styles were imported from China in the early history of Japan. Traditional Japanese music is also related to various tales and legends. Traditional Japanese music is sometimes performed with words and many times performed as an instrumental. Finally, some types of traditional music such as Yokyoku are types of theatrical plays in which the actors sing and chant.

The first type of traditional musical category is *Gagaku*, and it was music of the elites. The music style was performed in the imperial court and in religious ceremonies. Most *Gagaku* pieces use an orchestra of string, wind and percussion instruments accompanied by dance. These dances are very elaborate. Shomyo is another early musical style. This style is known as Buddhist chanting.

The *biwa* is an instrument that was described earlier, and this lute has its own category of music. At first, it was only performed in warrior households, and the musical style was very powerful. Then, at the end of the Meiji period in Tokyo, Nagata Kinshin developed and improved the *Satsuma biwa* into a modern concert instrument and composed a variety of new pieces for it. The *biwa* songs usually tell a story or legend and were traditionally performed by blind musicians.

One of the most important styles of Japanese music is *kabuki*, this was the popular theater of the Edo period. It was basically a puppet show with song and dance. It was a blend of all three arts; song, dance, and acting. In the theater, *nagauta* was the most important type of music. The word stands for "long song," which is why it was used for the kabuki theater.

There is a great diversity to traditional Japanese dance. Dance was associated with the court, religious situations, rituals, and theatrical dance. Japanese dance supposedly goes back to the mythical age to a famous Japanese myth. The Myth explains how Amenozume no Mikoto danced in front of the Amano Iwato to open the cave that she was trapped in. The kagura (dance of the gods) dancing originated from this myth and is very religious. Bugaku and Gagaku were brought over from China while Dengaku and Sarugaku sprang up as the entertainment of Japanese farmers. From all these dances the Nohgaku was formed and went on to have a great influence in Kabuki Theater. The Okuni is modeled after traditional dance and this style is credited as being the founder of Kabuki. Kabuki and dance were once synonymous, until it was performed by prostitutes. When this happened, Kabuki was banned, but the art was still passed down. Kabuki is performed by men, but women can be on stage for special circumstances.

The last style of dance that originated in Japan is a contemporary style that appeared in 1959. It is called butoh dancing and is different from both traditional Japanese styles and western styles. The dancers use white body make up like traditional dance, or they use other colors. Few do not use any make up, and they wear several different types of costumes. The dancing is related to meditation and martial arts. It is hard to explain this style, and it is said that the only way to grasp it is to watch it.

Contemporary Music

Modern Japanese music is very similar to that of the western societies. Like the United States, there are several different genres. In the 1950s through the 1990s, there were several different stages. Early on in this period, the rock/pop songs of the U.S. became very popular in Japan. Artists such as Elvis, The Beatles, and the Rolling Stones were an inspiration to several Japanese musicians. In the last 10 years, the music of Japan is very similar to the U.S. There is a major pop music trend going on with the young adults in Japan, and a few artists that mix the old with the new. The Yoshida brothers use the shamisen but mix it with pop music. Most of the music that seeps to the U.S. is done through popular anime and video games.

Conclusion

In summary, Japanese music is modeled around its great tradition based on imported cultures from Asia. Their music is spiritual and is traditionally focused in the theater. As Japan changed from era to era so did its musical trends. Today in Japan, the culture is very similar to that of western society, but Japan still holds on to its own traditional identity.

References

Deschenes, Bruno (2006). The Music of Japan. The All Music Guide. November 22, 2006, http://www.allmusic.com/cg/amg.dll?p=amg&sql=J339.

Fujie, Linda (2001). Japanese Taiko Drumming in International Performance: Converging Musical Ideas in the Search for Success on Stage. *The World of Music* 43(2-3), 93-101.

Gen'ichi, Tsuge (1983). Raiment of Traditional Japanese Musicians: Its Social and Musical Significance. *The World of Music* 25(1), 55-69.

Gen'ichi, Tsuge (2004). Coercively Standardized or Not: Romanization Systems of the Japanese Language in Music Literature. *The World of Music* 46(2), 137-43.

Groemer, Gerald (2004). The Rise of Japanese Music. *The World of Music* 46(2), 9-33.

Halliwell, Patrick (2004). Groupism and Individualism in Japanese Traditional Music. *The World of Music* 46(2), 35-46.

Harich-Schneider, Eta (1983). Dances and Songs of the Japanese Shintô Cult. *The World of Music* 25(1), 16-29.

Hughes, David W. (1992). Esashi Oiwake' and the Beginnings of Modern Japanese Folk Song. *The World of Music* 34(1), 35-56.

Ishii, Maki (1983). Japan's Music of Encounter: Historical Background and Present Role. *The World of Music* 25(1), 80-90.

Japanese Culture (2006). Japan Zone. November 22, 2006, http://www.japan-zone.com/culture/index.html.

Japanese Traditional Instrumental Music (2006). November 22, 2006, http://www.mustrad.org.uk/articles/japan.htm.

Johnson, Henry (2004). To and from an Island Periphery: Tradition, Travel and Transforming Identity in the Music of Ogasawara, Japan. *The World of Music* 46(2), 79-98.

Malm, Joyce R. (1983). The World of Japanese Classical Dance. *The World of Music* 25(1), 70-9.

Malm, William P. (1978). Japanese Music: A Brief Survey. *The World of Music* 20(2), 64-8.

Malm, William P. (1983). Japanese Music and its Relations to Other Musical Traditions. *The World of Music* 25(1), 5-15.

Nattiez, Jean-Jacques (1983). The Rekkukara of the Ainu (Japan) and the Katajjaq of the Inuit (Canada): A Comparison. *The World of Music* 25(2), 33-44.

Tamba, Akira (1980). The Use of Masks in the Nô Theatre. *The World of Music* 22(1), 39-52.

Tamba, Akira (1983). Confluence of Spiritual and Aesthetic Research in Traditional Japanese Music. *The World of Music* 25(1), 30-43.

Thornbury, Barbara E. (2004). Cultural Policy and Private Initiative: The Performing Arts at The Japan Society, New York. *The World of Music* 46(2), 123-36.

Vos, F. (1978). Background to Japanese Culture. *The World of Music* 20(2), 61-3.

Part IV: South Pacific

30. The Kapa Haka Dance Tradition of New Zealand

Kapa Haka is the term for the traditional performing arts of the Maori people of New Zealand. It is a centuries old style that has essentially, been around ever since pre-colonial times. There are, of course, modern-day interpretations but it still remains the most basic kind of Maori performance art. A combination of dance and song, it can be likened to sign language in that specific moves represent different ideas. The accompanying music to these performances is at times haunting due to the focus on wind instruments.

Intricacies of the Kapa Haka

Regardless of the performance art in question, there are four key characteristics of *Kapa Haka*: timing, footwork, stance, and *wiri*. First, the timing is important because it ensures accuracy. The change from one action to another is part of the timing, and the sign of a harmonious group is synchronized actions. Due to the variety of tempo changes in some dance, it is of the utmost importance to keep up with the particular beats and the overall speed of a performance. Next, footwork ties in with timing as the two seem to depend upon each other. The performer must know exactly when to carry out a specific set of steps or jumps or else he or she risks throwing off the timing of the performance. The differences in footwork reflect both different customs and traditions in the varying parts of New Zealand. While some areas feature the lifting of the foot in performances, others don't.

The stance, or the way the performers carry themselves, is not always actively considered in Western culture, but it is very important to the Maori.

Confidence is a reflection of the pride one takes in one's art and, thus, the way one presents himself is always examined. Finally, *wiri* is the trembling side to side movement of the whole hand. Rather than a wriggling of the fingers, it is a more focused movement that is said to represent the world around us.

Four different kinds of performances are performed under the holistic term of *Kapa Haka*, one of which is a song, one a dance, and two a sort of game. The song, called *Waita a Ringa*, can be classified as an action song that is typically accompanied by a distinctive type of music, unlike the other three *Kapa Hakas*. The *Waita a Ringa* usually recounts the actions of a past event or communicates a story, which is instead depicted as a challenge that the performer may have faced. The *Haka* dance is traditionally performed by males and most *Hakas* were typically done before warriors left for battle. Many *Hakas* tend to involve weapons, a considerable degree of footwork, such as jumping or foot stamping, and *wiri*, the trembling of the hands.

Titi Torea is the name for the game in which sticks are skillfully, quickly, and accurately passed between performers. Often struck on the ground or floor to the time or beat of the actions, it can be seen as a means to improve speed and accuracy. Similarly, *Poi*, small and long flax balls, are swung on the end of a flax cord. This fourth and final type of *Kapa Haka* is similar to *Titi Torea*, in that both require dexterity and coordination. The *Poi*, in particular, require a large amount of skill to manipulate since performers often may use four *Poi* at once. This sort of challenge to test one's self was once a means by which warriors trained for battle. In order to improve their agility, they would swing *Poi* balls on long flax cords and aim for accuracy and coordination. This shows that although nowadays *Titi Torea* and *Poi* are typically not seen as particularly applicable in the lives of present-day New Zealanders, they still represent a large part of the history and traditions of the Maori people.

History of the Kapa Haka

The *Haka* dance has been a part of Maori culture since first relations between Maori natives and early European explorers, missionaries, and settlers. Although, recent tradition implies that the *Haka* was solely performed by men, there is history of female involvement. This is especially clear in the most popular origin myth of the *Haka*. The first use of the dance in the natural world is typically attributed to the Chief Tinirau and some of his womenfolk. It is said that Tinirau wanted revenge for the killing of one of his pet whales so he sent a hunting party of women to find the man responsible, an old priest, or *Tohunga*, called Kae. Although the women did not know what Kae looked like, they knew he had uneven teeth that overlapped. Upon arriving at Kae's village, they performed the *Haka* to get the men of the village to smile and, thus, for Kae to reveal himself. The plan worked, and when the old *Tohunga* smiled, the women found him out and brought him back to Tinirau's village where Kae was killed. This myth thus reveals women's involvement in the development of the *Haka* and ensures their place in the history of the dance.

More historically, the *Haka* was used as a part of the formal communication process in pre–European times and when two separate Maori parties came together. First, the area tribe, or *tangata whenua*, would issue a challenge. Then the visiting party, or *manuhiri*, would respond. The *tangata whenua* would then perform a *Haka Peruperu* and the *manuhiri* would respond with their own version of *Haka*. Finally, after speeches from both sides, the two groups would participate in *hongi*, or the traditional greeting of pressing noses. Although such an elaborate form of greeting is not commonly seen, it is still used on special occasions, such as visits from government officials.

Haka Today

Typically seen as a war dance, the word "*Haka*" actually means a dance or a song accompanied by a dance. Despite many variations, all *Hakas* feature the use of weapons, such as spears, as well as fierce gestures and motions. It is interesting to note that this sort of ferocity has carried over to the sporting teams of New Zealand, which nowadays perform *Hakas* before each match or game. The rugby team All Blacks is particularly known for their passionate and prideful performance and have, as a result, made the *Haka* a dignified and mystical symbol of New Zealand.

Additionally, the New Zealand Army has its own unique *Haka*, which begins and ends with female soldiers. They acknowledge their special place in the armed forces in this manner since traditionally only men could become warriors. As a result of these two instances of its performance, the *Haka* has become a unique form of national expression. So much so does it unite New Zealanders living abroad that trade delegation nowadays often travel to official meetings overseas with *Haka* groups. The globalization of the dance is truly an incredible phenomenon, which exemplifies the versatility of the *Haka*.

The social and historical contexts of the *Kapa Haka* performing arts are intertwined in the sense that both are still valid even today. Historically, warriors improved their agility by practicing with long *Poi* and performed the *Haka* dance before leaving for battle. Additionally, both historically and socially, *Kapa Haka* songs and chants have been significant parts of wedding and funeral ceremonies, which also incorporate dances. Since there is a considerable disparity between a wedding and a funeral, it is necessary to note that the Maori celebrate key points in their lives by using the best form of expression they have which is their *Kapa Haka*, or performance arts.

Waita a Ringa music is usually performed to tell about past events or to illustrate stories and this use of it has not changed a great deal historically. Finally, in modern times, *Titi Torea* and *Poi* are performed at festivals and social events for entertainment and to exhibit the abilities of the performers. Thus, over time, the *Waita a Ringa* is the only singular part of the *Kapa Haka* to have stayed the same. The *Haka dance*, as well as *Titi Torea* and *Poi*, are currently performed for reasons that differ from historical ones but the meaning behind the various art forms is still the same as it ever was in celebrating Maori culture.

Instruments and Costumes

Similarly, the same sort of traditional instruments are still used for the *Kapa Haka* performances. Made of Maori wood, whalebone, and stone, the wind instruments have distinct shapes and sounds. A *Koauau* is a rotund flute that can only be played in one way, while the *Putorino* is a small flute that sounds different when played three different ways. The *Nguru,* or nose flute, is longer in shape than the others and is often quite elaborately carved. The *Pukaea* is a type of trumpet that is used for louder sounds. Finally, the *Pututara* is a conch shell whose sound deepens as its size increases. With the exception of stages and microphones, Maori instruments have essentially stayed the same over an extended period of time.

Although only members of *Kapa Haka* groups and tourist guides wear full traditional costumes nowadays, the tradition of how they are made is still preserved. *Harakeke*, or the Maori term for flax, is one of the most common materials along with fur, wool, and linen are used to make Maori costumes. The *Kahu* or *Korowai* is a cloak commonly worn by people who are of high rank within a tribe or during a *Kapa Haka*, by the two *Kaea*, or male and female leaders. Typically made of either *harakeke* or animal hide, the *Kahu* is decorated with feathers in a more ornate fashion. The *Pari* is a bodice of linen or tapestry that is usually based on a square shape. Intricately designed and decorated, it is the same for both men and women. The *Tatua* is a body band made of linen or tapestry and wool. Part of a ceremonial costume for men, the *Tatua* is worn over the left shoulder with the ends meeting at the right hip. The *Piupiu* is a *harakeke* skirt, which women wear long and men wear short. Finally, the *Tipare* is a headband of plaited *harakeke*, which is woven in patterns that match the *Pari*.

Ta Moko, which means to strike or tap, is the traditional art of Maori tattooing. Most often done on the face, it is also seen on other body parts. Essentially, the carving of ink into the wearer's skin, it has been practiced for more than a millennium. Although originally *Ta Moko* could only be afforded by chiefs and warriors, it was essentially used as a form of identification, rank, genealogy, tribal history, eligibility to marry, and a mark of either beauty (on women) or ferocity (on men).

Conclusion

In today's modern world, every two years *Kapa Haka* groups gather from all over New Zealand to compete in *Te Matatini* or the *Aotearoa* Traditional Performing Arts Festival. It is seen as the most well-known national Maori performing arts competition, as thousands of Maori gather during the event to view and cheer the competitors. In addition to the planned competition in New Zealand, the *Kapa Haka* is a way for New Zealanders around the world to unite and celebrate their heritage. Both the formal and informal practices of the *Kapa Haka* arts reflect not only the meaning behind the performances themselves, but also the continual evolution and growth of the Maori tradition.

References

Bunk, S. (1989). Rockin' with the Ancestors. [Yothu Yindi]. *Territory Digest* 11 (1): 2–5.
Carmody, Kevin. (1988). The Bitter Cake. *Social Alternatives* 1: 3–6.
Chryssides, M. (1993). Mandawuy Yunupingu. In *Local Heroes,* ed. Helen Chryssides. North Blackburn, Victoria: Collins Dove.

Cox, Peter (2001). *Spinning Round: The Festival Records Story*. Sydney: Powerhouse.
Davies, Chris Law (1993). Black Rock and Broome: Musical and Cultural Specificities. *Perfect Beat: The Journal of Research into Contemporary Music and Popular Culture 1/2* (January): 48–59.
Ellis, C., M. Brunton, and L. Barwick (1988). From the Dreaming Rock to Reggae Rock. In *From Colonel Light into the Footlights: The Performing Arts in S.A. from 1836 to the Present*, ed. A.D. McCredie, 151–172. Adelaide, South Australia: Pagel.
Hayward, Philip (1998). *Sound Alliances: Indigenous Peoples, Cultural Politics and Popular Music in the Pacific*. London and New York: Cassell.
Hayward, Philip (2001). *Tide Lines: Music, Tourism and Cultural Transition in the Whitsunday Islands (and Adjacent Coast)*. Lismore, NSW: Music Archive for the Pacific Press, Southern Cross University.
Keir, Phillip (1992). Yothu Yindi. *Rolling Stone* 466: 72–77.
Lawe Davies, Chris. (1993). Aboriginal Rock Music: Place and Space. In *Rock and Popular Music: Politics, Policies, Institutions*, ed. T. Bennett, S. Frith, L. Grossberg, J. Shepherd, G. Turner, 249–265. London, New York: Routledge.
Lawe Davies, Chris (1993). Black Rock and Broome: Musical and Cultural Specificities. *Perfect Beat: The Journal of Research into Contemporary Music and Popular Culture* 1(2), January: 48–59.
Malm, William (1967). *Music Cultures of the Pacific, the Near East and Asia*. Englewood Cliffs, NJ: Prentice-Hall.
Mitchell, Tony (1996). Real Wild Child: Australian Popular Music and National Identity. In *Popular Music and Local Identity: Rock, Pop and Rap in Europe and Oceania*, 173–214. Leicester: University of Leicester Press.
Poignant, Roslyn (1967). *Mythology: Polynesia, Micronesia, Melanesia, Australia*. London, New York, Sydney, Toronto: Paul Hamlyn.
Shepherd, John, David Horn, Dave Laing, Paul Oliver, Peter Wicke, eds. (2003). *Continuum Encyclopedia of Popular Music of the World. Vol. 1: Media, Industry and Society*. London, New York: Continuum.
Shepherd, John, David Horn, Dave Laing, Paul Oliver, Peter Wicke, eds. (2003). *Continuum Encyclopedia of Popular Music of the World. Vol. 2: Performance and Production*. London, New York: Continuum.
Skelly, S. (1991). Voice from the Wilderness. [Archie Roach]. *HQ Magazine* (March): 82–86.
Streit-Warburton, J. (1993). Smashing the Silence: A Review of "With Open Eyes—the First National Aboriginal and Torres Strait Islander Contemporary Women's Music Festival." *Perfect Beat: The Journal of Research into Contemporary Music and Popular Culture* 1(3): 86–90.
Walker, Clinton (1993). Archie Roach. *Rolling Stone* (March): 78–81.
Yunupingu, Mandawuy (1992). Black and White. *Rolling Stone* 471: 33–34.
Yunupingu, Mandawuy (1994). Yothu Yindi—Finding Balance. In *Voices From The Land: 1993 Boyer Lectures*, 1–11. Sydney, NSW: ABC.

31. Australian Aboriginal Music and Dances

Today, few cultural remnants of past civilizations remain unscathed by the influence of an increasingly westernized global society. Ancient artifacts pass between museum displays under tight security for the limited viewing pleasures of a select few. In reality, the majority of citizens never experience or witness the remains of truly ancient cultures and traditions that predate and underlie those of the various communities today. Therefore, it is indeed a priceless opportunity to study a living artifact such as the Aboriginal culture still thriving in Australia, one of the most fascinating, primitive and isolated peoples left to date.

Dwelling in the harsh environments of the island continent of Australia, the Aborigines may well be the last living examples of an ancient, prehistoric human civilization with their unique and mysterious cultural traditions. Despite the westernization of modern day Australia, the Aboriginal tribes still survive as stark naked hunters and gatherers across their native, arid continent with relatively little foreign influence. For this reason, their religious, social, philosophical, and musical traditions have remained intact for millennia. As arguably the most primitive civilization, studying their numerous rituals and belief systems presents everyone with a glimpse into their own history as human beings. However, truly comprehending a community so ancient and far-removed from those of today's society can prove difficult. Fortunately, the art of music, shared and experienced by all peoples of the world, creates an even playing field to study, compare, and contrast modem ideas and traditions with those of the Aboriginal Australians.

Aboriginal Anthropology

Before exploring the unique musical customs of the Aboriginal Australians, it is necessary to become educated a bit about their basic history, culture, and lifestyle. The Aboriginal peoples are alone unique in their physical characteristics and initially presented scientists with a difficult task in categorizing them within the human race. Until the discovery of the remote Aboriginal tribes, there existed only three physiological divisions of humans under which every race could be classified. The Aborigines clearly did not follow the classic European form, characterized by the features of the indigenous people of Scandinavia, the Alpine country, and the Mediterranean region. Nor was it difficult to rule out the Aborigines' place within the Mongoloid division, which encompasses the physical traits of the Japanese, Chinese, Siamese, American Indians and Micronesians, etc. Researchers naturally believed the Aborigines to belong to the third, Negroid class of humans, marked by their brown to black skin, wooly or frizzy hair, large lips, bulging forehead, and medium to tall stature. However, further examination produced an image of the Aborigines noticeably distinct from their African cousins with less dark skin, curly or wavy hair, less everted lips, and profuse amounts of body hair. The Aboriginal Australians seemed to possess qualities of all three human forms; hence, anthropologists accurately classified them as living examples of another ancestral group of humans, yet neither Neanderthal nor Cro-Magnon. As a result, the "Australian Aborigine was classified in a special group: the Australoid" (Elkin, 1964, p. 4).

Content with the classification of the primitive Aboriginal peoples in the new Australoid division, the anthropologists focus then shifted to their origins. Preliminary studies claiming their direct migration from the north were eventually dismissed out in light of new evidence and research techniques. More appropriate models described Aborigines as spawning directly from the earliest human ancestor. In accordance with tectonic and drift theories, the first true Australoid diversified from the common human after becoming isolated on the islands north of modem day Australia. This position, near the island of Java, has since been referred to as the epicenter of Aboriginal migration. With evidence of their existence in the islands dating back to the last Ice Age, researchers believed the Aborigines to have first landed on the northern coast of Australia some ten thousand years ago. The Aborigines successfully crossed the narrow straits of northern Australia by using quite advanced tide maneuvers in areas where tide shifts were as great as thirty meters per day.

By the late eighteenth century, the Aboriginal population had reached 300,000; a small number considering their origins several thousands of years ago. Population size, however, was drastically limited due to their primitive methods of hunting and gathering, restricted food sources, and even some cultural practices such as infanticide and abortion. By this time as well, there were roughly some five hundred distinct tribes segregated by clear territorial boundaries and natural structures. Over the centuries each tribe developed their own exclusive dialect of the Aboriginal language, which researchers today still cannot completely decipher. Yet despite the abundance of different idioms, their common origin is undeniable. Similar sounds and words appear throughout every dialect and each one contains another very critical element; each and every dialect of the Aboriginal tribes relates back to their uniform cultural belief system. Try as they might, no outsider has yet to truly master the Aboriginal tongue due to their misunderstanding of Aboriginal thought and custom, which every dialect strives to express. According to famous Aboriginal researcher A.P. Elkins, "an Australian (Aboriginal) language is an adequate means of expressing thought in Aboriginal life … their languages belong to their own cultural world and the words, phrases and methods of expression derive their meaning from it" (Elkins, 1964, p. 16).

Researchers have also struggled with methods for distinguishing tribal groups. One system very simply states a tribe to be a group of neighboring natives who inhabited and owned a definite area of land. Other methods group the Aborigines by their regional dialects or namesakes and lineages; or even segregate the tribes by the unique customs and laws that certain groups of Aborigines shared. The last systematic method divides the tribes by their individual rites and beliefs, which differed from those of other groups of natives. Though territory is important for the true definition of a tribe to the Aborigines, the real roots to each of the five hundred tribes lie within their unique mythology. "Home" to any Aborigine is defined by the dwelling place of ancient heroes and ancestors. In Aboriginal culture, spirits never die and the essences of the unborn reside amongst the tribe for eternity as well. As a result, the Aborigines segregate their tribes according to the territory where their personal heroic spirits roam. Consequently, all neighboring spirits and tribal groups are viewed as inherently evil.

This mythological view of spirits also serves as the basis for Aboriginal religious beliefs and social practices. Aborigines view the world as a timeless exchange between several key spirits that they refer to as the "Great Ancestors." Interacting in "dreamtime," the boundaries between life and death, nature and man, and the past, present, and future did not exist as the Great Ancestors laid the foundation for life thereafter. For this reason, the Aborigines see meaning and purpose in every aspect of life as predestined by the elements and spirits in "dreamtime."

Individual tribes or clans may possess slightly different interpretations of the "dreamtime" code since each tribal community is viewed as present day descendent of a particular spirit once involved in "dreamtime."

Nonetheless, the dissimilarities are minor and the "dreamtime" influence on Aboriginal life ultimately remains the same. All Aboriginal Australians live their daily lives according to the relationships defined in the ancient spiritual transactions, commonly referred to as "dreamings." Even though it is debated by many anthropologists whether it is appropriate to use such words as "dreamings," "tribe" or "nomad" for the sake of this book, respect is given to the human emotions the aboriginals experience in their livelihood. Glowczewsci (1999) has observed that

> Teaching manuals of Aboriginal studies at the primary and secondary levels recommend, for instance, avoidance of the terms "tribe," "myth," "nomad" or "dreaming," even if the Aboriginals use the terms themselves—on the grounds that they are derogatory [Glowczewsci, 1999, p. 3].

The dreamings mean our identity as people. The cultural teaching and everything, that's part of their lives and the understanding of what they have around them. As a result, the "dreamings" are mirrored in the daily, temporal, and ceremonial activities of the Aborigines and echo throughout their entire culture. Music, in particular, serves to remind tribal members of the "dreamings" and pass them on to the newly initiated.

Musical Tradition

Song and dance plays a vital role in the life of tribal Aborigines. As the "dreamings" dictate the life and activities of every native, so do the arts provide the content and inspiration for many of their indigenous musical traditions. Be it for social gatherings or religious ceremonies, there exist songs for every occasion, supplemented by a unique yet appropriate text, rhythm, and melody. The musical tradition of the Aborigines serves to inform them of the ever present relationships defined in "dreamtime" long ago as well as reiterate the presence of the "dreamings" in the tribesmen as the current carriers of their message and authority on earth.

The songs of the Aborigines mark specific moments in the overall story of the "dreamings." The texts for each song are what Kleinert refers to as, locally specific: they make sense in relation to a particular geographical, cosmological, and social context (Kleinert, 2000). In addition, the Aboriginal Australians believe all song origins to be non-human, old, and having spawned in the country. New songs and texts can only be created by individuals in altered states on consciousness interacting with their spirits' "dreamings," similar to the participants of medicinal dance rituals

31. Australian Aboriginal Music and Dances

in Africa. Still, it is often difficult to understand the text or message proclaimed through the song texts. First of all, the complexity and belief oriented language of the Aboriginal people makes comprehension of the normal dialect difficult. Couple an indecipherable language with the phonetic changes and ambiguities commonly introduced in musical performance and understanding the song becomes near impossible.

The Aborigines possess songs for many of the same ceremonies and ritual traditions found else in the world. The journey song for example, or *bunggul* to the natives, retells the epics and journeys of the spirits in "dreamtime" or some present day hero as imagined in altered consciousness by a tribal member. Another common song, the death wail, is performed rightly during burial rituals telling of the late victim's life and "dreamtime" ancestor. Other traditional songs include: the *karma*, for religious storytelling, the *krill* in its round style, and *kun-borrk* and *wangga*, both similar in style to modern day responsorial pieces.

Regardless of the setting, every song contains common textual, rhythmic, and melodic traits. Aboriginal song texts not only present problems to foreign listeners in their complex language, implications, and dialect, but also in their sheer size. Due to their role in portraying the stories and relationships in the "dreamings," the depth of knowledge and mere word count necessary to understand traditional Aboriginal song is astounding. Beyond the actual text, all forms of Aboriginal song are characterized by definite cyclical patterns found in their rhythms and melodies. The rhythms, in particular, contain repeating patterns and cadences, which can be either lengthened or shortened by indivisible rhythmic sections depending on the text. The text and rhythm together as well, may pick up or stop anywhere throughout the score so long as the piece ends where it began, thus completing the cyclical pattern. The melodies as well represent this cyclical feeling with two or three repetitions of a specific series of pitches. However, the melodic variations in pitch do not necessarily coincide with the repetitions of the text/rhythm cycles and thus improvisation may be required by the performers.

Traditional songs of the Aborigines are many times accompanied by various dances. The vibrant arm and foot movements of these spirited dances pertain directly to the content of the song or music, most often the story of the "dreamings." Such Aboriginal dances are identifiable by their jumpy character and overuse of a "foot stamping" technique where the performer continually strikes his foot or heel on the ground in specific rhythmic patterns. The dances, aside from their role in the story-telling of "dreamtime," often imitate the movements of wild animals, many times birds. Whether for sacred or social settings, performed by men or women and children, the numerous dances of the Aboriginal Australians help proclaim the message of the Great Ancestors in the "dreamtime" along with music and song.

Despite the length and insight of Aboriginal song texts and fanatically expressive movements of their dance traditions, the repertoire of native Aboriginal instruments is surprisingly small. Beyond their generic drum instruments, used to maintain the repeating beat in their rhythmic cycles, the Aboriginal people possess one truly unique instrument, now famous around the world. Named according to its distinctive sound, the *didgeridoo* is the hallmark instrument of Aboriginal music and culture. Known to the natives as the *Yidaki, Yirdaki, Gurrmurr,* or *Gindjunggang*, legends suggest the birth of this famous instrument occurring, when the Great Ancestors gave the native people fire, man took up a burning, hallow branch, and blew the termites out of it. The termites flew into the heavens, and became stars. Out of the strong, deep sound of the breath through the branch the didgeridoo was born (Aboriginal Culture, 2000).

Naturally, construction of more modern didgeridoo's is carried out in a manner very similar to that which the "dreamings" entail. Thick branches of *Eucalyptus cinerea* or eucalyptus trees are simply yet crudely allowed to be hallowed out by termites. The sound of the didgeridoo is as primitive as its construction and design, commonly described as droning and "rough around the edges." However, to the Aboriginal man, the didgeridoo carries the essence of all sounds found in nature as assigned by the "dreamings" from the flapping of wings to the running of water.

The spiritual, mythological, social, and least not musical aspects of Aboriginal culture are truly unique unto the world. So matchless are the Aborigines that they claim their own division of physical form within the human race. No other racial community on earth clings so strongly to the roots of their cultural identity as the Aboriginal Australians, still practicing their "dreaming" ceremonies in honor and remembrance of the Great Ancestors in "dreamtime."

Conclusion

Much respect and adoration is due to a culture, which, for the most part, has survived the pressures of Western society, remaining true to ancient tradition. For this reason, the uniqueness of the Aborigines stretches beyond their position as living examples of modern human ancestors, to their unmatched faith and loyalty to tradition and Aboriginal thought. The way of the Aborigine stands as a testament to the ancestry of all humans, in most instances still untouched by the outside world. The spirit of the Aborigines seems to surpass all worldly boundaries ... into the realm of dreams.

References

Elkin, A.P. (1964). *The Australian Aborigines*. New York. Doubleday.
Global Volunteers (2002). Aboriginal Culture. "Origins in Dreamtime." http://www.globalvolunteers.ora/l main/australia/australiaculture.htrn 2005.
Glowczewsci, Barbara (1999). Dynamic Cosmologies and Aboriginal Heritage. In *Anthropology Today* 5(1), 3–9.
Kleinert, Sylvia, and Margo Neale (2000). *Aboriginal Art and Culture*. New York: Oxford University Press.
Spencer, Baldwin, and F.J. Gillen (1938). *The Native Tribes of Central Australia*. London: Macmillan.
Tunstill, Guy, and Arthur Lampton (1994). Aboriginal Music Students' Views on Aboriginal in Music Research. *The World of Music* 36(1), 21–40.

Part V: Europe

32. The Ballet of Europe

The ballet dance style that we are familiar with today has come a long way since its beginnings in the sixteenth century. Not only has the dance style evolved, but so have the costumes and even the social context of the dance. As time has progressed, ballet has become more technically challenging and has influenced many other forms of dance.

There are two different types of ballet: classical and modern. Classical ballet is highly structured. It comes from the traditional techniques of the seventeenth and eighteenth centuries created in France and nineteenth century Italian ballet (Andros, 2005). Modern ballet arose around the twentieth century as choreographers became opposed to the strict rules of classical ballet.

The History of Ballet

The earliest forms of ballet can be traced all the way back to Italy during the Renaissance period (Andros, 2005). It is thought that ballet rose out of the sixteenth-century European *balletti*. *Ballettis* were ideally the social court dances of the time. The dance style was brought to France by Catherine De Medici from Italy. At this point in time, there were no professional dancers (Andros, 2005). The dancers were members of the court, and they danced in order to please their leaders. The dances did not emphasize difficult technical moves, but focused more on intricate floor patterns and group work, since the audience viewed the performance from above (Andros, 2005). The performances included music, singing, and dancing, all to honor the king or another important person (Paskevska, 1992).

Only men were allowed to dance in the works at this time, so men played the part of both men and women (Andros, 2005). The social and moral views of the sixteenth-century strongly influenced the characters of the ballets. Men were portrayed as strong and heroic and danced with dignity. Female characters were to be modest and gracious and were conveyed as such through the men dancing their parts (Paskevska, 1992).

The first known surviving ballet was *Le Ballet Comique de la Reine*, or, *The Queen's Ballet Comedy*. It was choreographed by Balthasar de Beaujoyeulx in 1581 (Andros, 2005) for the wedding of Catherine De Medici's son (Andros, 2005). Five and a half hours long, it told the story of the Greek mythological character Circe. What the dance lacked in its pedagogy, Beaujoyeulx made up for in costumes and set design. Beaujoyeulx created ballets that would satisfy "the eye, the ear, and the intellect."

Ballet increased in popularity and technique in the seventeenth-century with the help of strong supporters such as King Louis XIV. The king was known for his love of ballet. Not only was he a strong supporter, he was also a dancer himself. He danced in *Cassandre* and Le *Ballet de la Nuit*, among many others. It was thought that the king used ballet as a way to show all of Europe his "prestige as a heroic prince" during the time of the insurrection of the Fronde ("Louis XIV" 229). He is credited with opening the Academie Royale de Danse in Paris in 1661. This dance school was used to train dancers professionally. Now that there was a way to train, dancers could practice and create skills and moves that amateurs could not. Because there were now skilled professional dancers, ballets were moved from the courts to the theater stage. Although the location moved, the ballets still centered on Greek and Roman mythology (Paskevska, 1992).

The Dance Movements

During this time of pedagogical advancement, the five basic feet positions were established. The positions were founded by choreographer Pierre Beauchamp. All these five positions are still in use today and are based on a position commonly referred to as "turn out" or the *en dehors* position (Andros, 2005) In this position, the legs are rotated at the hip as much to the side as possible. The turned out position provides the dancer more movement freedom, a stable base for jumping, and a more pleasing body-line. It also makes spinning easier. One of the five basic positions always begins and ends every move or pose in the dance (Andros, 2005). In first position, the dancer stands with his/her feet touching heel to heel in a straight line. Second position is similar to first position except that the feet are apart. While in third position the dancer's feet touch, one in front of the other and overlapping by about half a foot. In opened fourth position, the feet are turned out and apart with one foot in front of the other. The closed fourth position is similar to the open position; however, in this position, the feet fully overlap. While in fifth position, the dancer's feet completely usually overlap and touch with one foot in front of the other.

The seventeenth-century also marked a turning point for women as dancers. The first women dancers performed in the ballet *Le Triomphe de l'Amour*, or *The Triumph of Love*, in 1681 (Andros, 2005). Produced by Jean Baptiste Lully, the ballet was the first in which the girl's part was actually played by a female, Mlle. Lafontaine (Andros, 2005).

Though movements were more advanced, they were still hindered by the elaborate costumes of the time. Dancers wore big, bulky costumes with masks and wigs (Andros, 2005). When women began dancing professionally, they were required to dance in court dress, which consisted of hoop skirts and corsets. The outfits were so heavy and physically demanding to wear that the women would *only* wear them for the short time that they were in a formal setting. Men wore knee-length kilts along with helmets and boots ("Costume" 238).

The eighteenth-century saw major changes to ballet costumes. Dancer Marie Camargo is famous for shortening her skirt and removing the heels from her dance shoes, in order to show off her beautiful technique and moves (Andros, 2005). Also during this time, corsets were no longer worn, and some women did not even wear shoes ("Costumes" 239). Jean Georges Noverre, author of *Letters on Dancing and Ballets*, had a strong influence on costumes during the eighteenth-century. He pushed for getting rid of the masks that the dancers wore. The masks, he said, took away from dancers' ability to use facial forms of expression (Andros, 2005).

Noverre was a major supporter of expression. He felt that dancers should use movements to convey the storyline and explain the characters and not by using costumes or any other source. He created the *ballet d'action*, a ballet that told a story using only movements. By using natural looking movements, the dancer could then express emotions such as anger or love (Andros, 2005).

The Beginning of Today's Ballet

Near the end of the eighteenth-century, a new style of ballet developed. Created by Charles-Louis Didelot, this type of ballet was made up of a much more clear-cut storyline that was explained in the program notes so that dance and expression could convey the plot entirely. Technique and expression boundaries were expanded while the courtly structure remained (Paskevska, 1992). In his ballets, Didelot used the earliest forms of toe dancing. For example, in his ballet *Metamorphose*, the dancers used advanced (for the time) "flying machinery" to allow them to stand on their toes for a few moments before being swept up into the air (Paskevska, 1992).

Many changes took place in the nineteenth-century. This century was known as the Romantic period of ballet. Ballets moved away from the mythological themes. As more people wanted to escape from the real world, ballets became centered on the idea of fantasies and dream worlds (Andros, 2005). Most of the changes that occurred were brought about because of the ballet *Le Sylphide*. This ballet not only had a fantasy-like theme but also included different style costumes and an entirely new technique. Also in the nineteenth-century, women took on a greater role in the ballets than men ("History of Ballet"). At this time, the main role of the men was to be dance partners with the women, to lift the women as a way to show their delicate and light characteristics. It was a time when the ballerinas were the stars and the men were there mainly to show off the female's capabilities (Andros, 2005).

The main ballerina in *Le Sylphide* Marie Taglioni, became the standard to which other ballerinas were examined and placed. Choreographed by her father, Filippo Taglioni, the ballet made use of a new style of dance; toe dancing. As one of the first dancers to dance *sur les pointes*, Marie Taglioni became famous. Going along with the dream world theme, dancing on pointe made the ballerinas look as if they were heavenly beings just barely touching the earth (Andros, 2005). Taglioni was known for dancing without showing any signs of strain; so much so that it even earned her the nickname "Marie full of grace." Her sublime character became archetypical of the light and delicate heroines that became popular in the ballets of the generations that followed.

Not only did the techniques of *Le Sylphide* change ballet immensely, the main costume, the Sylphide dress also became the standard uniform for future ballerinas to come. All the dancers wore white not only for the heavenly illusions but also for the symbolism: White symbolizing virginity. All these symbolisms and illusions were not only used to create beautiful décor and costumes, but they also played a major role in expressing an idea in the ballet. The floating skirt flowed around the dancer and would remain suspended in the air moments after the dancer would jump to provide the illusion that the dancer landed slower than she actually had adding to the esthetics of beauty in and from a heavenly illusion.

The Sylphide's dress began transformed into the tutu in the late 1860s. As ballerinas increased their technique difficulty and began to use higher leg extensions, they shortened their skirts, to show the movement completely. In the 1890s, the ballet skirt was made up of numerous ruffles that took the form of a mushroom. It was stiff and rigid and made to keep its shape as intact and as flamboyant as possible as the ballerina danced. This is what is now referred to as the "tutu."

It was not until the middle of the nineteenth century that Paris was the center for ballet. As dancers began to move around to other countries, so did the capital of the ballet to St. Petersburg in Russia. Michael Fokine, a Russian choreographer, played a major role in changes to ballet in the twentieth century. He is responsible for ending the use of pantomime or mixing gestures used to explain the story with the dancing. Like Noverre, Fokine felt that technique and the dancer's body language should be used to express the idea of the story.

Ballet as We Know It

The birth of modern dance occurred in the twentieth century. Choreographers wanted to make their own statements, and to do this they had to come up with their own dance movements and move away from the strict defined moves of classical ballet. This opened up a variety of new dance styles. Because of World War I, audiences wanted to see dances that expressed more realistic emotions and themes. Choreographers such as Isadora Duncan and Ruth St. Denis were inspired by more realistic ideas such as nature and the Orient, respectively. Movements were no longer picked from a defined. Instead, inspiration came from the idea or feeling being expressed. The Postmodern era began in the 1960s and expression was no longer as important in dance; instead the skills of the dancers were much more pronounced. During this period, ballet was also becoming popular with the younger audience. Because of this youthful influence, popular music began to accompany the ballet. In this era we saw more of such genres as Rock and Roll and jazz (Andros, 2005).

Ballet was influenced by and also influenced many different dance styles in the twentieth century. For example, Jerome Robbin's ballet *Fancy Free* included some jazz style dance along with tap dancing (Andros, 2005). While most choreographers of the time rejected the strict set of dance movements that comes with ballet, they recognized and assimilated the disciplined training that is involved with ballet. The twentieth century led to the openings of two famous American ballet companies in New York City, American Ballet Theatre and New York City Ballet.

> Today, the average ballet dancer begins practicing when he or she is very young. The best age to begin learning the art of ballet is around eight to ten years old. Because it is nearly impossible to practice the techniques at home, to be successful dancers must put in many hours in the studio practicing. The ideal dancer has a specific body type that is "flexible, slim, and strong" which can be achieved with the right training. Not only must they have the right body, ballet dancers today must also have a strong understanding for rhythm and music. A successful ballet dancer must absolutely love the art and be totally dedicated to the dance [Andros, 2005].

Conclusion

What started as a court dance performed by amateurs to honor the king is now a highly respectable dance performed by professional dancers in a theatrical atmosphere for anyone who wants to see it. As time has passed, costumes have become more functional for the performers to dance in. Technique has become more and more difficult; so much so that in order for a dancer to become professional, they must begin taking multiple dance classes at a very young age. Even though it originated in Europe, the art of ballet has grown and evolved so much that we now see its popularity throughout the entire world.

References

Andros, Dick (2005). "Early Ballet." Andros on Ballet. October 2, 2005, http://michaelminn.net/andros/index.html.
"Ballet History" (2005). The History of Ballet. Retrieved October 2, 2005, from http://www.dance4it.com/ballethistory.htm.
"History of Ballet." Dancing Online, History of Ballet. Retrieved October 2, 2005, from http://www.ccs.neu.edu/home/yiannis/dance/history.html.
International Encyclopedia of Dance (2004). Costume in Western Traditions: An Overview; Genres of Western Theatrical Dance; Louis XIV; Taglioni Family. Edited by Selma Jeanne Cohen, et al. New York: Oxford University Press.
Paskevska, A. (1992). *Both Sides of the Mirror: The Science and Art of Ballet.* Pennington, NJ: Princeton Book.
Principles of Ballet. Retrieved October 2, 2005, from http://www.dgillan.screaming.net/stage/th-ballet3.html.

33. Igor Stravinsky and the Ballets Russes

Igor Stravinsky's long-term association with Serge Diaghilev's *Ballets Russes* dramatically influenced his style as a composer and the world of theater, set design, and ballet choreography. The *Russian Opera and Ballet* as well as the *Ballets Russes* in 1909 as a summer theater in Paris. It soon became an official ballet company named the *Ballets Russes*, or the Russian Ballet, in 1911. Serge Diaghilev, an important figure in Russian art, managed the *Ballets Russes*. His collaboration with the era's most talented and accomplished designers, composers, dancers, and choreographers brought a cultured superiority to the *Ballets Russes*. It became an elite company that refreshed the traditional ballet forms and further popularized ballet in Russia and all of Europe.

The Beginning of Ballet Russes

By the time Stravinsky became involved with Diaghilev, he had already established himself as a promising composer with brilliant orchestral works such as *Fireworks* and *Scherzo fantastique*. As a pupil of the famous orchestrator and Russian nationalist composer Nikolai Rimsky-Korsakov, Stravinsky was largely influenced by his teacher, from whom he learned invaluable methods of instrumentation and orchestration. Under Rimsky's instruction, Stravinsky developed a distinct Russian style, which was largely based on traditional Russian folk songs.

While Diaghilev was organizing and preparing for the *Ballets Russes'* 1909 season, he heard performances of both *Fireworks* and *Scherzo Fantastique* in St. Petersburg. Alexander Ziloti led the first performance of *Scherzo Fantastique* with the orchestra of the Mariyinski Theatre in the Assembly of the Nobles on January 24, 1909. This performance left the strongest impression on the impresario, who was so inspired by the young composer's talent that he immediately invited him to join the *Ballets Russes*. Stravinsky began his relationship with Diaghilev's ballet company by orchestrating two piano works by Frederic Chopin for *Les Sylphides*. This short, non-narrative ballet was followed by *The Firebird* for the 1910 season, *Petrushka* in 1911, and the historic *Le sacre du printemps*, also known as *The Rite of Spring* in 1913. These three ballets have become landmarks in twentieth century music and dance; for they challenged and modernized traditional Western forms of composition and ballet. To analyze the development of Stravinsky as a composer, and the influence of his ballet scores in the realm of music and dance, we must discuss the many artists that he was affiliated with and inspired by.

Stravinsky's Role Models

Serge Diaghilev belonged to a circle of distinguished artists and writers who began the *Mir iskusstva*, or World of Art, movement in Russia. This group of revolutionary artists created a newspaper known as *World of Art* through which they fought the *Peredvizhniki*, or The Wanderers, school of Russian realist art and promoted the individualist Art Nouveau movement. Diaghilev's involvement with this newspaper led to many influential performances and exhibits of Russian music and art.

The first of these events was the large exhibition of Russian portraiture in the Tauride Palace of St. Petersburg in 1905. The wild success of this exhibition led to the launching of an even greater exhibition of Russian artwork in the Grand Palais of Paris in 1906. In exposing the Parisians to Russian art, Diaghilev became inspired to organize a series of concerts featuring Russian music in France for the following season. Thus, in 1907, the World of Art presented Paris with concerts of "Russian Music Down the Ages" which featured Fyodor Chaliapin performing excerpts from Mussorgsky's opera, *Boris Godunov*. These short Chaliapin performances led to the complete production of *Boris* in the 1908 season at the Paris Opera. This was the opera's first performance outside of Russia and it featured Chaliapin in the lead role.

In 1909, the World of Art introduced ballet into its performance repertoire. The first World of Art ballet was Nikolay Tcherepnin's *Le Pavillon d'Armide*, which became the main performance of Diaghilev's 1909 Paris season. Other performances of the season included *Cléopâtre, Le Festin*, and Stravinsky's *Les Sylphides*. For the *Armide* production, Alexander Benois designed the sets and Mikhail Fokine choreographed the dance. Benois was the most enthusiastic about the production of this ballet; his infectious love for ballet as an art form soon affected other World of Art artists. The influence of Fokine, Benois' production partner, came from his concept of ballet choreography, which was largely based on Isadora Duncan's free-movement style of dance. This original outlook on ballet dance form "turned out to be the real catalyst through which the World of Art became the Ballets Russes." (Walsh 130).

The successful production and reception of this ballet aroused Diaghilev and his audience's interest in possible ballet performances by the *Ballets Russes* in the future. Diaghilev's primary concern with the start of the next season became securing a composer for a new ballet score and commissioning it. *Daphnis and Chloe* was undertaken by Ravel, Fokine, and Léon Bakst, a painter who was one of the founding members of the *World of Art* newspaper. For Alexander Benois' ballet, *The Firebird,* Diaghilev searched amongst the era's most popular composers and finally commissioned the work from the young Igor Stravinsky, his Chopin arranger.

The Firebird

The Firebird would be the first of much collaboration between Stravinsky and the *Ballets Russes*. Its libretto was a synthesis of ideas by Fokine, Benois, and other past World of Art members. It was the realization of one of Benois' life-long dreams- "a ballet based on authentic Slav mythology... a painstakingly reconstructed ethnology in the spirit of art nouveau" (Walsh 134). The plot embodies the Romantic preoccupation with the supernatural while capturing a sense of the mysticism that characterized old Russian fairy tales.

The Firebird is the tale of Prince Ivan, who discovers a beautiful creature named Firebird while strolling through a forest at night. He finds Firebird in a magical garden filled with silver trees while she is picking golden apples from their branches. The Firebird is a creature who is covered with feathers that resemble shining flames. She roams through this enchanted forest and performs good deeds. The captivated Prince Ivan captures her while she is picking the apples but releases her when she begs him to let her go. In return for his kindness, Firebird gives the prince one of her feathers, which will magically protect him from harm.

When the sun begins to rise, the enchanted forest becomes the park of an old castle and Prince Ivan finds himself in the company of thirteen princesses. They play with the apples and dance for the prince until the sun rose, which signifies the time at which they must hasten into the castle. Prince Ivan discovers that this castle is the home of an evil sorcerer known as Kaschei who holds the princesses as prisoners. This sorcerer is feared by all, for he has an army of evil monsters and the power to turn his enemies into stone. Prince Ivan heroically decides to save the beautiful princesses, and breaks into the castle, setting off the sorcerer's alarm of ringing bells. The monsters and Kaschei suddenly appear and capture the prince. The ill-fated prince suddenly remembers Firebird's magical feather and waves it out, causing Firebird to appear in his protection. With her powerful magic, she forces the monsters and Kaschei to dance wildly until the point of exhaustion, and sings a beautiful lullaby to put them into a state of unconsciousness.

With the evil sorcerer and his minions in deep sleep, the Firebird leads Price Ivan to the egg that Kaschei's evil soul is kept in. Prince Ivan destroys the egg and thereby makes the sorcerer, the monsters, and the ancient castles disappear. The princesses are saved, and all of Kaschei's victims are transformed from stone to human form. The ballet ends with good triumphing over evil.

Although Stravinsky did not initially show much enthusiasm for the conception of this work, he worked diligently and composed three-quarters of the entire work in less than six months. In the composition process, Stravinsky worked closely with the members of the ballet company and set a precedent for the collaboration that would characterize his future ballet scores. In one of Mikhail Fokine's reflections he reveals:

> Stravinsky visited me with his first sketches and basic ideas, he played them for me, I demonstrated the scenes for him... [He] played, and I interpreted the role of the Tsarevich, the piano substituting for the wall. I climbed over it, jumped down from it, and crawled, fear-struck, looking around my living room. Stravinsky, watching, accompanied me with patches of the Tsarevich melodies, playing mysterious tremolos as background to depict the garden of the sinister Immortal Kotschei. Later on I played the role of the Tsarevna (Princess) and hesitantly took the golden apple from the hands of the imaginary Tsarevich. Then I became Kotschei, his evil entourage- and so on [Walsh, 1999, p. 135].

This working relationship between the choreographer and the composer led many critics to refer to *The Firebird* as a "danced symphony," which set it apart from the typical ballet, where the dance merely illustrated the music. Stravinsky expanded the improvisation that he had made for Fokine's movements and effectively captured the spirit of each character in his orchestration. In reviewing the ballet, Ghéon observed, "When the bird passes, it is truly the music that bears it aloft. Stravinsky, Fokine... in my eyes, are but one name" (Pasler, 1986, p. 2).

The score became a rustic collection of Russian folk music that resounded with the richness of a full-sounding orchestra. Stravinsky achieved this sonority through the teachings of his old professor, Rimsky-Korsakov, with whom he had developed an affinity for ingenious instrumentation. He was so influenced by his teacher that Stravinsky dedicated *The Firebird* to Rimsky-Korsakov.

With the completion of *The Firebird* score, the *Ballets Russes* began rehearsing at the beginning of June 1910. Although the dancers and the orchestra found the new music challenging, the level headed Diaghilev and the dedicated Stravinsky who attended every rehearsal maintained control in the last-minute preparations for its official premier. To facilitate the stressful rehearsals, Stravinsky played his piano reduction of the score for the dancers in order to emphasize and clarify the trickier rhythms. Through his coaching, they eventually mastered their cues. *The Firebird* premiered at the Opéra in Paris on June 25, 1910, and it experienced immediate success. The Parisians were swept away by the sense of equilibrium between dance, design, and music, which was to become the signature characteristic of future *Ballets Russes* productions. Stravinsky was immediately hailed as the next significant Russian composer of the Russian nationalist school, for he had successfully conveyed the Russian spirit through his popular folk-inspired melodies.

While composing *The Firebird,* Stravinsky received an incredible vision of "a solemn pagan rite: wise elders, seated in a circle, watching a young girl dance herself to death. They were sacrificing her to propitiate the god of spring." Upon envisioning this scene, Stravinsky began collaborating with his friend Nikolay Roerich, an artist, ethnographer, and amateur archaeologist, to realize it. Although he had already begun the initial sketches for *The Rite of Spring* by the spring of 1910, Stravinsky was interrupted by other works that had already been commissioned, and was not able to compose for it *seriously* until he completed *Petrushka* in 1911.

Petrushka

After experiencing his *Firebird* victory, Stravinsky was under pressure to compose another piece of equal merit. With his newfound popularity, Stravinsky began composing *Petrushka,* his next commissioned work for the 1911 season of *Ballets Russes*. This new commission allowed Stravinsky to exercise more control over the libretto. For *The Firebird*, the libretto had already been completed by the time Stravinsky became involved with the score. *Petrushka*, on the other hand, was born from Stravinsky's original vision of a frustrated Romantic poet rolling two objects on the black and white keys of a piano. He had originally intended it to become an orchestral work with an important part designated for the piano. However, with the encouragement of Diaghilev, this orchestral work developed into the ballet.

With the contributions of Benois in creating the libretto, *Petrushka* became the story of a puppet named Petrushka, who is simply made of straw and sawdust but has the capacity to love and show human emotions. The libretto is based on the love triangle between the Moor, the Ballerina, and Petrushka. The ballet begins at a celebration called the Shrovetide, which occurs a few days before a religious fast. The scene is an agile one—a dancing girl, an organ grinder, and a large crowd bustle around the set of a Russian city, which resembles St. Petersburg. An Old Wizard appears and introduces the carnival crowd to the lifeless and limp puppets Petrushka, the Ballerina and the Moor. The Old Wizard begins to play a magical flute to bring the puppets to life. They immediately awaken, jumping of the stage to perform a Russian dance for the charmed crowd.

The second scene of the ballet takes place in Petrushka's room after the performance. The audience is exposed to the dismal environment that Petrushka lives in. The walls are painted in dark colors and stars and a portrait of the frowning Old Wizard hangs above to remind him of his pathetic existence. The Old Wizard kicks Petrushka into his cell after the performance and he falls in with a loud crash. While he isn't performing, Petrushka lives a sad life, for he is plagued by both his love for the Ballerina and the taunting portrait of the Wizard. His unhappiness leads to his attempt to escape the cell; he fails as his depression deepens. The pathetic Petrushka suddenly brightens up when the Ballerina enters his cell, and he bravely professes his love for her. The flirtatious Ballerina rejects his advances, and Petrushka is devastated.

The next scene begins in the Moor's comfortable and decorated cell. The Moor lives in a much brighter and larger room than Petrushka and enjoys the comforts of a couch, colorfully decorated walls, and a cheerful red floor. In this scene, the Old Wizard places the Ballerina in the Moor's room. She is enchanted by his handsome features and begins to play a coquettish tune, which they dance to. The Old Wizard then interrupts the two enamored puppets and places Petrushka in the Moor's room. Petrushka sees them together and jealously attacks the Moor. Unfortunately, he is soon overpowered by the stronger, larger Moor and is chased out of the room.

The final scene returns to the carnival, where the humans continue to rejoice and enjoy performances by a peasant's dancing bear, gypsies, and masqueraders. The celebration is interrupted by an outcry from the puppet theater, from which Petrushka escapes as the Moor chases him down. To the shock of the humans, the Moor catches up to the doomed Petrushka and kills him with his sword. The Old Wizard and the police try to calm the crowd by reminding them that Petrushka is merely a lifeless puppet. As the festivities end and night sets in, the Wizard leaves the scene with Petrushka's once again slouching puppet body. Petrushka's ghost suddenly appears on the roof of the puppet theater and angrily shouts at the Wizard. He thumbs his nose at his cruel master and spooks the Wizard into running off. The ballet ends and the audience is left questioning who is the real Petrushka.

The procedure in creating this ballet was very detailed and involved much intimacy in the communication between the artists of the *Ballets Russes*. Much of the music was composed before the remainder of the libretto was completed. A distinct characteristic of the score is the hodgepodge of melodies that are used to differentiate the many groups of people in the city scenes. Each puppet also has a distinct musical theme that complements its personality. According to Pasler (1986), a musicology professor at the University of California, San Diego,

> the melodic fragments associated with the characters not only create tension, direction, and drive in the music; they also condition the audience to *look for* the character whose music it *hears*. Stravinsky's music thus elicits a visual, as well as an aural response [p. 13].

Most of the main melodies in the score are once again Russian folk songs, which are almost used verbatim and without much modification. The so-called "Petrushka chord" is an example of Stravinsky's technique of associating a part of the music with a certain character. The chord is a combination of the C major and F-sharp major triads. The unification is very dissonant because the triads are a tri-tone apart; it creates a bitonal effect. This bitonality represents the inner conflict of Petrushka—he is a puppet, but he has human emotions and desires.

The staging and choreography influenced much of the composition process. Benois contributed to the libretto and managed the design of the sets and costumes while Fokine choreographed the dance. Benois' childhood fascination with puppets and puppet theaters helped enliven the sets for the ballets. For Benois, the staging of this ballet was particularly difficult, for it featured a great number of props. It also used large-scale sets to switch between a busy city filled with two-story buildings and a life-size puppet theater. In addition to creating the sets, Benois also conducted much research on the clothing of the 1830s and 1840s for the design of the characters' elaborate costumes.

Fokine faced similar obstacles in the choreography, which were caused by the frequent changes in meter and complicated rhythms in the score. According to Fokine, Walsh (1999) has concurred that with Stravinsky's music, composition cannot progress so rapidly as with Chopin or Schumann. It was necessary to explain the musical counts to the dancers. At times it was especially difficult to remember the rapid changes of the counts. The two soloists were the famed dancers Tamara Karsavina, who danced the part of the Ballerina, and Vaslav Nijinksy, who danced the Petrushka part. Fokine gave each of the three puppets a very distinct personality, through their movements to develop them as characters further.

Fokine had Petrushka's toes pointed in with his heels pointed outwards for most of the ballet. This gave him a very puppet-like appearance. Fokine choreographed doll-like, mechanical movements that were stiff, yet natural, for Petrushka. Nijinsky's interpretation of this role turned out to be one of the leading contributions to the ballet's success. For the Ballerina, Fokine choreographed a fairly simple role, which Karsavina performed exquisitely. Her interpretation of the Ballerina is still considered to be definitive. Fokine described the Ballerina as an "attractive, stupid doll" that displays certain life-like characteristics but never fully becomes human. The Moor's movements are, on the contrary, very strong and clumsy. His toes are always pointed out and he makes large, leaping motions when he chases the weak Petrushka. The Moor is generally depicted as a stupid and comical character until he murders Petrushka.

Despite the complexities of this demanding ballet, the enthusiasm of the audience at the premier was overwhelming. It was first performed in Paris on June 13, 1911, under the baton of Pierre Monteaux, who proclaimed that "in many respects [it] surpassed *Firebird*" (Walsh, 1999, p. 163). The boldness of the ballet lay in the colorfully written score, which reflected the brightly designed sets and agile dances. The *Petrushka* premier was monumental in Stravinsky's career, and it caught the attention of prominent French composers such as Maurice Ravel and Claude Debussy, who had just become familiar with Stravinsky's name through *The Firebird*. As his popularity grew, Stravinsky leaned more toward the ballet as an inspiration for composition. He was becoming more comfortable and well-versed in integrating the staging and choreography into his music. The *Ballets Russes* performances were becoming musically historic spectacles in which all art forms existed as highly innovative entities that were still closely related.

With the completion of *Petrushka*, Stravinsky was free to continue his work on *Le sacre du printemps*. Upon reading an essay by George Fuchs, the German stage director and theatrical revolutionary, Stravinsky became part of the following that supported "a new approach to theatre in which dance and the cult of the body played a pre-eminent role alongside music" (Walsh, 1999, p. 170). This new concept would become extensively apparent in his compositions.

Le sacre

Although interrupted by additional rehearsals and performances of his other ballets, Stravinsky was always mentally preoccupied with the composition of *Le sacre*. In between the ballet performances, Stravinsky was able to play excerpts of his new ballet for Pierre Monteaux, who had become the *Ballets Russes'* regular conductor. Monteaux reacted to Stravinsky's piano reduction of the orchestra part by proclaiming that the ballet would surely cause a scandal. In composing for this particular ballet, Stravinsky appeared to have abandoned all traditional forms of theory and composition. Much of the score was written by ear. Stravinsky claimed, "I was guided by no system whatever in *Le scare du printemps*.... I had only my ear to help me; I heard and wrote what I heard. I am the vessel through which *Le sacre* passed." In reflecting upon his creative process, Stravinsky discusses the composition of his revolutionary Sacrificial Dance, which he could only play on the piano, "but did not, at first, know who to write" (Walsh 187). This new technique of composing is one of the elements that sets this score apart from *The Firebird* and *Petrushka*.

Vaslav Nijinsky choreographed this ballet. For *Le sacre*, Nijinksy was deeply influenced by Emile Jacques-Dalcroze's method of eurythmics, which he came across when he met Dalcroze in 1911 while the instructor was visiting St. Petersburg. With his newfound interest in this dance movement, Nijinsky hired a eurythmics teacher to provide instruction for the *Ballets Russes'* dancers. Eurythmics techniques promoted the concept "that experiencing meaningful rhythmic movement associated with ear-training and improvisation facilitates and reinforces the understanding of music concepts, enhances musicianship and focuses awareness on the physical demands of artistic performance" (Dalcroze Training Center 1). Nijinsky's refreshing concept of this rhythmic form of movement was especially relevant because Stravinsky and Roerich had come to the conclusion that rhythm connected man with nature; it would become an underlying theme for the ballet.

For the design aspects, Roerich energized the stage with his simple sets, which featured bold and clean lines that paralleled the striking rhythmic passages of *Le sacre*. The backdrops became visual representations of the music, which was dramatic and forward moving. At the rise of the curtain, for example, Stravinsky's score opens with thirty-two repeated percussive chords to highlight the first visual event. Roerich's close relationship with Stravinsky yielded highly musically related sets, which displayed "the purest forms of nature" in their stark images (Pasler 16).

The rehearsals for the premier of *Le sacre* were stressful and difficult. The music's discontinuity, dissonance, and unpredictability made it extremely difficult for the orchestra to learn. The complexities of the score also affected the dancers' abilities to understand its rhythms and to feel at one with the music. For this ballet, Stravinsky carried his bold style of composition to another level with sharp meter changes, surprising accents, strange instrumental sounds and discontinuous themes. These characteristics sometimes make the work difficult to understand as a whole. Its intellectual depth makes it very challenging to perform.

With *Le sacre*, Stravinsky was freer with his use of folk songs. Many themes of this ballet were inspired by Slavic and Lithuanian folk music, which complemented the pagan basis of the libretto. A particularly Lithuanian tune appears as the main theme of the Introduction. Because of Stravinsky's unique form of instrumentation, this theme is written for a bassoon playing at an abnormally high register. It produces a haunting sound like no other. According to musicologist Richard Taruskin, "Stravinsky, by seeking in folk songs something far more basic to his musical vocabulary and technique, was to use them as part of his self-liberation from that artistic mainstream, and as things turned out, it's downright subversion" (Taruskin 1). Instead of assimilating folk music into traditional Western literature like Rimsky-Korsakov, Stravinsky adopted it into his personal musical vocabulary to shake the very foundations of Western twentieth century music.

The ballet is composed of a series of dances depicting the wild pagan nature of the spring, which ultimately results in human sacrifice. The plot begins with the start of spring. A Slavonic tribe gathers at the bottom of a hill for a celebration, which includes a witch telling the future, round dances, games, and a procession of the "oldest-wisest" elders of the tribe. The ballet follows with a group of virgins dancing at the foot of the hill. One virgin is chosen by the elders to be sacrificed to the sun god Yarillo. She dances herself to death in "The Chose One."

The Rite premiered on May 23, 1913, at Paris's Théâtre des Champs-Élysées by the *Ballets Russes* with Pierre Monteaux as the conductor.

Parisian audiences were anticipating another ballet more akin with Stravinsky's last two ballets. His audience "could not comprehend why the composer would turn from the fantastic imagery of these ballets to the ugly primitivism of *The Rite* or, as Jacques Riviére put it, from 'poetry' to 'prose'" (Pasler 1). With the rise of the curtain, the audience experienced a historic culture shock that culminated into a large-scale riot. In 1913, Stravinsky's ballet was too radical for the ordinarily unshakeable Parisian audience. Nijinsky's provocative choreography, the scantily clad dancers, the harshly dissonant music, and the primitivism combined to cause such an unexpectedly chaotic reaction. The crowd began with catcalls but soon began yelling and becoming violent in the aisles. Fistfights broke out between arguing audience members as the commotion escalated into a riot. The police arrived by the intermission but were unable to make the agitated crowd sufficiently phlegmatic. The orchestra had trouble staying together amidst the noise and the dancers kept missing their cues. Nijinksy shouted the beats out to his dancers from the wings of the stage while the musicians struggled to hold together.

Although the initial reaction of the majority of the audience was negative, *Le sacre* also received positive reviews. The overall response was mixed. After the ballet premiered in England in 1913, a critic named H. Colles wrote:

> The functions of the composer and producer are so balanced that it is possible to see every movement on the stage and at the same time hear every note of the music. But the fusion goes deeper than this. The combination of the two elements of music and dancing does actually produce a new compound result, expressible in terms of rhythm—much as the combination of oxygen and hydrogen produces a totally different compound, water [Pasler 3].

The whole spectacle embodied simultaneity—developments in the music were instantaneously reflected in the movements of the dancers. Stravinsky was very detailed in his workings with the choreography; he even sketched instructions for his idea of choreography in the score. This detail appealed to a select group of members in his audience.

Conclusion

With the *Rite of Spring*, we therefore conclude our discussion pertaining to Stravinsky's collaboration with Diaghilev's *Ballets Russes* Company. In the years between 1909 and 1913, Stravinsky evolved dramatically as a composer. The remarkably original ballets he composed in this period attest to the idea that through the influence of the *Ballets Russes*, Stravinsky had created a style of his own. In liberating his own method of composing, Stravinsky inadvertently influenced the next generation of composers and performers. His commissioned scores left a great imprint upon the fabric of modern dance. In working together, the artists of the *Ballets Russes* inspired each other and adopted the other art forms to their own. As a group, the *Ballets Russes* had artistic vision of the highest standards and therefore yielded productions that changed the international arena of performing arts.

References

Dalcroze Training Center (2005). Carnegie Mellon University Dalcroze Training Center. November 25, 2005, http://www.cmu.edu/cfa/dalcroze/.
Pasler, Jann. (1986). Music and Spectacle in *Petrushka and The Rite of Spring*. In *Confronting Stravinsky*, ed. Jann Pasler, 2–16. Los Angeles: University of California Press.
Taruskin, Richard (1986). From Subject to Style: Stravinsky and the Painters. In *Confronting Stravinsky*, ed. Jann Pasler. Los Angeles: University of California Press.
Walsh, Stephen (1999). *Stravinsky: A Creative Spring*. New York: Alfred A. Knopf.

34. Traditional Music and Dance of Ireland

Irish culture is extremely diverse, especially in respect to its traditional music and dance). Music and dance in Éireann have been linked since the prehistoric era. These arts have evolved over time with the Irish people and have been central to Irish life throughout history. John Waters summed up this central importance by saying, "It's not all surprising that a nation whose language and culture was suppressed through centuries, should make music virtually the sole vehicle for its spirit, personality and aspiration" (Curtis, 1994, p. 7). The Irish have been spread throughout the world by the Diasporas of Gaelic emigrants that occurred during the Emerald Isle's history. This book examines the relationship between the island nation's turbulent history and the country's traditional music and dance. The evolving view of what constituted the Irish arts of expression in different time periods was intrinsically linked to the political and social climate of the era and the changes have accumulated to give the exciting, innovative perspective we have today.

The History of Irish Music and Dance

The Celtic warriors came to Ireland starting in the eighth century BC and continued up until first century BC. However, they imposed the brunt of their civilization on the native Irish during the fifth century (Ó hAllmhuráin, 1998). There is scare archeological evidence of the pre-Celtic Irish arts and little is known about the artistic abilities of the ancient Celts. Modern Celtic music has no known historical basis in regards to the warrior people (Ó hAllmhuráin, 1998). The few records describing Celt music in Gaul and Hungary emphasize the role of the lyre in musical activities, which included dancing, battles and religious ceremonies (Ó hAllmhuráin, 1998).

Romans visited Ireland around the first century AD calling it Hibernia. Even though they mapped its geography, they failed to record any evidence of the life and culture of the ancient Hibernians or the common people's traditions. Early Gaelic society was formed by assimilated Celts. In AD 434, St. Patrick influenced the migration of Christians to Éire. Even though the new religion brought with it the Latin traditions of learning and literacy, the Irish did not completely abandon their past pagan and druid traditions.

Musicians are mentioned in the 11th century *Book of Leinster* poem "Aonach Carman" that describes the Fair of Carmen that was held on the first of August every three years to mark the Celtic Festival of Lughnasa (MacNeil, 1962). The poem describes the pipes and other instruments of Early Ireland. It differentiated between the *píopaí* (pipes) and *cuisleannaigh* (pipe blowers). Other instruments referred to were the *timpán*, a *fidil* (similar but not the same as the modern Italian violin), a *buinne* (a horn-like trumpet), and a whistle called the *feadán* (MacNeil, 1962).

The hypnotic music of the early Irish sagas remained prevalent in the Irish culture. The tales featured the musicians conspicuously. The sagas were grouped into four "cycles"; the Mythological, the Ulster, the Fianna, and the Kings (Ó hAllmhuráin, 1998). Before being written down, these sagas were an oral tradition for centuries. They focus a great deal on the powers of music that were divided into *geantraí* (music of happiness), *goltraí* (music of sadness), and *suantraí* (the music of sleep and meditation) that were hypnotic states produced by harp strings of brass, silver and iron (Ó hAllmhuráin, 1998). The Mythological Cycle chronicled the "Battle of Magh Tuireadh" in which Dagda the deity fought the Fomorians for the release of his captured harper Uaithne. It is believed that Dagda crept into the Fomorians camp using the three powers of Irish music on the harp to make the entire camp cry bitterly (*goltraí*), burst out laughing (*geantraí*) and finally fall asleep (*suantraí*) so he and his beloved harpist could escape unharmed.

The Irish learning centers were established in the Early Christian time period and housed scribes. These learned men also offered some commentaries on Irish music and dance in addition to translating scriptures. Due to the male dominance in Latin society (Maria, 2004), the few accounts of Early Irish music refer exclusively to male performers. Given women's equality in Celtic society, it is presumed that female performers also existed.

The laws of the late 8th century recorded by the scribes highlight the important role of the harpers. The Brehon Laws explains in the *Crith Gabhlach* that the social standing of a *cruitire*, harpist, is superior to that of all other musicians but equal to the status of a skilled craftsman (Markale, 1999). A teacher of the harp and *timpán,* a string instrument played with a bow, was considered part of the same social class as strong farmers, *bó-aire*, who was highly valued in an agricultural society such as Ireland. Both jobs held an honor price of four cows (Matthews, 1996). Musicians' high standings were a result of the important roles they played in the courts of Lords (Markale, 1999). As a member of the Lord's retinue, musicians had to eulogize and prolong the political clout of their aristocratic benefactor (Matthews, 1996). Additional laws that highlighted the high standing of musicians subscribed severe penalties for borrowing a harp's tuning key, *crann gleasa,* and failing to return it on time (MacNeil, 1962).

The new centers of learning which were often monasteries, also created their own unique Irish monastic music. These communities of religious most likely sang psalms and ecclesiastical orders similar to other communities in Early Medieval Europe (Williams, 1984). No transcripts of the monastic chants exist from this time period yet it is believed that chants similar to those of the Coptic Church existed. This assumption is based on the *sean nós* singing that survives in remote parts of Western Ireland today (Williams, 1984). *Sean nós* is a unique and highly personal form of modal singing in Gaelic that is said to be handed down from the chanting of monks in olden times (Bodley, 1973).

By declaring himself High King of Ireland, Brian Boru tried to unite the Irish nations in AD 1002. And in AD 1014, he defeated the Dane Sigurd the Stout in the Battle of Clontarf. However, after his death, the country returned to the political geography of Early Ireland that had consisted of numerous small kingdoms. The period between Boru's death and the Norman invasion in 1169 was a time of Irish artistic renaissance, due largely to ambitions of the rival provincial kings who had men of learning compiling new pseudo-histories, which highlighted the influences of musicians (Ó hAllmhuráin, 1998).

The Norman Invasion was a result of the political misfortune of the King of Leinster, which quickly resulted in an invasion of Ireland due to the weakening provincial leadership. The Normans helped fortify changes into the feudal governments that were already taking place, yet did little to change the music of the country (Golding, 2001). One of the few musical impacts of the Normans was they did bolster the popularity of the Gaelic courtly love songs in amhrám style of stressed meter (Ó hAllmhuráin, 1998). The Welsh cleric Giraldus Cambrensis visited Ireland in 1183 and wrote in his *Topographica Hiberniae* that Irish musicians were "more skilled than any other nation" with "quick and lively style" (Golding, 2001). Normans soon became more "Irish than the Irish themselves" through marrying the natives as well as Gaelicising their surnames (Ó hAllmhuráin, 1998).

During the period from 1200–1600 AD, a great tradition of bards, also called *files*, was sustained throughout the Gaelic world (Ó hAllmhuráin, 1998). The *file* received a fourteen year education to aid in composing pieces for the noble courts (Ó hAllmhuráin, 1998). In the Gaelic court, the *files*' eulogies were sung by the *reacaire*, who was accompanied by harp music played by the *cruitire*, harper (Henebry, 1928).

In early Irish culture, music and dance were most likely considered one in the same. No written accounts exist of dancing before the Norman conquests. However, given the plethora of Irish festivals combined with the native love of music, it is highly unlikely dance forms did not exist (Henebry, 1928). There was not even a Gaelic word for dance before the sixteenth century when rince and damsha were used (Ó hAllmhuráin, 1998). A scribe's translation of the Latin *"Passion of St. John the Baptist"* to the Irish did not have a word for Salome's dance before Herod, so he explained that Salome excelled in "feats of leaping and activity" (Ó hAllmhuráin, 1998). A fourteenth century Southern English song invited the audience to "come ant daunce wyt me in Irlaunde," suggesting the Irish were known for their dancing (Henebry, 1928). The mayor of Waterford recounted the first native account of a Christmas celebration that "took to the floor," emphasizing the social nature of Irish dance (Ó hAllmhuráin, 1998). The Normans affinity for French carol dances probably led to the development of Irish square and round dances (Henebry, 1928).

The Bruce invasion from 1315 to 1318 from Scotland disrupted the relatively peaceful cooperation between the Normans and Gaels (Barrow, 1965). The Crown passed the Statutes of Kilkenny: in 1366 that prohibited the alliances between Norman and Gael requiring Gaels in Norman communities to speak English (Ó hAllmhuráin, 1998). The initial vigorous enforcement also hurt the musicians, yet, luckily, the statutes were a failure in the long-term (Barrow, 1965).

Unfortunately, by the early 1500, Ireland had a weak infrastructure that had been formed by incomplete conquests (Ó hAllmhuráin, 1998). The 9th Earl of Kildare gave King Henry the VIII of England an opportunity to gain complete control of the entire Emerald Isle, which he had seized, declaring himself King of Ireland in 1541. English rule had a profound impact on Irish culture, suppressing the Catholic faith, Gaelic language and Irish Music (MacFarlane, 1925). King Henry VIII realized the immense political power held by musicians and therefore initiated laws to destroy the instruments, especially harps, and to suppress the activities of the artistic class known as *aois ealadhn* (Graves, 1967). Despite his strong dislike of the native Irish musicians, Henry did include Irish pipers in the Tudor military.

Elizabeth I followed in her father's footsteps by declaring that Irish bards and harpers were to be executed when found (MacFarlane, 1925). The Spanish allied with the rebel Irish in the Nine Years' War, however, after defeat in the Battle of Kinsale in 1601, the entire landscape of Ireland changed. Within a century, more than 85 percent of Irish land was transferred from the Old Gaelic order to the new English colonists when the noble native Irish class fled to Catholic Europe, taking with them the traditional system of artistic patronage (Graves, 1967). The Flight of the Earls led to the demise of the triumvirate of the *file, reacaire, and cruitire,* as they lacked financial support (Ó hAllmhuráin, 1998).

The revolt of 1641 against the Stuarts, had a great effect in the unification of the Old English and native Irish Catholic Confederates against the new Protestant settlers. These activities led to Oliver Cromwell's revenge in 1649 to crush the royalist cause in Ireland (Ó hAllmhuráin, 1998). Cromwell's victory relocated many native rebels to the west coast to separate them further from the Catholic Irish nation that was waiting in mainland Europe. Many Irish priests and musicians were sold into slavery in the West Indies and elsewhere, taking Irish traditions with them (MacFarlane, 1925). In 1650, more than 40,000 Irish were deported to the Caribbean plantations and Southern states to work alongside the African slaves (Curtis 81). They not only shared their misery, but also, their music. An Irish American author of the time wrote, "You got Ibo men playing bodhráns and fiddles and Kerrymen playing *jubi* drums. You got set-dances becoming syncopated to African rhythms and so your basic *céilí* turned into a full-blown voodoo ritual" (Curtis 81–82).

The Irishmen at home rallied for the Catholic English King James II in 1689 against William of Orange (Ó hAllmhuráin, 1998). The failed Irish battles against Orange's General Ginkel were immortalized into traditional Irish music, especially the Battle of Aughrim, referred to as the *Aughrims dread disaster*. The Treaty of Limerick allowed 14,000 Irish soldiers to flee to France after defeat, yet some stayed as rebels and were popular heroes in songs such as "Éamonn an Chnuic" (Troost, 1993). Poetic ballads called Fenian lays were extremely popular at this time and highlighted the mythological adventures of Fionn Mae Cumhail, who led the Fianna Éireann, the soldiers of Ireland (Troost, 1993). Laments are some of the oldest surviving songs sung at this time, with Marian laments being the most prominent (Graves, 1967). Love songs became in the popular mainstream popular beginning in the late seventeenth century and have dominated Irish traditional folk music to this day (Ó hAllmhuráin, 1998).

Starting in the sixteenth century, dancing in Ireland became well mentioned by many English sources who wrote generally about the "Hay," "Fading" and "Trenchmore" dances without leaving details about the actual steps (Graves, 1967). Jigs were first mentioned in the 1674 scandal involving Friar Peter ignoring his poverty vows by having a good time dancing "gigs and country dances" at the local pub (Ó hAllmhuráin, 1998). The British saw dancing as a harmless pastime. However, starting around this time, the Catholic Clergy began thundering against the national pastime of dance (Curtis 71). A parish priest in 1670 said, "Dancing is a thing that leads to bad thoughts and evil actions ... by dancing thousands will go to the black hell" (Curtis 71). The Church's conservative view would hold until the 1940s (Curtis 72).

Penal laws went into effect after William's success excluding Catholics from government, schools, and land ownership, giving musicians much to reflect on (Ó hAllmhuráin, 1998). *Sean nós* airs such as "The Priest's Lament," *Caoineadh an tSagairt,* chronicle the oppression of the time. Irish harp that had been barely sustained on the remnants of the Old Gaelic order further crumbled amidst Ireland's abject poverty, the popular advent of musical literacy and the presence of piano-forte (Ó hAllmhuráin, 1998). By 1730 when efforts were made to preserve the harpers tradition using the "Contention of the Bards" and other harp festivals, the harp had already lost most of its connection to the ancient Gaelic Éireann (Ó hAllmhuráin, 1998).

At the beginning of the eighteenth century, *aisling* vision poetic songs and Jacobite music both envisioned the Irish triumphant. The *aisling* songs dealt with the political injustice of the English and were spread throughout the communities by the changing order of poets (O'Boyle, 1976). The Jacobites believed in a utopian idea that the Gaelic aristocracy would be restored and Catholicism would be freely practiced without Penal laws (Ó hAllmhuráin, 1998).

The better off Irish were able to smuggle items illegally from the European mainland and helped introduce the modern Italian violin to traveling dancing masters who used the fiddle to teach all social classes how to dance (Graves, 1967). Dancing masters considered viewed themselves as gentlemen and tried to instill this spirit into their students (Ó hAllmhuráin, 1998). One would stay in a community for a six week "quarter" and charge pupils about a sixpence in the eighteenth century for this session (Ó hAllmhuráin, 1998). A dancing master's success rested on his ability to invent new dance steps for solo reels, jigs, and hornpipes, as well as set dances such as "St. Patrick's Day" and "The Blackbird" that still exist to this day. The *rince fada* was also a popular dance at this time that included marching and was often danced on May Eve until it was superseded by French dances at the end of the eighteenth century (Ó hAllmhuráin, 1998).

During the 1790s, the politics as well as the culture of the era were influenced by the Enlightenment ideals and Romantic movements that were sweeping Europe (Graves, 1967). United Irishmen formed under the leadership of Wolfe Tone to oppose the British (Ó hAllmhuráin, 1998). The Celtic revival began at this time also to discover the authentic Gaelic traditions with the main focus on the harp (Graves, 1967). The Belfast Harper's Festival was held in July 1792 with one blind nonagenarian, Dennis Hempson, playing in the old style with long fingernails on brass strings (Ó hAllmhuráin, 1998). Edward Bunting compiled three collections of ancient Irish music. However, when written in musical scores, it reflected Mozart's style than the traditional Gaelic compositions.

The Industrial Revolution introduced new instruments to Ireland, including the free-reed accordion and the concertina (Ó hAllmhuráin, 1998). The *uilleann* pipes, union pipes, also reached their completed state in this era (Ashton, 1961). Unlike the previous instruments of Ireland, the *uilleann* pipes had published music from their conception including O'Farrell's popular *Collection of National Irish Music for the Union Pipes* in 1800. The piper superseded the disappearing harper's elite musical status and became the keeper of the traditional tunes (Ó hAllmhuráin, 1998).

The failed United Irishmen rebellion of 1798 strengthened English rule over Ireland and led to the merging of the Irish parliament with the British parliament in 1801 by the Act of Union (Ó hAllmhuráin, 1998). These events once again caught the attention of the musicians. The most popular hornpipe of the period was "The Rights of Man" that was most likely inspired by the political atmosphere (Graves, 1967). Dancing during this time was characterized by the introduction of quadrilles that were brought by soldiers returning from the Napoleonic Wars (Donal, 1974).

After the conclusion of the Napoleonic Wars of the nineteenth century, the rural landscape changed from tillage to pastures that favored large estates and required less labor, thereby increasing greatly the number of landless and unemployed native Irish. The Irish population of over more than eight million lived mostly below the poverty level in crowded conditions, relying primarily on potatoes for nourishment (Donal, 1974). Late in 1845, the population was rocked to its core by the emergence of the potato blight of a deadly fungus that ruined the peasants' potato food source (online source 2). The Great Famine lasted until 1849 (Daly, 1986). The lack of British assistance resulted in 1.5 million dead due to starvation and over millions more fleeing the country in the short four years (Donal, 1974).

The Famine forever changed the landscape of Ireland. Music and dance also suffered. Folklore tells of pipers, fiddlers and dancing masters ending their days in workhouses while silence fell on the "land of song" (Donal, 1974). Anguish was clearly expressed in the folk songs such as "Amhrán na bPrataí Dubha," the "Song of the Black Potatoes" (Graves, 1967). One of the saddest cultural impacts of the Great Famine on musicians was the loss of the Gaelic language by most Irish. It was accompanied by the loss of much of the folklore that went with it (Ó hAllmhuráin, 1998). Following the Great Famine, almost 30 percent of the population emigrated, spreading their music and dance with them (Shaw, 1986).

A Second Chance

The Second Celtic revival took place in the 1890s with the establishment of the Gaelic League, *Conradh na Gaeilge*, with the goal of a romantic reconstruction of Irish music and dance (Graves, 1967). The movement grew rapidly and held its first céilí in England in 1897 called the *Feis Ceoil* (Ó hAllmhuráin, 1998). The league also laid down rules for dancing and initiated competitions for music; both practices unheard of before in the Irish performing arts (Graves, 1967). The Gaelic League also tried to revive the native language (Ó hAllmhuráin 98). The revival's cultural renaissance of urban Ireland was very different from the rural Irish culture that retained some regional traditions and was less structured (Donal, 1974).

In the early twentieth century, Ireland's traditional music was marked by loss of rural traditions and towns experiencing renewed interest in Gaelic culture (Ó hAllmhuráin, 1998). Ireland experienced a period of economic stability from the end of the Boer War in 1898 until World War I that further helped the revival efforts spread throughout Ireland (Daly, 1986). The league set up traveling teachers, *timirí*, to instruct Gaelic language classes all over the country (Ó hAllmhuráin, 1998). They continued to transform dancing with their league rules being transferred from the *feis* competitions to other social events (Ó hAllmhuráin 98). They even altered the dancer's costume of plain cloaks and sashes to include silver buckle shoes, brooches and added additional national emblems (Donal, 1974).

Politics of the times were also rapidly changing with the return of the local Irish government in 1898 (Ó hAllmhuráin, 1998). The Sinn Féin, "ourselves alone," party was founded in 1905 and attracted the attention of separatist groups such as the Irish Republican Brotherhood (Ó hAllmhuráin, 1998). The Sinn Féin rebellion in 1916, as well as their success at the polls in 1918 helped lead to the War of Independence and the 1921 Anglo-Irish treaty that created the Irish Free State of the British Commonwealth from 26 Southern counties. Northern Ireland remained part of the United Kingdom (online source 2; Ó hAllmhuráin 100–101).

A conservative wave of policies was enacted in the Free State supported by the Catholic Church that limited dancing and music (Ó hAllmhuráin, 1998). In 1926, radio was introduced in the Free State that popularized some traditional musicians (Donal, 1974). The Gaelic League set up the *An Coimuisiún le Rincí Gaelacha*, the Irish Dancing Commission, that codified Irish dancing as a competitive process in 1930 (Ó hAllmhuráin, 1998). The commission was given authority in 1935 when the Public

Dance Hall Act required all public dances to be licensed (Curtis 73). *An Coimuisiún le Rincí Gaelacha* certified teachers, oversaw competitions, regulated dances and laid down precise rules for national dance costumes (Donal, 1974).

The Fianna Fáil party was formed by Eamon de Valera in 1932 and dominated Irish politics for many years (Ó hAllmhuráin, 1998). The economic situation was bleak in Ireland, as it was in America and Britain (Ó hAllmhuráin 110). Music and dance greatly suffered under the oppressive watch of the clergy, police, and judiciary trinity (Shaw, 1986). Ireland remained out of World War II, and in 1949 the Irish Republic Act was initiated by the new government of the Inter-Party, led by John A. Costello, which withdrew the country from the British Commonwealth (Ó hAllmhuráin, 1998).

The unstable government of the 1940s allowed the church to dominate politics, and the traditional music had a lower status than its "high art" counterparts (Ó hAllmhuráin, 1998). The Fleadh Cheoil Movement, which was started in 1951 by the Dublin's Piper's Club helped raise the status of the traditional players of all Irish instruments by offering a competitive venue, *fleadh cheoil*, (Ó hAllmhuráin, 1998). The renamed Comhalltas Ceoltóirí Éireann made the *fleadh cheoil* an annual event in County Clare that had immense effect on traditional music in the 1950s and 1960s (Ó hAllmhuráin, 1998). This era was marked by the emergence of performers playing professionally on stages, in céilí bands and in lounge bars (Ó hAllmhuráin, 1998). As Ireland became a global player in business, the music of lounge bars became more eclectic, with jigs and ballads mixed with jives and waltzes (Donal, 1974). The Chieftains formed in 1963 and became an immensely popular recording ensemble in 1975 that brought Irish traditional music up to par with other music genres in world entertainment (Ó hAllmhuráin, 1998).

In the 1970s when Ireland entered into the European Economic Community, it left behind the self-conscious feelings of the 1940s and truly became an urban nation (Ó hAllmhuráin 134). The Arts Council of Ireland was founded in 1973 and had the position of Traditional Music Officer added in 1980 to aid in the preservation and promotion of traditional Irish music (Donal, 1974). Musicians gained new found notoriety in the 1970s and 1980s, proving that Irish Traditional music was no longer stuck in its old communal setting and was now part of popular culture (Ó hAllmhuráin, 1998). The commercialism of music since the 1980s has had an impact on traditional Irish music because copyrights have infringed on the traditional process of the musicians sharing songs and modifying them (Donal, 1974).

Irish dancing has undergone several developmental stages since the 1970s with the formation of dance and Feis commissions around the globe (Graves, 1967). In the 1980s, set dancing gained wide support in urban Irish middle class with the formation of set dance classes and clubs in many parts of the world. The 1990s had a large revival of Irish step dancing after the 1994 Eurovision performance of *Riverdance* set off a worldwide phenomenon (Ó hAllmhuráin, 1998). The costumes of dancers have become flashier, and the competitions more fierce with the increased popularity.

Conclusion

Ireland is very different country today than a century ago. It has the second highest GDP in the European Union and the entire Island is more peaceful as the IRA officially disarmed only in the summer of 2006. Despite these changes, traditional Irish music and dance seem set on remaining an important factor in the lives of the Irish people for many years to come. Preservation organizations and the engagement of the youth bonds well for traditional Irish music and dance (Graves, 1967). However, the political and social events of Irish culture are bound to continue the cycle of evolution, despite effort to preserve the old ways. The traditional dance and music of the Emerald Isle has always followed its people through good times and bad. The "land of song" will continue to use music and dance to carry on its spirit for centuries to come.

References

Ashton, T. S. (1961). *The Industrial Revolution, 1760–1830*. London: Oxford University Press.
Barrow, G.W.S. (1965). *Robert Bruce and the Community of the Realm of Scotland*. London: Eyre & Spottiswoode.
Bodley, Seoirse (1973). Technique and Structure in Sean-nós Singing. *Éigse Ceol Tíre* 1:44–54.
Breatnach, Liam (1987) *Uraicecht Na Riar*. Dublin: Dublin Institute for Advanced Studies.
CBS News (2005). IRA Says It Will Disarm, and News Tools Ireland: Retrieved November 11, 2005, from http://www.cbsnews.com/stories/2005/07/28/world/main712424.shtml.
Cowdery, James (1990). *The Melodic Tradition of Ireland*. Kent, Ohio: Kent State University Press.

Curtis, P.J. (1994). *Notes from the Heart: A Celebration of Traditional Irish Music.* Dublin, Ireland; Torc.
Daly, M. E. (1986). *The Famine in Ireland.* Dublin: Dundalgan.
Golding, B. (2001). *Conquest and Colonization: The Normans in Britain, 1066–1100.* New York: Palgrave.
Graves, A. P. (1967). *Irish Literary and Musical Studies.* Freeport, NY: Books for Libraries.
Hadjiapvlou, Maria (2004). *Women in the Cypriot Communities Interpreting Women's Lives.* Nicosia: PC.
Henebry, Richard (1928). *A Handbook of Irish Music.* Cork, Ireland: Cork University Press.
The History of Irish Dance (2004). Retrieved November 11, 2005, from: http://www.irelandseye.com/dance.html.
Hopman, Ellen Evert (1995). *A Druids Herbal.* Rochester, VT: Destiny.
Kelly, Fergus (1976). *Audacht Morainn.* Dublin: Dublin Institute for Advanced Studies.
Kelly, Fergus (1991). *A Guide to Early Irish Law.* Dublin: Dublin Institute for Advanced Studies.
MacFarlane, Malcolm (1925). Half a Century of Vocal Gaelic Music. In *Transactions of the Gaelic Society of Inverness* XXXII.
MacNeil, Máire (1962). *The Festival of Lughnasa: A Study of the Survival of the Celtic Festival of the Beginning of Harvest.* London: Oxford University Press.
Markale, Jean (1999). *The Druids, Celtic Priests of Nature.* Rochester, VT: Inner Traditions.
Matthews, John (1996). *The Druid Source Book.* London: Blanford.
O'Boyle, Seán (1976). *The Irish Song Tradition.* Toronto: Macmillan.
Ó Canainn, Tomas. (1978). *Traditional Music in Ireland.* Boston: Routledge and Kegan Paul.
Ó Canainn, Tomás (1993). *Traditional Music in Ireland.* Cork: Ossian.
Ó Faracháin, Róibeárd (1947). *The Course of Irish Verse in English.* New York: Sheed and Ward.
Ó hAllmhuráin, Gearóid. (1998). *A Pocket History of Irish Traditional Music.* Dublin, Ireland: O'Brien.
O Madagàin, Breandàin (1993). Song for Emotional Release in the Gaelic Tradition. In *Irish Musical Studies,* vol. 2, ed. Gerard Gillen & Harry White. Dublin: Irish Academic Press.
O'Sullivan, Donal (1974). *Irish Folk Music: Song and Dance.* Cork: Mercier.
Shaw, Margaret Fay (1986). *Folksongs and Folklore of South Uist,* 3d ed. Aberdeen, UK: Aberdeen University Press.
Shields, Hugh (1973). Supplementary Syllables in Anglo-Irish Folk Singing. In *Yearbook of the International Folk Music Council* 5, 62–71.
Shields, Hugh (1993). *Narrative Singing in Ireland.* Dublin: Irish Academic.
Troost, W. (1983). *William III and the Treaty of Limerick (1691–1697): A Study of His Irish Policy.* Unpublished Ph.D. thesis, Leiden University.
Williams, Sean (1984). Joe Heaney Sean-nós: the singing of Joe Heaney, and An Tighearna Randal: an Irish-Gaelic version of Lord Randall. *Seattle Folklore Society Journal* 2(1)2, 4–7.

35. The Flamenco Dance Tradition of Spain

Originating in the southernmost region of Spain, *Flamenco* is known as the music of Andalusia (Totton, 2003). Clearly a genuine Spanish art form, Flamenco is the music of the people (Don Quijote, 2005; Totton, 2003). Today, Flamenco can be seen throughout the world. But, before one can appreciate it in its entirety, one must discover its secrets of origin as well as its elements of artistry.

The Origin of Flamenco

The Gypsies played an important part in the evolution of Flamenco, but the musical style is not exclusively theirs. Although often credited for originating the style, the Gypsies did not bring their own music to the different countries where they settled. Instead, they adopted a country's music and incorporated their own particular musical style and rhythmic sense into the music (Totton, 2003). Gypsies have acted more so as catalysts of Flamenco and are known for being largely responsible for its survival (Totton, 2003).

Flamenco dance developed from the "melting pot of Andalusia" (Totton, 2003, p. 14). Andalusia was ruled for nearly eight centuries by the Moors, a Muslim people. Because they were a mixture of different cultures themselves, the Moors were a tolerant people, accepting many into their civilization (Totton, 2003). Those accepted by the Moor society were Christians, descendants of Greek colonists, retired Roman legionaries, Sephardic Jews, Tartessians, Carthaginians, and Phoenicians (Totton, 2003). However, the Christian intolerance of the Moors and the Jews following the Christian Reconquest in 1492 caused the Christians to force them out and to move underground to survive in hills or caves. The Moors and the Jews also found refuge by living with the Gypsies, who commonly gave hospitality to those escaping the law (Totton, 2003).

This migration brought their music underground as well. They performed it in houses or caves, where it stayed until the end of the eighteenth century (Totton, 2003). The Moors and the Jews probably shared much of their music with the Gypsies with whom many of them lived.

35. The Flamenco Dance Tradition of Spain

This is perhaps why Gypsies were believed to be the sole creators of Flamenco. However, it was most likely their stylistic additions and renditions of the music of the Moors and Jews that helped shape Flamenco. In addition, all of the different cultures that the Moors accepted into their society prior to the Christian Reconquest left an imprint on Andalusian culture and directly and indirectly influenced Flamenco (Don Quijote, 2005). The music of the "melting pot of Andalusia" began to be heard in taverns and other public places at the beginning of the nineteenth century (Totton, 2003, p. 14). This was when Flamenco as it is known today started and began to be recognized as an art form.

It was in *Las Cartas Marreucas* of *Cadalso* in 1774 that Flamenco was first mentioned in literature (Don Quijote, 2005). The towns of Cádiz, Jerez de la Frontera, and Seville are probably the birthplace of Flamenco. These are the places where the first Flamenco schools arose between the years of 1765 and 1860. In the beginning, Flamenco seemed to be purely vocal, and it was accompanied only by clapping of the hands (*toque de palmas*). The guitar playing or dance was introduced as a form of Flamenco much later.

Flamenco began developing into its definitive form during its Golden Age between the years of 1869 and 1910 (Don Quijote, 2005). During this period, Flamenco was performed in music cafes known as *cafes cantantes*. Also dating from the Golden Age is Flamenco's most intense form, *cante jondo*, which expresses deep feelings. In the *cafés cantantes* of the Golden Age, Flamenco dancers became major attractions of Flamenco as the art of its dance rose to new heights. Finally, the role of the guitar reached its peak during these years and began developing into an essential part of the Flamenco art form (don Quijote, 2005).

The appearance of *ópera flamenca* marked the style of Flamenco singing during the period between the years of 1910 and 1955 (don Quijote, 2005). *Opera flamenca* was an easier kind of music, unlike *cante jondo*, and had evidence of South American influence. Beginning in the year 1915, shows featuring Flamenco began being organized and performed around the world (don Quijote, 2005).

The year 1955 sparked a sort of Flamenco Renaissance with Antonio Mairena being its key figure and performer (don Quijote, 2005). During this time, Flamenco made its way out of the *tablaos*, successors of the *cafés cantantes*, as its dancers and soloists began performing in theaters and concert houses. In addition, guitar players began acquiring increasing positive attention and recognition as important components of Flamenco, and, therefore, guitar playing arrived at mastery (don Quijote, 2005).

The Music and Movement of Flamenco

Flamenco exists in three forms: the song (*el cante*), the dance (*el baile*), and the guitar playing (*la guitarra*) (don Quijote, 2005). A fourth, very important component of Flamenco is its rhythmic pattern called the *compas* (Martinez, 2003). In Flamenco, the *compas* is a "rhythmic cycle, a recurring pattern, with accents in certain places" (Martinez, 2003, p. 7). Rhythm in Flamenco is found first and foremost in the song, with the rhythm itself disguised as "potential dance" (Totton, 2003, p. 43). The rhythm also comes from the guitar, from clapping (*palmas*), finger snapping (*pitos*), and from the dancer's own feet. In addition, the guitar gives the meter, and the feet of the dancer generate the shape of the dance as the clapping reinforces the rhythm and beat variations within the performance (Totton, 2003). Robin Totton (2003) notes, "All these are a part of the art" (p. 43).

Because re-creation is one of Flamenco's central defining characteristics, Flamenco constantly changes (Totton, 2003). A second characteristic of Flamenco is that, even when a group performs together, it is essentially a solo art. While true Flamenco dancers can perform in groups, their movements may be synchronized, but they won't be the same, or even symmetrical. A third characteristic of Flamenco is that it communicates strong, uninhibited feeling. Just as Totton (2003) points out "Grace is a quality of dance the world over, and that Force is a Flamenco quality" (p. 48). Flamenco is also built on strong and complicated rhythms. The art of Flamenco is described most elegantly and accurately by Totton (2003) as:

> A form of communication generated by emotion unrelated to intellect; complicated rhythms; an art that is essentially individual, and expresses that individuality; the forceful expression of strong feeling, rather than prettiness of sound and movement; and a musical form that is re-created at each performance: these are the main characteristics of an art that evolved as the music of outcasts, of people harassed by the law or hounded by the Spanish Inquisition and living outside the pale of society [pp. 25–26].

Totton (2003) continues his description by adding that it is "Not surprising, then, that it is primarily a tragic expression of the human condition.... Flamenco is tragic—or else, by reaction, festive" (p. 26). It is believed that Flamenco performances exist as ways to remember and reenact the essence of the social life of the Andulasian people of Spain (Washabaugh, 1996). Through Flamenco, the twists and turns of Andulasian cultural history are preserved and celebrated. Washabaugh (1996) expands on this idea by noting that "the extraordinary variety of Flamenco performances in the twentieth century results, in part, from artists' creative handling of these elemental experiences" (p. 3).

Creative handling of the Flamenco has allowed it to remain essentially an improvised art (Totton, 2003). Flamenco depends on the mood and form of the performer for its quality during a performance. In addition, Flamenco is, in essence, folk music. Totton (2003) adds, "It [Flamenco] is folk music in the sense that it is of the people, not an art learned as classical music is learned" (p. 16). Even today, many performers of Flamenco cannot read a note of music. Instead, they learn from one another by listening (Totton, 2003). Also, for many people of Andulasia, Flamenco is an everyday part of their lives. Totton (2003) notes, "And it is more flourishing now in the beginning of the twenty-first century than it was ten or twenty years ago" (p. 17).

Three fundamental elements that help define whether or not a dance belongs to the Flamenco genre are the presence of a Flamenco mode (musical tonality), *compas*, and a Flamenco performer (Martinez, 2003). These three elements contribute to the authenticity of a Flamenco performance also known as *flamencura* (Martinez, 2003). There is also no such thing as a passive audience during Flamenco performances. The audience joins in the performance by clapping their hands and even sometimes singing along (Totton, 2003).

Additionally, there are four general characteristics of Flamenco dance: 1) downward; 2) introvert; 3) abstract; and 4) ecstatic (Totton, 2003). The downward characteristic of the dance can be seen in the *zapateado*. The *zapateado* is the "creation of rhythms by drumming on the ground with the feet" (Totton, 2003, p. 54). Although the dance uses the whole body, Flamenco dance is largely dependent on the drummed rhythms created by a dancer's feet. The patterns and rhythms of the *zapateado* are created when the dancer uses the heel, the whole foot, the sole, and the point of the toe to make variations in the quality and intensity of the sound (Totton, 2003). The *zapateado* patterns can also be created by scraping the sole on the ground in a brush-drum effect. The *zapateado* and its associated movements place much attention of the dance downward (Totton, 2003). The downwardness of the dance can also be seen in the downward placement of the eyes. Even when the face is turned up, the eyes are still directed downward (Totton, 2003).

Because Flamenco is basically a solo art, the dancer does not have to relate to anyone else. This in itself forces introversion of the dancers as they look inside themselves for the emotion to use as artistic expression.

In addition, the downward placement of the eyes reinforces introversion, allowing the dancer to place her focus inside herself (Totton, 2003). The abstract characteristic of the dance stems from the notion that the dancer only expresses himself or herself (Totton, 2003). The ecstatic characteristic of the Flamenco arises from the force and intensity of the continuous movement and repetition of the *compas* (Totton, 2003). Totton (2003) describes the ecstatic nature of the dance as seeming "understated at first, then slowly, gradually, it rises in intensity until it reaches a climax" (p. 59).

Flamenco as a Mixed-Gender Dance

The Flamenco is danced by both men and women. The male Flamenco dancer is called a *bailaor*, and the female dancer is called a *bailaora* (Martinez, 2003). Both the man's dance and the woman's dance incorporate the *zapateado* as the foundation of the dance (Totton, 2003). Although only the man's dance had the presence of *zapateado* in the past, in the 1920s, when the great Carmen Amaya began incorporating *zapateado* into her dances, *zapateado* began taking over the dance for both men and women (Totton, 2003). The woman's dance is characterized by ornamental wrist and finger movement. The woman's arms, hands, and fingers move in a continuous flow, seemingly independent of her other movements (Totton, 2003). However, in the man's dance, his fingers are "held together, straight or cupped, and the twirling at the wrist is usually done as an inward motion rather than both in and out" (Totton, 2003, p. 62). Men usually have a more rigid stance while dancing as well. Other differences can be found between the man's dance and the woman's dance, most being to the man's disadvantage. This is apparent in that women can add to their constant arm and hand movement by swirling their skirts (Totton, 2003). The man is left with only a jacket, waistcoat, or kerchief to manipulate during a performance. He is able to hold it and turn it back or take it off and swing it over his shoulder, but it is not comparable to the audacity of a woman's dress (Totton, 2003).

Conclusion

Influences of other kinds of music including jazz, salsa, and Bossa Nova, are shown in modern day Flamenco. Today's Flamenco dancing has also changed somewhat in that female dancers are more likely to showcase their temperament more than their artistry (Don Quijote). In addition, the Flamenco guitar that was usually used for featuring Flamenco dancers has become a solo art form in itself (All About Spain). However, although Flamenco has been an art form acknowledged and accepted on the world stage, it will always remain an intimate, genuinely southern Spanish style of music.

References

All About Spain. (n.d.). Flamenco. Retrieved November 7, 2005, from http://www.red2000.com/spain/flamenco/.

don Quijote. (1996–2005). Flamenco. Retrieved November 7, 2005, from http://www.donquijote.org/culture/spain/flamenco/.

Manuel, Peter (1989) Andalusian, Gypsy, and Class Identity in the Contemporary Flamenco Complex. *Ethnomusicology 33*(1), 47–65.

Martinez, Emma. (2003). *Flamenco.... All You Wanted to Know*. Pacific, MO: Mel Bay.

Mitchell, Timothy (1994). *Flamenco Deep Song*. New Haven, CT: Yale University Press.

Taylor, Roger L. (1978) *Art, an Enemy of the People*. Atlantic Highlands, NJ: Humanities.

Totton, Robin (2003). *Song of the Outcasts: An Introduction to Flamenco*. Portland, OR: Amadeus.

Washabaugh, William (1996). *Flamenco: Passion, Politics, and Popular Culture*. Washington, D.C.: Berg.

Woodall, James (1992). *In Search of the Firedance*. London: Sinclair-Stevenson.

Part VI: Middle East

36. The Music and Dances of Afghanistan

Afghanistan is one of the many countries that everyone in America has been affected by in the past few years. Even through its extensive media coverage and the many stories circulated, Afghanistan as a country is shrouded in mystery and misnomers. One of these misunderstandings is that of Afghanistan's culture and music. Does Afghanistan have music? Are their children's heads permeated with the latest pop song as many in America are? The answers to these questions do not contain simple straightforward answers, but instead need context. The history and traditions of the Afghani people combined with their present day music tell the full tale of their musical heritage.

The Background

Before any conjectures can be made on present-day Afghanistan and its music, it is crucial to understand the people of the country and their complex past. Before "Afghanistan" came into existence, the land was home to a wide variety of settlers. These travelers would collect and form ethnic-based tribes throughout the land. Some of these groups included Jewish, Sunni, Shia, Ismaili, Sikh, and Hindu (Dupree, 2002). These tribes helped form the value system that Afghanis stand by to this day. This emphasized the importance of honor in every situation. Honoring ones name comes in many forms. That belief in honor is reflected in the works of Pashto poet Khushal Khan Khattak. Loyalty to tribe, family, and friends are of the utmost importance. Also is the protection and respect of guests and tolerance of others. These values and senses of patriotism would continue through the countries founding in 1880 (Dupree, 2002).

In a country with so many different ethnic groups and such avid patriotism, small scale strife was always present. In the 1940s, the central government tried to use radio to unify a fractioned country. Radio Kabul, later Radio Afghanistan, turned out to be one of the greatest unifying tools at the government's disposal: "there were some 500,000 radios in Afghanistan by 1976, or one radio for each 36 persons," (Dupree, 2002). This new creative medium sparked a rise in musical talent and industry.

This circulation of both popular and traditional music did much to promote the unity of the nation, but had some inherent problems. The Islamic faith recognizes music with mixed opinion. The Koran at one instance views it as being a tool of corruption, but in another refers to it as a way to express the joys of the heart (Mayar, 2006). It is in this contradiction that contains the fate of Afghanistan's music. The progressive music and culture of Kabul did not satisfy all of Afghanistan. In fact, many of the rural dwellers were resentful about what they perceived as corruption in their cities. In the late 1970s, this gap between Afghanistan's people spurred a coup d'état, starting a long spiral of conflicts that dominate the regions current history.

The Soviets were the first to capitalize on this civil unrest. The Soviet rule forced millions into exile and wreaked havoc on the culture of the country. With the cities as their basis of existence, the new administration started eliminating forces of opposition and remodeling society after that of Russia. Meanwhile, millions of refugees were forced to exist outside of their homeland and raise three generations of Afghans who had never been home. In this period, much of the music and tradition faded from the hardships faced in exile. The only haven of Afghani art would be the poetry expressing the turmoil of the people.

It would be to a rising group of Islamic purists to fight back against the Soviet oppressors. Up until the withdrawal of Soviet troops in 1989, the "Reagan Doctrine" allowed for the spending on an estimated 3.5 billion dollars for the war effort. The vacuum left by the sudden lapse in government allowed for these Islamic purists to take control of their homeland. It was then the Taliban regime was created (Misra, 2002).

The Taliban has been a near household name in the past few years. With the war in Afghanistan, the media was consumed with the stories of their violent oppression and extremist views. The Taliban government failed for two reasons: it did not represent the will of the people, and it utilized flawed interpretations of the Koran to empower its laws. Saidel Mayar, a native of Afghanistan, had this to say about the Taliban's effect on culture and music when asked what kinds of censorship was enforced under the Taliban: "There was not any censorship; there just was no music at all."

With jailing and harsh penalties, the bias interpretation of Islam was enforced, causing another mortal blow to the Afghani musical culture. Among these harsh punishments were also extreme views on the rights of women. It wouldn't be until the downfall of the Taliban when Afghanis would have the opportunity to have their own musical culture once again.

After the destruction of the Taliban government, culture was slow to return to the harshly Taliban ruled cities. Kabul, the most liberal of the cities, was the first to shed new life into the country. After rebuilding, music shops and cultural stores of many types opened in Kabul. Music, although not quite acceptable in public areas, was no longer taboo (Mayar, 2006). Even Radio Kabul slowly resumed its airing of musical talents. Saidel made mention that much of the music on the radio was nothing compared to pre-Taliban radio, but it just needed time to improve. At the present, music has become a strong industry and cultural focal point of Afghanistan.

The Music

Despite the large strains put on the culture of Afghanistan, the people still managed to keep many of the musical traditions alive. From the radios and music stores of Kabul to the musical prayer of Sufi Islam, music today is a part of everyone's life there. Like in the days before the Soviet and Taliban oppression, celebration and festivities were accompanied by music. This created not only another unifying source of patriotism but a market for the advancement of Afghan culture.

Music and dance are not a usual public affair but everyone does dances at weddings and special ceremonies (Yousuf, 2006). In many festivities, professionally trained musicians are hired from the Court of Kabul. This institution can be compared to the United States Julliard. Graduates of this prestigious school go on to be musical performers of every category: traditional, neo-traditional, and the contemporary or pop music genres. In particular, the Attan is a dance specifically performed at many formal celebrations, such as weddings or birthdays. This traditional dance can be accompanied by a variety of *Attan* songs. It is performed by forming large circles, one male one female, and dancing traditional dances (Mayar, 2006). These styles vary from location to location but usually include spinning and a variety of other motions.

Music from Afghanistan shares many commonalities among the other Middle-Eastern countries. Many of the melodies of the traditional music are sung in a solo format with a variety of simple string or drums accompanying. Some commonly recognized instruments used in traditional Afghani music are the harmonium, a hand-organ type instrument, and the Tabla, a smaller hand drum (Mayar, 2006). Other instruments commonly used are *Dolak* (drum), *Shashtar* (long-necked guitar) and a variety of other drum and guitar-like instruments. Many traditional songs only use two or three of these instruments with a vocal line to complete the song. Their music uses several different meters to give the Middle-Eastern feel. The most noticeable of these is the 9/8 time signature. This pattern is very different from our 4/4 common time signature in nearly every way. The odd beat causes a disorienting scheme to be present in the music and usually casts the song into obscurity to the untrained ear.

The songs subjects cover a broad spectrum of emotion. Many of the songs are about love or faith (Mayar, 2006). Other songs are made to prepare men for battle. Like any society, music takes many functions. Now in Afghanistan, many contemporary groups are playing with a new blend of music, fusing the western world. Using guitars and synthesizers along with few traditional instruments, popular contemporary artists like Ahmad Zahir win over new audiences in Afghanistan.

Even though the large majority of Afghanistan is cautious about the overuse of music in life, there is one religious group who incorporates song into their prayer. The *Sufi's* are a mystic intellectual group that predates the coming of Islam in the area. These people are known for their poetry and music. After the conversion to Islam they used their poetry for prayer. Many of these songs are adapted directly from Sufi poems of praise to their God (Mayar, 2006).

This form of prayer was of the greatest controversy when the Taliban was in power. With the new interpretation of the Koran, Sufi could no longer use their religious poetry as song to praise their God (Mayar, 2006). But since the freedom from the Taliban rule, the Sufi people have been able to return to worship in their own characteristic way.

Conclusion

Afghanistan is a complex country with a myriad of factors making its cultural identity. It is only after looking at the background of the Afghan people that their music and culture can start to be understood and appreciated. From the refugee poetry, to the code of honor, this nation had produced not only a unique style of music and culture, but a unique way of life. From the wondering settlers of old to the unique blend of today, it is hard not to respect the origins of the Afghan sound. Traditional Afghani Instruments include Dolak, Shashtar, Zerbagali, Dhamboura, Tambur, Tula, Richak, Daira, and Waj.

References

Baily John (1979). Professional and Amateur Musicians in Afghanistan. *The World of Music* 21(2), 46–64.

Baily, John (1988). *Music of Afghanistan: Professional Musicians in the City of Heart*. Cambridge: Cambridge University Press.

Barahami, Yousuf (2006). Personal interview. November 3, 2006.

Dupree, Nancy (2002). Cultural Heritage and National Identity in Afghanistan. *Third World Quarterly* 23(5), 977–989.

Mayar, Saidel (2006). Personal interview. November 16, 2006.

Misra, Amalendu (2002). The Taliban, Radical Islam and Afghanistan. *Third World Quarterly* 23(3), 577–589.

Sakata, Hiromi Lorraine (1986). The Complementary Opposition of Music and Religion in Afghanistan. *The World of Music* 28(3), 33–41.

Touma, Habib Hassan (1978). Present State and Problems in the Study and Research of Arabian Music Heritage. *The World of Music* 20(1), 110–6.

Touma, Habib Hassan (1980). World History of Music—History of Arabian Music: A Study. *The World of Music* 22(3), 66–75.

37. The Saray Court Dance of the Turkish People

Turkey, or the Republic of Turkey, is a Eurasian country that stretches from Southwest Asia to the Southeast Europe. Turkey is bordered by eight countries: Georgia, Greece, Bulgaria, Armenia, Iraq, Syria, Iran, and Azerbaijan. Since the demise of the Ottoman Empire in 1923, Turkey has been a democratic republic. The capital of Turkey is Ankara; however, its largest city is Istanbul, which was once known as Constantinople, capital of the Roman Empire from 330 to 395. Turkey's current President is Ahmet

Necdet Sezer, and its current Prime Minister is Recep Tayyip Erdogan. Turkey's total area is 302,534 square miles, making it the 37th largest country in the world. Turkey's population, according to the 2005 census, is 73,193,000, with a population density of 24 per square mile, making Turkey the seventeenth most populated country in the world. Turkey's GDP as of 2006 is approximately $612.3 Billion, the seventeenth highest in the world. Turkey's currency is the New Turkish Lira. Turkey is one of the largest and most powerful countries in the world; it was even one of the founding countries of the United Nations.

History of Turkey

Modern Turkey is one of the oldest inhabited places in the world. Some of the earliest Neolithic sites can be found within Turkey such as *Gobekli Tepe, cayonii, Mersin catalhoyuk, Hacilar,* and *Nevali Cori.* The city of Troy began in the Neolithic Era and continued onward until the Iron Age. Although Turkey had many settlements within it, it was not until the eighteenth century until it had a major empire. From the eighteenth to the thirteenth century, the Hittites dominated the Turkish area. The Phrygians then succeeded the Hittites in their decline. After the demise of the Phrygians in the 7th century, the Cimmerians took control. The Greeks, meanwhile, settled in Anatolia. Anatolia was controlled by the Persians until 334 BC when Alexander the Great conquered the area. Most of the Turkish areas, however, fell into Roman rule in the first century BC. In 324 BC, Constantinople I chose Constantinople as the capital of the Roman Empire. It later became the capital of the Eastern Roman Empire, or otherwise known as the Byzantine Empire. The Byzantine Empire gradually declined until the 11th century BC, when the Seljuk Empire came to be. The Seljuks were a Muslim tribal people in the Anatolia area. The Seljuk Empire, however, gave way to the Ottoman Empire that arose in 1299. The Ottoman Empire was able to interact with both Eastern and Western cultures nearby. In the sixteenth and seventeenth centuries, the Ottoman Empire was one of the world's most powerful entities. In World War I, the Ottoman Empire joined the German side. When the Axis lost, the Allied forces broke apart the Ottoman Empire through the Treaty of Sevres. On May 19, 1919, Mustafa Kemal Pasha, a military commander, began the Turkish national movement. The movement aimed at the dissolution of the Treaty of Sevres by involving every available person in the Turkish War of Independence. The occupying armies were defeated and a new state was created in September 18, 1922. The office of the sultan was abolished in November 1, 1922, ending the 631 year rule of the Ottoman Empire. The Republic of Turkey was officially recognized in 1923 by the Treaty of Lausanne. Mustafa Kemal Pasha became the republic's first president and sought to bring Turkey into the modern realm. He was later given the name "Ataturk" which meant "father of the Turks." During World War II, Turkey joined the Allied side and became a charter member of the United Nations. In 1947, the Truman Doctrine gave Turkey large economic support from the United States. During the 1950s and 1960s, Turkey experienced many coups: the Coup of 1960, the Coup of 1980, the Coup of Memorandum, etc. During the 1970s and 1980s, Turkey's political system was very unstable. However, during this period, Turkey experienced spurts of economic growth. The 1990s brought in political stability when the Justice and Development party came into power. In 2005, Turkey became a candidate to become a part of the European Union.

Music of Turkey

Because of Turkey's location, it became a crossroads for the cultures in Europe, Asia, and Africa. This has affected the music of Turkey greatly and can be seen in the elements evident in Turkish music. There are various elements taken from Byzantine, Central Asian, Balkan, Persian, Arabic, and even American music. However, that is not to say that Turkish music is not influential. Many other cultures have been influenced by the music of the Ottoman Empire. Traditional Turkish music has its origins from the Seljuk tribes of the Anatolia area in the 11th century. However, modern Turkish music takes its influences from the 1930s when the Republic first began. The traditional Turkish music can be divided into two main areas: Turkish classical music and Turkish folk music.

Turkish Classical Music

Turkish classical music can be characterized by the culture of the Ottoman Empire and was influenced lyrically by the Persian and Byzantine vocal traditions. The earlier form of this classical music is called *saray music*, which, in Turkish means royal court music, indicative of its origin in the Ottoman royal courts. From these royal courts came *Mehter takama*, or Ottoman military band, considered to be the oldest military marching band in the world.

Classical music has copious amount of scales of which can be used to write music. These scales known as *makams* can be arranged to make a *fasil*, which is a composition comprised of a prelude, postlude, and a primary section that begins with a taksim, an improvised piece or pieces. A full fast/ concert involves four instrumental parts and three vocal parts including a parka format that has the same makam, or scales, throughout the song starting with the prelude and usually ending with an *oyun havas*, or dance. Some of the shorter, *sarka* songs date back to the fourteenth century, but still influence modem day Turkish music.

Famous composers and performers of this era of Turkish music from the past are Sufi Dede Efendi, Prince Cantemir and Sultan Suleyman the Magnificent. Some popular modem Turkish classical performers are Munir Nurettin Seleuk, Biilent Ersoy, Zeki Muren, Muzeyyen Senar and Zekai Tunca. Turkish classical music can be taught to anyone who wants to learn the genre in conservatories and clubs all over Turkey. The largest and most respected of these conservatories is in Istanbul and is known as the *Uskiidar Musiki Cemiyet*.

Ottoman Harem Music (Belly Dancing)

From the melodies of the royal courts, a type of dance music emerged that was different from the oyun havast of fasil music. In the Ottoman Empire, the *harem* was that part of a house set apart for the women of the family. It was a place in which non-family males were not allowed. Eunuchs guarded the sultan's harems, which were quite large, including several hundred women who were wives and concubines. There, female dancers and musicians entertained the women living in the harem. Belly dance was performed by women for women. The female dancers, known as *rakkase*, hardly appeared in public; because of this the belly dance was exclusive to that of the sultan's harem. However, the dance was taken out to the street by male entertainers, *rakkas*, who performed the dance in wedding celebrations, feasts, festivals, and in the presence of the sultans.

Military Music

The Mehter Talcum, or Janissary bands, is considered to be the oldest military marching band of the world. Individual performers were mentioned in the Orhun inscriptions, which are believed to be the oldest written sources of Turkish history, dating to the eighth century. However, they were not mentioned as bands until the thirteenth century. Other cultures borrowed the notion of military marching bands from Turkey from the sixteenth century forward.

Western Influences on Turkish Classical Music

The Istanbul Conservatory was created in 1926 to instruct Turkish musicians and composers on the Western style of music. The school would send talented musicians abroad to learn more of Western musical theory. These illustrious students included such composers as Cemal Reşit Rey, Ulvi Cemal Erkin, Ahmet Adnan Saygun, Necil Kazim Akses and Hasan Ferit Alnar, also known as the Turkish Five. More conservatories teaching the Western style of music were made thereafter, showing Turkey's affinity for becoming more Western. This, however, went against the orders of Atatürk. His belief was to "take from the West but to remain Turkish in essence," and thus an archiving of Turkish classical and folk music began in 1924 and ended in 1953 with an archive of 10,000 Turkish songs.

Turkish Folk Music

Traditional Turkish folk music has its meaning about daily life, usually about more humble subjects than Ottoman classical music. Most of the Turkish folk songs speak of real-life stories or sometimes Turkish folklore. Some of these folk songs have developed from "song contests" between musical poets. Folk songs are usually played at weddings, funerals, and festivals, depending on the region the song came from.

Usually each folk song is accompanied by a folk dance, which can differ greatly between different regions. The people of the Aegean region at wedding receptions will dance the *Zeybek*, while *Rumeli* guests will dance to the more upbeat music of the *ciftetelli*. The folk songs can also be affected by "regional mood." Songs from the south have more melodies with more sadness, whereas in the east there are more songs with a joyous beat about them.

The instruments used in traditional Turkish folk music are a wide array of native Turkish instruments. The *baglama* and the *kemence*, for instance, are bow instruments, whereas the *zurna*, *ney*, and *davul* are percussion instruments. Instruments can vary between different regions as well.

Most of these folk songs are taken from the *ozan*, or minstrels. These poets have been adding on to the body of Turkish literature since the 11th century. The baglama was the usual instrument of choice these minstrels used. The musical knowledge was passed down by older ozan. The lessons these teachers gave usually took place in coffeehouses around Turkey. After the apprentices, *alayh*, became experts they took apprentices themselves to pass on the knowledge. Usually, the poets would get into "contests" with other poets, where they each would musically rhyme against each other until one could not find a *quatrain* that fit the story.

Conclusion

Turkish music has an abundant amount of traditions and elements that have been kept throughout the years. Turkish culture has been able to keep its long-standing traditions for the most part and still infuse other cultures into theirs. That is not to say that Turkey is in anyway not influential, on the contrary, the Ottoman Period was a very important cultural period for Turkey and the world. Turkey was able to influence and be influence because of its location in the world. Turkey was called the crossroads of the Middle East, when in fact it was the crossroads of three countries, and not just the Middle East.

References

Bartok, Bela, & Benjamin Suchoff (1976). Turkish Folk Music from Asia Minor. The New York Bartok Archive Studies in Musicology, no. 7. Princeton, NJ: Princeton University Press.
Bellman, Jonathan (1993). *The Style Hongrois in the Music of Western Europe.* Boston: Northeastern University Press.
Erderner, Y. (1987). The Song Contests of Turkish Minstrels: Improvised Poetry Sung to Traditional Music. Milman Parry Studies in Oral Tradition.
Head, M. (2000). Orientalism, Masquerade and Mozart's Turkish Music. London: Royal Musical Association.
Janissary Band (Mehter) (2003). Retrieved 2003 from http://www.cankan.com/gturkishfolks/12mehter_janissary%20band.htm.
The Music of Turkey (2006). Retrieved 2004 from http://tarkandeluxe.blogspot.com/2006/02/music-of-turkey.html.
Popescu-Judetz, Eugenia (1999). *Prince Dimitrie Cantemir: Theorist and Composer of Turkish music.* Istanbul: Pan.
Stokes, M. (2000). Sounds of Anatolia. In *Rough Guide to World Music.* London: Penguin.
Tietze, Andreas & Joseph Yahalom (1995). *Ottoman Melodies—Hebrew Hymns: A*

16th Century Cross-Cultural Adventure. Akademiai Kiado, Bibliotheca Orientalis Hungarica.

Yildiray, E. (1995). *The Song Contests of Turkish Minstrels: Improvised Poetry Sung to Traditional Music*. New York: Garland.

Yildirim, A. (2004). Turkish Music and Artists. Retrieved 2004 from http://tarkandeluxe.blogspot.com/2004/05/turkishmusic-and-artists.html.

38. Traditional Music of Iraq

Iraq's music represents an ancient, highly developed, and multifaceted culture. The diverse culture and deep multiethnic civilizations of Iraq have created a rich heritage of music. Baghdad was the capital of West Asia between the 7th and the fourteenth century, with people immigrating to Baghdad from various parts of the world. This interaction brought different nations together to make unique and distinct musical traditions. Arabic musical styles form the majority of Iraq's music, but with strong influences from Kurdish, Turkish, and Persian music thus creating a unique mix. Iraqi music has been around for a number of years and although it is strongly influenced by the rest of the Arabic world, it still has many of its own musicians, instruments, genres, and dance.

Maqamat

Iraqi singers enjoy great popularity in the Arab world. Jewish singers and musicians also made an important contribution to Baghdad's culture from the 1920s until 1950s, when most of them left the country for various reasons. Among them were the two famous brothers Saleh and Da'ud al-Kuwaiti. In the 1940s and 1950s, the four most important types of music in Baghdad were *Maqamat, Monologat, Pestat,* and *Budhiyat. Maqamat*, the most popular form of classical Arab music, is a kind of high-pitched, sophisticated Arab blues, accompanied by *oud*, violins, and drums. Across the Arab world, *maqam* refers to specific musical scales, whereas in Iraq, it can also refer to a specific kind of rule-based improvised performance. There are 50 to 70 different maqams, each with its own mood and characteristics. In the Iraqi maqam form, the introduction and finale surround set musical and melodic passages performed alternately by the vocalist and instrumentalists. *Monologat* consists of non-classical songs that include elements of humor and cynicism. *Pestat* is popular poetry sung to music. *Budhiyat* is a hymn like type of music reminiscent of Buddhist chanting.

Contemporary Music

From the late 1940s to the late 1970s, tastes in music shifted from traditional Maqamat to a mix of Maqamat and songs based on lighter, more popular Arab music. Uniquely Iraqi styles blended gradually with other Arab styles, mainly under Egyptian influence. Nazim al-Ghazali, who was popular in the 1950s and 1960s, was the main representative of this trend, although most of his songs were in the classical Maqamat style. Beginning in the late 1970s, a combination of Arab and European music was introduced, creating Arab pop music.

Important singers since the late twentieth century have included Ilham al-Madfa'i, Kazim al-Sahir, Sa'dun Jaber, Fu'ad Salem, and Haytham Yusuf Ilham al-Madfa'i usually accompanies his singing with a Spanish guitar. His main contribution is in modernizing old Maqamat songs. Kazim al-Sahir combines traditional Arab and modern Western singing styles. Most of his songs are personal, but some of them are political. The music of the late Nazim al-Ghazali is still popular, as are the songs of his wife, Salima Murad.

Bedouin songs, accompanied by a simple string instrument, the *rababah*, a two-string spike fiddle whose sound box is made from a coconut shell, are popular in the countryside. Since the late twentieth century, Bedouin music, songs, and dance became popular in Baghdad under Hussein's regime, owing to the rural background of the former ruler (Bedouin).

Instruments

Many of the composers, artists, and singers of Iraqi and Arab music use many of the same instruments. A large number of the instruments used through the years have been around for hundreds of decades. The oud (or ud) is one of the most popular instruments in Middle Eastern music. Its name derives from the Arabic word for "wood," and this refers to the strips of wood used to make its body, which is rounded. This instrument is also played in Greece, where it is known as the *outi* and in Iran, where it is known as the *barbat*. The neck of the oud, which is short in comparison to the body, has no frets, which contributes to its unique sound. The most common string combination is five pairs of strings tuned in unison and a single bass string, although up to 13 strings may be found. Strings are generally made of nylon or sheep or catgut and are plucked with a plectrum known as a *mizrap* or *risha*. Another distinctive feature of the oud is its head, with the tuning pegs bent back at an angle to the neck.

The oud used in the Arab world (including Iraq) is slightly different to that found in Turkey, Armenia and Greece. Different tunings are used, and the Turkish-style oud has a brighter tone than its Arab counterpart. Many musicians have become famous for their playing of the oud: Jamil Bashir, Munir Bashir, Naseer Shamma, Rahim Al Haj, and Ahmed Mukhtar (Oud). Probably the most famous oud player is Munir Bashir. He learned to play the instrument from his father at a very young age and then went on to study and learn much more about it at the Baghdad Institute of Music. His music is used in different advertisements in the Arab world. In his later years, Bashir traveled the world doing a one-man recital show.

Another popular instrument in Iraq and the Arabic world is the *rebab*. The rebab is a two-stringed fiddle. It has an almost heart-shaped body made of wood. The body is covered with a thin layer of skin taken from the intestine or bladder of a buffalo, or sheep skin. The two strings are usually made of copper. In fact, what appears to be two strings is actually a single long string wound around the bottom of the stick and ending in two pegs at the upper part of the stick. These two strings pass over a wide wooden bridge. Unlike other Asian fiddles, the two tuning pegs of the rebab are excessively long. These two long tuning pegs will break easily if they are not gripped closer to the neck of the instrument. This instrument is usually played in the classical music genre but has been known to step outside of its boundaries and play in current genres of music.

The *qanun*, a classical instrument of the Arab world and Turkey, is a plucked box with a trapezoidal body with one rectangular side. It reached its current basic form in the Abbasid period, AD 750 to 1258. It is usually strung with 87 nylon strings (formerly gut) in groups of three that run across a bridge resting on five patches of fish or cow skin. The instrument has a range of four octaves. The strings are plucked by ring-shaped plectra of buffalo horn on both index fingers (Qanun).

Dance

Many of these instruments are used in playing music for the main dance in Iraq and Arab society: the famous belly dance. Belly dancing has a long history and it is hard to say when it actually started. The belly dance is believed to have started in ancient times for women in the midst of childbirth, it was to instruct pregnant women on how to strengthen and roll their abdominal muscles for birth. Women also danced in the absence of men; some sort of goddess worship. Eventually, the dance became commonly known to not just men, but the rest of the world. The belly dance is a spiritual connection between mind and body. Belly dancing is as majestic and regal as classical plays, but differs because it offers its practitioners a total experience, a sense of well-being, joy, freedom and most importantly, is a celebration of the feminine soul and inner spirit through movement. Women say the Goddess within emerges every time they dance. They get entranced by their craft and become totally engulfed with the art and can slip into a "dance trance." When they enter their dance space, their presence and energy is immediately communicated to the audience. They speak to their audience with strong Egyptian technique, intricate and precise movements mirrored with a playful personality. The glue that holds it all together is a vivacious theatrical presence and professionalism. This is still very much the case today, but belly dancing has spread through the entire world and has become an entertainment dance. Many Iraqis do belly dancing to keep the pounds off and to release stress.

The War's Effect on Music and Dance

Unfortunately today, music and dance is very limited because of the war that is taking place in the country. Many of the large cities that were home to music and dance are the most violent cities, and those types of activities can get people killed. But as a result of the music and dance being hushed in certain cities, they have started to flourish in other, less violent cities. Erbil, the Kurdish capital, was able to hold a music festival in October of 2006. Most of the music that was played was traditional music; some pieces were as old as 400 years. The festival was a huge success (Sand).

Conclusion

Before all of the violence in Iraq, music and dance was a huge part of the everyday culture. Although the war has dampened this, it is not ruined and once the war is over, things may go back to the way they were. People will hopefully start to hear familiar instruments such as the oud, rababah, and qanun again. Familiar and new voices will come and unite the country once again. But until this war is over, unfortunately there will not be much music or dancing taking place in Iraq. Hopefully, one day they will return to their musical and dancing traditions.

References

Alexander, Tobias (1995). On the Musical Instruments in the Psalms. *Jewish Bible Quarterly 23*, 53–55.
Al-Khalesi, Yasin Mahmoud (1966). Clay Figurines in the Iraq Museum. Unpublished Master's Degree Thesis, Dept. of History and Archaeology, University of Baghdad.
Avenary, H. (1997). The Discrepancy between Iconographic and Literary Presentations of Ancient Eastern Musical Instruments. *Orbis Musicae 3-4* (1973-74), 121–127.
Badley, Bill, and Zein al Jundi (2000). Europe Meets Asia. In *World Music, Vol. 1: Africa, Europe and the Middle East*, ed. Simon Broughton and Mark Ellingham with James McConnachie and Orla Duane, 391–395. London: Rough Guides/Penguin.
Barnett, R.D. (1969). New Facts about Musical Instruments. *Ur. Iraq 31*, 96–103.
Braun, Joachim (1970). Musical Instruments. *The Oxford Encyclopedia of Archaeology in the Near East*, vol. 4, ed. Eric M. Myers. New York: Oxford University Press.
Cerny, M. K. (1994). Some Musicological Remarks on the Old Mesopotamian Music and its Terminology. *Archiv Orientalni 62*, 17–26.
Collon, D., and A. D. Kilmer (1980). The Lute in Ancient Mesopotamia. *Music and Civilization. The British Museum Yearbook 4*, 13–28.
Cooper, J. (1970). A Sumerian U-I LA from Nimrud with a Prayer for Sin-ar-iskun. *Iraq 32*, 51–67.
Crocker, R. (1997). Mesopotamian Tonal Systems. *Iraq 59*, 189–202.
Crocker, R. L., and A. D. Kilmer (1997). The Fragmentary Music Text from Nippur. *Iraq 46*, 81–85.
Duchesne-Guillemin, M. (1981). Music in Ancient Mesopotamia and Egypt. *World Archaeology 12*, 287–297.
Duchesne-Guillemin, M. (1982). Pukku and Mekku. *Iraq 45*, 151–156.
Dumbrill, R. J. (1998). *The Musicology and Organology of the Ancient Near East*. London: Green.
Dumbrill, R. J. (2005). *The Archaeomusicology of the Ancient Near East*. London: Trafford.

Dyk, P. J. van (1991). Music in Old Testament Times. *Old Testament Essays 4*, 373–380.

Farmer, Henry George (1957). The Music of Ancient Mesopotamia. In *New Oxford History of Music*, vol. 1, ed. J. A. Westrup, et al., ed., 228–256. London: Oxford University Press.

Gurney, O.R. (1968). An Old Babylonian Treatise on the Tuning of the Harp. *Iraq 30*, 229–233.

Gurney, O.R. (1994). Babylon Music Again. *Iraq 56*, 101–106.

Gurney, O. R., and M. West (1998). Mesopotamian Tonal Systems: A Reply. *Iraq 60*, 223–227.

Jenkins, J. (1969). A Short Note on African Lyres in Use Today. *Iraq 31*, 103.

Kilmer, A., D. (1984). Music Tablet from Sippar: BM 65217+66616. *Iraq 46*, 69–80.

Lawergren, B., and O. R. Gurney (1987). Sound Holes and Geometrical Figures: Clues to the Terminology of Ancient Mesopotamian Harps. *Iraq 49*, 37–52.

Shaffer, A. (1981). A New Musical Term in Ancient Mesopotamian Music. *Iraq 43*, 79–83.

Spycket, A. (1998). Le carnaval des animeaux: On Some Musician Monkeys from the Ancient Near East. *Iraq 60*, 1–10.

Wulstan, D. (1968). The Tuning of the Babylonian Harp. *Iraq 30*, 215–228.

Index

aboriginal music 203, 205, 207–209
Afghanistan 247–251
Africa 4–10, 12–36, 38, 40, 42–43, 53, 69, 74, 76, 81, 84, 115, 119–120, 124, 126, 131, 134, 137, 207, 253, 261; *see also* Botswana; Côte d[apost]Ivoire
The Americas 13, 45–46, 48, 50, 52, 54, 56, 58, 60, 62, 64, 66, 68, 70, 72, 74, 76, 78, 80, 82, 84, 86, 88, 90, 92, 94, 96, 98, 100, 102, 104, 106, 108, 110, 112, 114, 116, 118–120, 122, 124, 126, 128, 130, 132, 134, 136, 138, 140, 142, 144, 146, 148; *see also* Brazilian music; Dominican Republic; Latin America; Mexico; tango
animals 16, 41, 90, 96, 121, 207
anthropology 19, 35–36, 58, 66, 100, 149, 203, 209
Argentina 125, 127–136
Armstrong, Louis 106, 108, 110; *see also* jazz; jazz age
Asia 80, 151–152, 154, 156–158, 160, 162, 164, 166, 168, 170, 172–174, 176–178, 180, 182, 184–186, 188, 190–192, 194–196, 202, 251, 253, 256–257, 261; *see also* China
Australia 13, 117–118, 202–204, 209
Aztecs 112–114, 117

bachata dance 45, 47–49
Ballet Russes 217
Baule 15
bebop 109–110
belly dancing 254, 260
Bharata Natyam 152–154, 158–164; *see also* India
Bikutsi dance 5, 7; *see also* Africa; Cameroon
bossa nova 143, 146–149, 244
Botswana 29–36
Brazil 9, 13, 117, 136–149; music 143–149
Buenos Aires hardcore 131–132

Cameroon 4–8
Capoeira 136–142, 147–148; *see also* Brazil
carnival 57–58, 66, 123, 138, 146, 222
Chacarera 131, 133–135; *see also* Argentina
China 180–191, 193–195
Chinese art 189
Choro 143–146, 148
clothing 21, 24, 80, 135, 155, 192, 223
costume 10, 16, 95, 142, 155, 162, 164, 169, 201, 213–214, 216, 236
Côte d[apost]Ivoire 14–15, 17, 19–20
Cuba 6, 9, 13, 57, 66, 76, 80–88
culture 4, 7–11, 13–15, 18–21, 23, 26–27, 29, 31–42, 45–47, 49–50, 53–54, 56, 58–59, 62–63, 65, 67–69, 73–75, 79–81, 85–87, 94, 98–100, 104–106, 110–114, 116–118, 124–125, 134, 142–144, 146–149, 151, 153, 155–157, 164–165, 168, 173–174, 176–180, 182, 184–193, 196–198, 200, 202–203, 205–206, 208–209, 227–229, 231–232, 234, 236–238, 241, 245, 247–251, 253, 256–257, 261
Cumbia 116, 131–133

Democratic Republic of Congo 15, 36–37
demographics 30–31, 37
Diaghilev, Sergei 217–219, 221–222, 227
Dominican Republic 45–53, 55–61, 63–67

economy 4, 14, 32–33, 37, 112, 152, 181, 185
education 4, 29–30, 33, 35, 74, 168, 173, 231
Egungun dance 8–9, 11, 13; *see also* Nigeria
Europe 6, 28, 33–34, 49, 105, 128–129, 131–132, 134, 143, 177, 202, 211–218, 220, 222, 224, 226, 228, 230, 232–234,

263

Index

236, 238, 240, 242, 244, 251, 253, 256, 261; *see also* Ireland; Spain; Stravinsky, Igor
Evita 127–128, 135

festivals 10, 18, 48, 52, 85, 123, 172, 194, 200, 231, 234, 254–255
flamenco 240–245
folk music 30, 59, 68, 70–74, 110–111, 122, 131, 133–134, 136, 175, 188, 220, 226, 233, 239, 243, 253, 255–256
folk songs 67, 69, 73, 88, 168, 175, 189, 217, 223, 226, 235, 255–256

geography 8, 30, 32, 37–38, 60, 177, 181, 229, 231
gumboot dance 20–28
Gur people 15

Hawaii 94–100, 174
hip-hop 178
hula dance 94–95, 97, 99; *see also* Hawaii

India 80, 151–159, 161, 163–165
Indian dance 151, 153, 155–159, 164–165
instruments 6, 9–12, 17, 22, 24, 34, 39–40, 46, 52, 55, 60, 63–64, 69–72, 83–85, 90, 96–97, 103, 107–109, 113–117, 122–123, 126, 133–134, 141–142, 145, 148, 163, 166, 174–175, 180, 187–194, 197, 200, 208, 229, 232, 235, 237, 250–251, 255, 257–258, 260–261
Iraq 251, 257, 259–262
Ireland 35, 228–239
Ivory Coast 14–19, 80; *see also* Africa; Baule; Gur people

Jamaica 13, 68–80, 88
Japan 29, 184, 191–196
jazz 6, 12, 34–35, 55, 63, 72, 76–77, 101, 103, 106–111, 124, 147, 154, 176, 190, 215, 244; *see also* Armstrong, Louis
jazz age 106, 108

Kapa Haka 197–201; *see also* New Zealand
Kathak 158–159, 161–164; *see also* India
Khalkas people 180–181, 183, 185; *see also* Mongolia
Kundiman 165–167, 169, 171, 173, 176; *see also* Philippines

Latin America 51, 53, 55–58, 62, 67–68, 88
Lesacre 225

Maqamat 257–258
Marley, Bob 78–79; *see also* Jamaica
Mayan instruments 113–114
Mbuti people 36–37, 39, 41, 43; *see also* Republic of Congo
merchants 180–182, 185
merengue 48–49, 51–68
Mexico 111–118
Middle East 247–248, 250, 252, 254, 256, 258, 260–262; *see also* Afghanistan; Iraq
Molimo 40–42
Mongolia 180–181, 183–185

New York 8, 19–20, 35, 43, 51, 54–55, 57–58, 62–63, 65–67, 88, 100–103, 105–106, 110, 124–125, 127, 131–132, 135–136, 142, 157, 164–165, 173, 179, 185–186, 196, 202, 209, 216, 228, 239, 256–257, 261
New Zealand 197, 199, 201
Nigeria 8–9, 11–13, 81, 126
North America 45, 74, 80, 118–119, 121, 123, 128

Odissi 151–157; *see also* Indian dance
opera 176, 189–190, 217–218, 241
Ottoman harem music 254

peasants 180–181, 185, 188, 235
Petrushka 217, 221–225, 228
Philippines 165–169, 171–180
Plains Indians 88–89, 91, 93
punk 105, 131–132, 190
pygmies 36–41, 43

reggae 17, 34, 50, 68, 73–75, 77–80, 202; *see also* Jamaica
religion 8, 10–11, 18, 30, 38, 41–42, 57, 66, 76, 78, 98, 152, 158, 180, 182–183, 185, 192, 229, 251
Republic of Congo 15, 36–37
rock 12, 28, 55, 58, 62, 64, 67–68, 73, 76, 79, 104, 110, 116–117, 128, 131–132, 176–178, 190, 193, 195, 202, 215
rumba 13, 49–50, 56, 58, 68, 70, 80–88; *see also* The Americas; Cuba

samba 11, 70, 81, 143, 145–148
Santacruzan dance 174–175, 177, 179; *see also* Philippines
Saray court dance 251, 253, 255; *see also* Turkey
shōmyō 191, 193–195; *see also* Japan
sinulog dance 165–166, 168; *see also* Philippines

Index

South Pacific 197–198, 200, 202, 204, 206, 208; *see also* aboriginal music; Australia; Kapa Haka
Spain 6, 81, 114–115, 165–166, 176, 240–243, 245
step dancing 26–27, 238
Stravinsky, Igor 217, 219, 221, 223, 225, 227
sun dance 88–93; *see also* Plains Indians
swing dancing 101–105; *see also* New York

tango 70, 125–131, 134–136; *see also* Argentina
Tinikling dance 165, 172; *see also* Philippines
Turkey 251–257, 259

United States of America 17–18, 27, 34, 45, 51, 53, 55–58, 61–62, 64, 67–68, 70, 74, 76, 78–80, 88, 104–106, 111, 118–119, 121, 123–124, 128–129, 131, 137, 143, 165, 167–168, 173, 177, 237, 247

Video Anthology of World Music and Dance 15, 29

Western influence 165, 189–190, 192

Yoruba 8–13, 17, 19–20; *see also* Nigeria

Zulu dance 24–25

www.ingramcontent.com/pod-product-compliance
Ingram Content Group UK Ltd.
Pitfield, Milton Keynes, MK11 3LW, UK
UKHW041931140426
5217IPUK00014B/428

9 780786 497157